The United States and the Gulf:
Shifting Pressures,
Strategies and Alignments

The Gulf Research Center Book Series at Gerlach Press

The GCC in the Global Economy
Ed. by Richard Youngs
ISBN 9783940924018, 2012

Resources Blessed: Diversification and the
Gulf Development Model
Ed. by Giacomo Luciani
ISBN 9783940924025, 2012

GCC Financial Markets:
The World's New Money Centers
Ed. by Eckart Woertz
ISBN 9783940924032, 2012

National Employment, Migration and
Education in the GCC
Ed. by Steffen Hertog
ISBN 9783940924049, 2012

Asia-Gulf Economic Relations in the 21st
Century The Local to Global Transformation
Ed. by Tim Niblock with Monica Malik
ISBN 9783940924100, 2013

A New Gulf Security Architecture
Prospects and Challenges for an Asian Role`
*Ed. by Ranjit Gupta, Abubaker Bagader, Talmiz
Ahmad and N. Janardhan*
ISBN 9783940924360, 2014

Gulf Charities and Islamic Philanthropy
in the 'Age of Terror' and Beyond
Ed. by Robert Lacey and Jonathan Benthall
ISBN 9783940924322, 2014

State-Society Relations in the
Arab Gulf States
Ed. by Mazhar Al-Zoby and Birol Baskan
ISBN 9783940924384, 2014

Political Economy of Energy Reform
The Clean Energy-Fossil Fuel Balance
in the Gulf
Ed. by Giacomo Luciani and Rabia Ferroukhi
ISBN 9783940924407, 2014

Security Dynamics of East Asia in the Gulf
Region
Ed. by Tim Niblock with Yang Guang
ISBN 9783940924483, 2014

Islamic Finance
Political Economy, Performance and Risk
Ed. by Mehmet Asutay and Abdullah Turkistani
ISBN 9783940924124, 3 vols set, 2015

Employment and Career Motivation
in the Arab Gulf States:
The Rentier Mentality Revisited
Ed. by Annika Kropf and Mohamed Ramady
ISBN 9783940924605, 2015

The Changing Energy Landscape in the Gulf:
Strategic Implications
Ed. by Gawdat Bahgat
ISBN 9783940924643, 2015

Sustainable Development Challenges
in the Arab Sates of the Gulf
*Ed. by David Bryde, Yusra Mouzughi and Turki
Al Rasheed*
ISBN 9783940924629, 2015

The United States and the Gulf:
Shifting Pressures, Strategies and Alignments
Ed. by Steven W. Hook and Tim Niblock
ISBN 9783940924667, 2015

Africa and the Gulf Region:
Blurred Boundaries and Shifting Ties
*Ed. by Rogaia Mustafa Abusharaf and Dale F.
Eickelman*
ISBN 9783940924704, 2015

Rebuilding Yemen:
Political, Economic and Social Challenges
Ed. by Noel Brehony and Saud Al-Sarhan
ISBN 9783940924681, 2015

Gulf Research Centre Cambridge
Knowledge for All

The United States and the Gulf: Shifting Pressures, Strategies and Alignments

*Edited by Steven W. Hook
and Tim Niblock*

 Gerlach Press

First published 2015
by Gerlach Press
Berlin, Germany
www.gerlach-press.de

Cover Design: www.brandnewdesign.de, Hamburg
Printed and bound in Germany by Hubert & Co., Göttingen

British Library Cataloguing in Publication Data.
A catalogue record for this book is available from the British Library.

Bibliographic data available from Deutsche Nationalbibliothek
http://d-nb.info/1070508918

ISBN: 978-3-940924-66-7 (hardcover)
ISBN: 978-3-940924-67-4 (ebook)

Contents

Introduction

Steven W. Hook and Tim Niblock

Security issues in the Gulf region have been of critical importance to global stability over a prolonged period. Seldom, however, have they reached as critical a turning-point as they have now. Three factors account for their current salience. First, shifts in the demand for Gulf oil have transformed the Gulf's economic relationships with outside countries. Rapidly increasing demand from Asian countries (especially China and India), declining demand from the United States and a static level of demand from the European Union, have propelled China and India into the positions of the Gulf's first and third largest trading partners. Second, developments in the Middle Eastern region have posed destabilising challenges and threats to all of the Gulf countries. The challenges and threats have been both external to the Gulf region and within it (or, at least, with a reach which directly affects Gulf regimes): the ongoing conflicts in Iraq, Syria, Yemen and Israel/Palestine in particular, and the nuclear issue in Iran. Finally, the shifting global balance of power, with China, India, and Russia (and to some extent the other two BRICS countries) pursuing more assertive foreign policies than before, the external presence in the Gulf becomes more open to debate and contest. Beyond the confines of the Gulf itself, moreover, there is the wider issue of control of the sea-lanes in the Indian Ocean, which are essential to the export of Gulf oil and the import of the critical needs of Gulf countries.

There has, in recent years, been an assumption among many of those monitoring the growing presence of Asian powers in the Gulf that China and/or India is likely to take up a strategic role in the region.[1] Conversely, the assumption has been that the United States, to which the Gulf's resources are no longer so critically important, will steadily reduce if not relinquish its strategic engagement there. US discussion of the rebalancing of US forces globally, with greater emphasis on Asia and the Pacific (the "Asian pivot"), have seemed to provide evidence of such an intention. This book seeks to examine these perceptions, not only with regard to US policy but also on whether other powers (Asian or European) have either the strategic ability or the desire/intention to become involved.

Chapter One (Tim Niblock: "Strategic Economic Relationships and Strategic Openings in the Gulf") sets out the framework within which changes in strategic alliances in the Gulf region need to be considered. The chapter examines the extent to which the Gulf's critical ties of mutual economic dependence have shifted from Western to Asian countries (specifically China and India); how Gulf states are likely to perceive their best interests strategically in the future; what capability to engage in the region is possessed by different external powers; and how such powers perceive the feasibility and desirability of strategic engagement. Special attention is given to the political aims and strategic objectives of China in the Gulf region. The chapter concludes that neither China nor other Asian powers are likely to have an interest in taking on a significant military engagement in the Gulf region, and that the interests of the Gulf populations are best served by seeking a resolution to existing inter-state conflicts in the region, lessening external security involvement, and working towards the creation of a Gulf-based collective security system.

Chapter Two (Steven W. Hook: "Hegemonic Stability and American Power") examines US global primacy through the prism of hegemonic stability theory, analysing the implications which this has for future US policy in the Gulf and the wider Middle East. A key element in US primacy is identified as the creation and maintenance of a liberal world order, where smaller states are drawn into a network of global government with established rules of cooperative behaviour. Primacy, in this setting, is undermined when the US turns away from the "hegemonic bargain" and takes actions which engender distrust or opposition among smaller states. It can be argued that this has happened in the Middle East, with George W. Bush's pre-emptive war against Iraq, documented reports of torture against suspected terrorists etc. Whether the US can reserve for itself a position of leadership even after it has lost its unipolar stature, therefore, will depend on the nature of authority which its leaders can provide.

Chapter Three (John Duke Anthony: "Arabia to Asia: The Myths and Merits of an American 'Pivot'") confronts directly the record of contemporary US policies in the Gulf region, the criticisms which can be made of these policies, the domestic US debate on the desirability of continued engagement, and the balance of positives and negatives which Gulf states have drawn and can still draw from US engagement in the region. Anthony ultimately warns of the dangers in abandoning commitments in the Gulf region, where policy has achieved some success, and focusing instead on a region (Asia-Pacific) where the alleged merits of engagement are questionable, the prospects dubious, and the potential implications and repercussions serious and far-reaching.

Chapter Four (David B. Des Roches: "The Evolving American Security Role in the Gulf") analyses the nature and extent of the US's security involvement in the Gulf, making a key distinction between the US's strategic interests and its operational presence. He maintains that the strategic interests are substantial and unchanging, and that it would be a mistake to assume that a decrease in the US physical presence indicates a correlating decrease in the strategic significance which the US attaches to the region. Indeed the lighter US operational presence which is currently emerging represents a return to the norm (in contrast to the build-up to confront Saddam Hussein and deal with other post-9/11 contingencies). The new posture is generated by political and technical developments in the US (requiring less *in situ* positioning of forces), as well as by partner states' increased willingness to collaborate on defence issues.

Chapter Five (Degang Sun and Yahia H. Zoubir: "The Eagle's Nest in the Gulf: Analysis of US Military Deployment in the GCC Countries") complements the analysis of Des Roches, emphasising not only the continued US strategic commitment but also its ongoing operational capability. Indeed, the chapter contends, the less visible US presence has been accompanied by increased capability, in so far as US bases are becoming stronger in mobility, and more multi-dimensional in their functions. Furthermore, they are gradually being interlinked with other US bases in Central Asia, Turkey, Djibouti and the Horn of Africa. Degang and Zoubir emphasise the dangers inherent in this strategy, warning that it will deepen Shi'a-Sunni rivalry, enhance competitive power struggles between Saudi Arabia and Iran, and invite further involvement from outside powers.

Chapter Six (Mohammed Turki Al-Sudairi: "The Future of a Critical Relationship in the Gulf: US-Saudi Relations and the Rise of the Saudi 'Garrison State'") looks at the other end of the US-Gulf relationship: the capacity of the key GCC state (the Kingdom of Saudi Arabia) to maintain a mutually beneficial and collaborative relationship with the US. Al-Sudairi focuses on the need for the Saudi regime to address the core issues of political and economic reforms rather than continuing to respond to challenges by intensifying security measures (reinforcing the existing "garrison state"). The time frame to pursue such a course is limited; similarly limited, therefore, is the hope of achieving a "soft landing" for the country. Unless this dilemma can be resolved, Saudi Arabia's relations with the US are unlikely to be stable. In the light of the past record, with the steady strengthening of the Saudi garrison state, the prospects are not bright.

Chapter Seven (Flynt Leverett and Hillary Mann Leverett: "America's Monetary Stake in the Gulf and the Looming Challenge of the Petro*yuan*") covers a critical foundation of the US' global geopolitical primacy, namely the dollar's standing as the world's leading transactional and reserve currency. The dollar's dominance as the invoice and settlement currency in international oil and gas sales – something which was engineered by the US in the early 1970s through its strategic links to the key Gulf oil producers – is a key element in this. China now has the economic leverage, as the leading market for Gulf energy producers, to challenge that dominance, thereby eroding the US' longstanding hegemonic position in the Gulf. China is now encouraging major Gulf oil producers to accept Chinese *renminbi* as a transactional currency. The writers do not expect the US to disengage from the Gulf, but China's currency strategy is poised to rebalance an element in the US-Gulf relationship.

Chapter Eight (Girijesh Pant: "Emerging Dynamics of US-Gulf Engagement: India's Policy Options") acknowledges that the US has re-affirmed its commitment to the current security architecture of the Gulf region, but maintains that there are long-term stresses which will threaten the stability of its relationships with GCC states. These centre, mainly, on the need for thorough-going structural reforms in the GCC, and on US contacts/relations with Iran. In this situation, the US will be seeking partners to shoulder responsibility for regional developments. Some have proposed that India should join a US-led alliance to pursue this objective. Pant, however, suggests an Asian alternative, where India would work together with other Asian powers to address the domestic dimensions of regional security in the Gulf, focusing not on regime threat or regime security, but rather on the empowerment of the public sphere. India and other Asian states, Pant contends, have the experience and value-empathy with Gulf states to succeed in such an undertaking.

Chapter Nine (Cinzia Bianco: "The European Union in the Gulf: New Opportunities for Cooperation") pursues a similar line to that of Pant, but in this case focusing on the role which the European Union could play. The context is again provided by the US's continued engagement co-existing with the need to draw in other external powers. Bianco examines the material interests and capacities of the EU, and concludes that it is the union's mediation capacity which constitutes the key contribution it could provide. This capacity could be employed to address the fierce sectarian violence and inter-state rivalries which have proved so destructive. The framework for this could be for the EU to initiate a Gulf-wide dialogue on cooperative security that puts together, under US auspices, discussions among GCC states, Iraq and Iran that confront common concerns and may create a new shared concept of regional security.

Chapter Ten (Saul Kelly and Gareth Stansfield: "On the Right Side of History? US Transitions and the Possibility of a British Strategic Role in the Gulf") addresses the key dilemma of values versus interests in British foreign policy. While the chapter focuses on the British case, it raises issues which apply to all external powers in their relations with Gulf countries. All make statements of high principle, but all have their own agendas of material interest to pursue. Kelly and Stansfield show that the Arab Spring gave rise to statements of principle in British foreign policy-making circles, emphasising the importance of placing human rights at the forefront of British policy in the Arab world. This trend was seen negatively by GCC governments. Within two years, however, policy had reverted to one of enhancing Britain's enduring legacy in the region and safeguarding its relationships with established governments. Britain is now well-placed to pursue a supportive role in the US's re-engagement in the Gulf, notwithstanding a significant degree of scepticism about such a policy in British domestic opinion.

The editors wish to thank the Gulf Research Centre for facilitating, within the context of the 2014 Gulf Research Meeting, the convening of the workshop which gave rise to the chapters of this book. It was through the discussions in this workshop, which involved others as well as the authors represented here, that some common perspectives were established – although not necessarily common conclusions.

Note

1   This has been evident in two earlier books which have come out in the same series as that to which this book belongs. All of the books have emerged from workshops held within the context of the Gulf Research Meetings in Cambridge. The two earlier books are: Niblock, Tim (ed) with Monica Malik, *Asia-Gulf Economic Relations in the 21st Century: the Local to Global Transformation* (Berlin: Gerlach Press, 2013), and Niblock, Tim (ed) with Yang Guang, *Security Dynamics of East Asia in the Gulf Region* (Berlin Gerlach Press, 2014).

1

Strategic Economic Relationships and Strategic Openings in the Gulf

Tim Niblock

1. Introduction

This chapter seeks to provide an overarching view of how economic factors are transforming the Gulf's relationship with the rest of the world, and assesses whether this creates the basis for new strategic alignments. The possibilities and implications of a changing US role in the Gulf, therefore, will be placed in the context of ongoing changes in the relationships between Asian powers and the Gulf states. Particular emphasis will be given to the role of China.

The chapter will begin by distinguishing between different meanings of "strategic", suggesting that the Chinese (and perhaps wider Asian) understanding of a strategic relationship differs from that normally accepted in the Western world. It will be suggested that the Chinese understanding of the term is of particular value in understanding how relations between Gulf countries and other countries are being transformed – with the Asian "strategic relationships" with Gulf countries growing stronger, while those with Western countries become less significant. The concept of acknowledged mutual dependence, focusing in particular on economic factors, is key to the Chinese use of the term.

Following this, updated information will be provided on the flows of trade and investment. Attention will be given to the significance of some of the latest trends. This will be used to assess the degree of mutual economic dependence which is present in the various relationships maintained by the Gulf states – and specifically the extent to which mutual dependence with Western countries is in the process of being replaced by mutual dependence with Asian countries. This is a factor not only of the level of trade and investment but also of its character, composition and significance to each economy.

The factors which will determine the shape of Gulf-Asian relations in the future will then be assessed. Specifically the focus will be on whether the developing relations between

Gulf and Asian states will be complemented by Western-style strategic relationships, with the heavier emphasis on political and defence-related engagement. This assessment requires some consideration of the character of the security roles where Gulf states may require external assistance in the future. The key factors identified as determining whether Asian powers will adopt major defence-related roles in the region are: how Gulf countries will perceive their best interests in the future; what capability different external powers have to cover the needs of "Gulf security"; and how external powers perceive their interests with regard to engagement in the Gulf.

The chapter concludes with an appraisal of the strategic role which China, in particular, could and is likely to play in the Gulf region. Some reference will also be made to the possible role of other Asian powers. The analysis suggests that there is complementarity between the roles which different Asian powers could play, rather than a dynamic where they would find themselves in conflict with one another. US policy will need to take this dimension into account.

2. Strategic Relationships and Gulf Security

"Strategic relationship" and the related term "strategic partnership" have been used loosely in international relations. This is particularly apparent when examining the "strategic relations" and "strategic partnerships" of Gulf countries. Insufficient attention has been given to the content of the terms. Journalistic reports and analyses of the relationship between Saudi Arabia and China have, ever since the late 1990s, described these as constituting a "strategic partnership". This, however, was not reflected in formal official discourse. It was only in March 2014 that Saudi Arabia and China announced – for the first time – that they were considering establishing a strategic partnership. In fact, prior to the March 2014 statement there had been no official mention from either the Saudi or the Chinese side of a strategic partnership existing.[1] Some of the confusion may stem from the signing by the Saudi and Chinese governments in 1999 of a "Strategic Oil Cooperation Agreement".[2] The use of the word "strategic" here, however, clearly relates exclusively to the field of hydrocarbons, and not to a wider political or military relationship.

It is important, therefore, to unpack the possible meanings of strategic relationship and strategic partnership, before examining possible changes in the strategic relationships of Gulf countries. The terms were used in the business field before they entered international relations vocabulary, and there "strategic relationship" referred to an understanding between two companies where each holds an economic facility which will help the other, and they agree to rely on eachother for the provision of that facility. In international relations, the use of the term is recent, with only very limited use prior to 2000. Although a number of theorists have sought to define it,[3] the governments which employ the term have seldom been specific about what it means.

It could be argued that the vagueness and pliability of the term is part of its value. It is not a straightjacket but rather a pliable framework which can be bent and adapted to the needs of a particular relationship.[4] It can indeed, in this respect, constitute a useful diplomatic tool. A country to which strategic partnership is offered can feel pleased to be deemed worthy of it. It indicates that the stronger power considers the country concerned a significant player in the global arena or in a significant regional sub-system – holding a position where it can help to shape international events. Yet the use of the words "strategic" and "strategic partnership" in describing relationships does require more precise formulation, as their differential use can cloak significant differences in what is envisaged.

It will be contended here that the Chinese (and to some extent wider Asian[5]) understanding of "strategic relationship" is distinctively different from Western understandings of the term. The latter understandings, as is clear with the European Union (at least in policy statements on strategic partnerships), suggest cooperation in fields which are primarily non-economic. The use of the term often implies a military dimension, although in the case of the European Union the emphasis is more on political coordination to counter global threats. In the case of China, the term refers primarily to an economic relationship. It is unlikely to include military dimensions and perhaps not even political dimensions.[6] This does not mean, however, that the reference is simply to a strong economic relationship. Rather, a strategic relationship (perhaps incorporated formally in a strategic partnership) implies mutual economic dependence: the two sides explicitly recognising that they are dependent on eachother for their own development, well-being and perhaps survival. In fact it is closer to the original business definition of strategic relationship, as mentioned above. Such a relationship may well require a strong underpinning of political and diplomatic contact to sustain it, but this is not core to the concept. Nor does it usually involve cooperation in the field of defence.

The Chinese understanding of strategic relationship, and the difference between this and Western understandings, is of key importance in the analysis presented here. The central theme is that the US and other Western countries have steadily moved away from strategic relationships with Gulf states, in the Chinese understanding of that term. Their relationships with Gulf states, in other words, no longer reflect (if they ever did) relationships of acknowledged mutual need and mutual dependence. This has come about in part by deliberate policy and in part through changes in the distribution of hydrocarbon resources and in the need for hydrocarbon imports. Asian countries, meanwhile, have steadily moved into relationships of acknowledged mutual dependence with Gulf states. This, however, does not necessarily mean that Asian powers are likely to move towards strategic relationships with Gulf countries of the kind found in Western understandings of that term. In fact it is unlikely to be in their interests to do that. Further, the interests of Gulf states themselves may be to move away from defence-related strategic relationships, and focus on working towards a framework of collective security in the Gulf. In such a framework, defence-related agreements with external powers would be mediated through a pan-Gulf collective security organisation.

3. The Economic Basis of a Strategic Economic Relationship: Shifting Trends in Trade, Investment and Contracting

The developing economic relations between the Gulf's major trading partners will now be examined, so that the development of their individual economic relations with Gulf states can be compared. The information provided here is an updating of material which this writer has previously published elsewhere.[7] Tables 1-4 present the data. However, it should be noted that the level of trade and investment between Gulf and external trading partners is not in itself an indication of how mutually-dependent economies are. That depends also on the character and composition of the trade and investment, and most importantly on whether both sides conceive the economic activity concerned as essential to their well-being and development. This dimension will be central to the subsequent analysis.

Table 1 Growth of Gulf Trade with Major Partners, 1990-2013

	1990	2000	2005	2008	2009	2012	2013
China	1.3	11.8	44.9	121.4	93.4	203.5	224.4
India	4.4	6.6	21.4	119.3	87.9	186.5	183.9
Japan	33.5	52.0	103.8	176.1	103.7	181.3	171.6
South Korea	6.1	25.6	53.4	109.7	71.9	142.4	136.1
EU	59.9	66.7	142.5	212.0	156.0	207.4	216.2
US	19.1	33.9	66.0	124.8	71.2	143.7	137.2

Source: International Monetary Fund, *Direction of Trade Statistics*, 1990-2013. Calculated by the writer.

Table 2 Rates of Growth of Trade with the Gulf (Major Partners), 2005-2013

India	759.3%
China	399.8%
South Korea	154.9%
United States	107.9%
Japan	65.3%
European Union	51.0%

Source: Calculated by the writer from IMF *Direction of Trade Statistics.*

Table 3 2013 Gulf Trade with Major Partners

$billion

	Bahrain	Saudi Arabia	UAE	Qatar	Oman	Kuwait	Iraq	Iran	TOTAL
China	1.7	69.2	48.3	9.6	21.2	11.6	23.9	38.9	224.4
India	1.3	46.1	65.5	14.0	6.1	17.1	19.4	14.5	183.9
Japan	1.2	52.8	48.0	35.0	8.5	14.3	3.2	6.5	171.6
South Korea	0.8	43.9	22.8	24.4	5.4	18.2	10.6	10.0	136.1
EU	3.0	77.6	69.6	18.6	5.6	13.0	20.1	8.7	216.2
US	1.7	68.5	29.2	6.8	1.8	14.5	14.6	0.3	137.2
World	49.6	509.2	515.8	154.4	81.2	126.4	131.9	171.3	1739.8

Source: International Monetary Fund, *Direction of Trade Statistics 2013*. Calculated by the writer.

Table 4 Percentages of Imports/Exports in Gulf Major Partners Trade, 2013

	Imports from Gulf	Exports to Gulf
EU	36.2	63.8
US	55.5	45.0
China	60.3	39.7
India	67.1	32.9
South Korea	80.5	19.5
Japan	83.9	16.1

Source: Calculated by the writer from IMF *Direction of Trade Statistics 2013*

The critical trends documented in these tables are clear. EU trade, which has been the predominant element in Gulf trade over the past two decades, has now (as of 2013) lost its leading position. China is now the leading trade partner of the 8 Gulf countries, taken collectively. India is firmly placed in third position, after the EU, although its trade with the Gulf fell slightly in 2013. Japan, which held the second position through the late 1980s, the 1990s and on to 2009, is now in fourth position. US and South Korean trade has been at a lower, and less consistent, level. A long-term shift in trading patterns is clearly under way. The rate of increase in the trade of India and China between 2005 and 2012 is shown to be well ahead of that of any of the other major trading partners.[8] The rates at which Japanese and South Korean trade are increasing are more similar to the rates of increase of fellow-industrialised Western economies than they are with those of China and India.

In terms of the composition of trade, it should not be assumed that growing Chinese-Indian dependence on oil imports alone accounts for trade growth. Despite the Asian trade being slightly skewed towards imports from the Gulf, rather than exports, China and India do nonetheless benefit from substantial export markets in the Gulf. In fact, the value of their exports has in recent years increased at a slightly higher rate than the value of their imports. The Gulf trading partners whose trade is most dependent on hydrocarbon imports are Japan and South Korea. The European Union is the only Gulf trading partner which has a positive trade balance with the Gulf.

Chinese and Indian trade is fairly well spread across the 8 Gulf countries. Although Saudi Arabia and the UAE are China's largest trading partners in the Gulf, Chinese trade with Iran is of considerable importance to Iran. This, of course, stems in part from the impact of the UN and US sanctions on Iran. China has interpreted the sanctions regulations more flexibly than have other great powers (although Asian countries in general have adopted a more flexible approach than have Western countries). China accounts for almost a quarter of all Iranian trade. China has also, however, been the major beneficiary of the gradual rehabilitation of the Iraqi economy, having now (in 2013) displaced the US as Iraq's largest trading partner. In contrast to the broad spread of Chinese and Indian trade, one-half of all US trade with the Gulf is with Saudi Arabia. The composition of US trade with the region, moreover, is relatively narrow in scope, consisting largely of imports of Gulf hydrocarbons and exports of US weaponry.

Overall, then, a substantial shift is taking place in the Gulf's trading patterns. This is changing fundamentally the character of the Gulf's economic relationship with the rest of the world. The Gulf's economic well-being is now closely intertwined with that of the newly-industrialising countries of Asia, especially China and India. The drift is not so much from West to East, but from the established industrial (OECD) countries to the two major newly-industrialising countries of Asia. The speed of the transformation has been remarkable.

To establish that there is the basis for a relationship of mutual dependence, it needs to be shown not only that there is a high level of trade but also that this is integral to long-term trends. Developments in the oil market provide clear evidence that a long-term trend is indeed present. As a result of the expansion of oil production in the Americas, through the development of production from the Canadian oil sands, tight oil (from hydraulic fracturing) in the United States, new conventional oil fields in Brazil, and possibly increased production from Venezuela,[9] imports into the Americas (in particular the United States, which up to 2013 had been the world's biggest oil importer) will decline sharply – and indeed did so in 2014. OECD demand for liquids[10] will decline as a result of conservation measures and increasing energy efficiency.[11] By 2035 the United States will have only minimal need for oil imports, and perhaps none of this need come from the Gulf region.[12] The US, moreover, will be able to export significant quantities of natural gas. China and India, on the other hand, will need to import substantially larger quantities of hydrocarbons. Recent estimates of Chinese demand for liquids are that this will grow from 8 million barrels a day (mb/d) in 2013 to 18 mb/d in 2035,[13] with Indian and Middle Eastern demand both growing by 4.6 mb/d.[14] China's imports will come to 14 mb/d in 2035, making up 75% of China's total liquids demand. The percentage of India's, Japan's and South Korea's total demand for liquids accounted for by imports will be even higher.

The overall pattern is clear: the United States will in the future have little need to import oil from the Gulf (what they need can come from the Western hemisphere); Europe, Japan and South Korea will have a still-substantial but marginally-reduced need for imports of Gulf oil; China and India will have a greatly-enhanced need for Gulf oil imports. The shifts in trade patterns which have been apparent since 2005 (as outlined earlier in this section) will therefore intensify in the period through to 2035.

For a strategic relationship to exist, however, there needs to be not only mutual dependence but also mutual acknowledgement of that dependence, accompanied usually (within the framework of a "strategic partnership") by joint consultation and planning between the two sides as to how they manage and develop their relationship. The contrast between Western powers and Asian powers (especially China) here, with regard to their relations with Gulf countries, is stark. The United States in particular, and in a less marked manner European countries,[15] have been eager to distance themselves from any "acknowledged mutual dependence". Indeed the objective of freeing their countries from "dependence on Arab oil" has been articulated by a number of Western leaders, and is often implicit in the energy policies pursued by Western governments. In January 2006, President Bush in his annual address to Congress, spoke of how technological breakthroughs would enable the US to "reach another great goal: to replace more than 75 percent of our oil imports from the Middle East by 2025".[16] Although other US presidents have omitted the direct reference to the Middle East, mention of the undesirability of dependence on oil imports has been a recurring theme. Asian governments, on the other hand, have tended to project their need for oil from the Gulf in terms of mutual need. Not only does the seller of oil need a buyer, but the trade necessarily leads to a broadening of the relationship. Wider dimensions of trade, investment and coordination are required so as to safeguard and buttress the critical oil transactions. Agreements following from this, therefore, are rightly described as strategic. A term which frequently occurs on the Chinese side with regard to such agreements is "win-win" cooperation.

The Strategic Oil Cooperation Partnership agreement which China and Saudi Arabia signed in 1999 is a good example of how China sees strategic relationships – even though in this case it was restricted to hydrocarbons-related activities. The agreement, and the outcomes which followed from it, covered not only a long-term framework for

Chinese imports of Saudi oil, but also Chinese involvement in upstream developments in Saudi Arabia (oil and gas exploration), cooperation in downstream developments in both countries (the construction and operation of refineries and petrochemicals industries etc), technology transfer, and cooperation in creating a strategic oil reserve capacity in China.[17] The broader strategic partnership, whose establishment was discussed between the two sides in January 2014 appears to be geared to taking the oil cooperation partnership further, bringing in more fields of cooperation.[18] There is no indication, however, that this would extend significantly into non-economic spheres.

Similarly, the Strategic Partnership agreement signed between the UAE and China in January 2014 covers wide-ranging cooperation in a range of fields, based on satisfying critical needs on both sides. Such fields range from "strategic cooperation" between the Abu Dhabi National Oil Company and the China National Petroleum Company, to currency swaps, cooperation in developing renewable energy and clean energy technology, and banking and securities. The agreement is described as "broadening the horizons of developing comprehensive cooperation" between the two countries, and representing a "benchmark document of bilateral relations in the future". There is explicit mention of increased high-level exchange visits, the forging of closer links between the foreign ministries, cooperation in areas like law-enforcement and anti-terrorism, coordination and cooperation within international organisations for safeguarding their mutual interests etc. The only directly political objective mentioned is the statement that "while China said it supported the policies and moves taken by the UAE with respect to national sovereignty and territorial integrity, the UAE backs the one-China policy". In January 2014 it was announced that China and the Gulf Cooperation Council would start negotiations for a strategic partnership agreement, and the indications at present are that this will be almost entirely economic in content.[19]

Although there are only limited examples of strategic partnerships between other East Asian countries and Gulf countries, those that there are tend to follow the Chinese model rather than the Western one. South Korea's one strategic partnership with a Middle Eastern country is with the United Arab Emirates, and that was established in 2009 in the context of South Korea winning the competition to construct civilian nuclear power installations in the UAE. There are military dimensions to the growing relationship between South Korea and the UAE, but these have entered into the relationship subsequent to rather than as integral elements in the strategic partnership.[20] Japan's partnerships in the region, sometimes termed "strategic", tend to eschew the term "strategic" in their titles, as in the Bahrain-Japan Partnership[21] and the Qatar-Japan Partnership for Stability and Prosperity. The only Asian power whose strategic partnerships mainly follow the Western pattern is India, but at present the only Gulf country with which India has a strategic partnership is Oman.[22] There was a strategic partnership between India and Iran, established in 2005, but this was terminated in 2013 under pressure from the US government.[23]

4. Assessing the Possibility that Asian Strategic Relationships May Transform into Western-Style Strategic Relationships: The Relevant Factors

As has been shown, the relationships developing between the major Asian powers and Gulf countries are substantial and significant. They have already changed, and will increasingly transform, how Gulf states relate to the outside world – especially as regards the balance between Asian and Western powers in Gulf external relationships. Whether these strategic relationships will in due course take on significant defence and military dimensions – leading to strategic relationships of the kind maintained by Western countries – depends on a number of factors. Before considering what those factors are, and (in the next section) how they may be applied to individual Asian powers, however, it necessary to examine the purposes and objectives of security and defence-related agreements between Gulf and external powers.

Security-related issues in the Gulf have, in Western governmental discourse, been swept together under the generic term "Gulf security". At the centre of the concerns of Western governments has been the desire to ensure the free flow of oil and other hydrocarbons to the Western world. The term "Gulf Security" is in itself, therefore, misleading: it is less concerned with the security of Gulf countries *per se* than with the security of oil supply to the Western world. Threats to the latter could emanate from three different sources: the overthrow of existing regimes (leading either to domestic instability, or to the emergence of regimes inimical to Western countries); external external attack (whether from within the Gulf or outside); and the cutting of the sea-lanes along which oil is transported to the rest of the world. In practice, threats would be most likely to straddle more than one of these dimensions at the same time.

While it may be apposite for Western governments to bundle all three sources of threat into one "problem" (Gulf security), Asian governments may not – and it will be argued here do not – have an interest in all the three aspects. In fact for most Asian countries, military engagement aimed at countering either of the first two sources of threat mentioned above would be problematic. For historical and ideological reasons, most Asian powers have pronounced themselves averse to external interference in the domestic politics of other states (at least outside of their regional environments). However alien the conduct and institutions of Gulf regimes may be to their own values, their foreign policies (reflecting their domestic concerns) are crafted around respect for the sovereign rights of governments. They have, in any case, fewer levers than Western countries to influence domestic politics in other countries. Nor have they seen it as being in their interest to align themselves with one Gulf state against another; they gain form peaceful cooperative relations with all of the states of the Gulf, and it makes no sense to alienate any one of them. This has, of course, sometimes been difficult when intra-Gulf conflicts have been at their most bitter.

The one dimension in which they have a clear interest in engaging with "Gulf security" is with the protection of the sea-routes into and out of the Gulf. In this regard, engagement with security issues is unproblematic – especially if the invitation to engage comes not from one Gulf state but a collection of them (and if possible all of them acting collectively). There is, moreover, a precedent for such engagement: Asian powers are already engaged in countering piracy in the Indian Ocean, as part of Combined Task Force 150 in the Maritime Security Patrol Area (MSPA) off the coasts of Somalia. The precedent, moreover, shows the viability of Asian powers acting collaboratively rather than in rivalry: the Chinese, Indian, South Korean and Japanese navies currently coordinate their anti-piracy naval operations in the MSPA.[24]

Three factors need to be taken into account in assessing whether Asian powers will develop security-based relationships (of any kind) with Gulf states. First is **the perceptions which Gulf governments have of their own best interests**. Over the past 40 years, it is clear that the Arab monarchies of the Gulf have conceived their security in terms of the whole range of Gulf security concerns outlined above. They (to different degrees) have seen one or more of their neighbouring Gulf states (Iran or Iraq), perhaps in alliance with external movements/powers, as a threat. The threat to the regimes has been elided with the threat to the state's existence and coherence. Clearly support to counter this threat requires engagement by powers which are prepared to take sides in Gulf politics – giving military support to one Gulf state against one or more others.

It should not be assumed, however, that this will always be the case. There is a growing, but still clearly minority (at least on the Arab side of the Gulf), view in the Gulf that the Gulf's problems can only be resolved through Gulf states acting pro-actively to resolve their differences and establishing collective security mechanisms and institutions to handle regional relations.[25] External support would only come in as agreed through the channels of collective security. This would, of course, mean that the kind of support which Western powers have provided in the past is no longer needed.

Second is **the capability of external powers.** Gulf states would, naturally, only want security to be provided by states which have a real capability to act decisively in their support. It has for long been assumed that only the United States would have the capability needed to protect the Arab monarchies of the Gulf. "Capability", however, depends on the uses for which force is needed. At present it is true that no Asian power has the capability to defend the regimes/states against an all-out attack by a major regional or global power. Asian powers, however, have an increasing ability to act in defence of the sea-lanes to and from the Gulf. Indian naval strength in the Indian Ocean seems likely to surpass that of the US in the near future.[26]

The final factor is **external powers' perceptions of their interests.** Global powers must balance their strategic involvement in different parts of the world according to perceptions of where their primary interests lie – and how much of their effort can be devoted outside of this arena. As is evident from the contents of this book, there are differing views on whether the United States will continue to see the Gulf as a primary area of interest or will need to "rebalance towards Asia". Within the US government itself there are differing assessments of the Gulf's significance to US interests. The outcome of debates on this (in US governing circles) will set the parameters of how much room there will be for others to come in.

5. China and the Possibility of a Security-Related Strategic Relationship with Gulf States

It would be impossible to cover adequately here the role which all of the major Asian powers could play in security-related strategic relationships in the Gulf region. As China is currently rising to a position of influence in global leadership, it seems apposite to take China as the primary focus. Some reference will be made to other Asian powers, to indicate a degree of complementarity in their positions.

The possibility of China playing a role in security issues in the Gulf region has already figured in regional and external speculative discourse. This stems in part from a spreading realisation of the extent and importance of China's economic stake in the area (as documented earlier in the chapter). It also comes, however, from the increasing activity/assertiveness of Chinese foreign policy, the declared intention of the Chinese leadership to "build China into a maritime power", and the adoption of a Chinese naval policy for the Indian Ocean.[27] The assumption is made that these developments could presage a more active security role for China in the Gulf. The undoubted importance of the region to China's economic interests would provide the rationale for, and justification of, such an engagement.

The perception that China has adopted a more assertive or active international posture in recent years (roughly since 2009) is one which is shared by both Chinese and external observers. Western observers, especially those worried by the new directions of policy, use the word "assertive" (implying the adoption of hard-line positions) to describe the new posture, while Chinese governmental spokesmen use the more positive term "active". Thus, the Chinese foreign minister, in an interview where he outlined the achievements of Chinese foreign policy since the 18th National Congress, emphasised that "a more active policy" was the underlying theme.[28] He described this in terms of China having become more engaged in international leadership, being more active in defending its interests, and opening up new links with governments around the world. Western observers, using the term "assertive", refer to the Chinese pursuit of sovereignty claims in the East and South China Seas, resistance to Western policies over Syria, Iran, Zimbabwe etc., and China's intensified involvement in organisations (such as the Shanghai Cooperation Organisation) and regional alliances which are outside the influence of the United States or other Western powers. Some would see the increasing use of the term "strategic" in agreements which China has reached with Gulf countries as evidence of enhanced assertiveness of Chinese policy in the Gulf.

Complementing the more active/assertive foreign policy has been the expansion, and intended development, of defence capability. Of key importance here has been the announcement that the Chinese leadership is intent on "building China into a maritime power", and the intensified programme of naval expansion currently under way. The ability of any power to project naval power beyond its coastal waters (a "brown water" facility) to the global oceanic environment (a "blue water" facility) is often described in terms of the availability of aircraft carrriers, although in practice what is important is not so much the carrier itself but the "carrier group" which includes accompanying destroyers, minesweepers, submarines etc. In September 2012 China's first aircraft carrier, a re-fitted and previously unused carrier purchased from Ukraine, became operational, and a carrier group is being developed to support it. A second aircraft carrier is currently under construction in the Dalian shipyards of North-East China. The intention to construct two more aircraft carriers "by 2020" has also been announced, but no indication has been given of when construction might begin. In practice, the possibility of China having four more aircraft carriers by 2020 is minimal, given that an aircraft carrier takes some 6 years to make and bring into operation. The attendant carrier groups, moreover, may take even longer to put in place. Nonetheless, it is clear that China is developing a blue water capacity, and the naval manoeuvres which have been held in the last two years in the vicinity of the Malacca Straits indicates that a blue water naval strategy is also being developed. Further evidence of the latter was the publication in June 2013 of the "Blue Book on the Indian Ocean", which lays out for the first time Chinese naval thinking on the Indian Ocean – and the role which China could play there; in addition to the increasing prominence given to the "maritime silk route" in Chinese public statements.[29]

In the light of the increasing activity/assertiveness of Chinese global policy, and of the developing capacity for China to act as a maritime power (with an indication that China sees itself with a role to play in the Indian Ocean), it seems rational to envisage a possible role for China in security issues in the Gulf. It will be argued here, however, that this is not likely – at least in terms of the "Gulf Security" activities which the United States and other Western powers have undertaken. Before developing this argument, it is important to "unpack" the notion of Gulf Security, so that its different components can be considered separately. As noted before, Western use of the term comprises three elements: the protection of regimes against unwelcome domestic political change; the prevention of external attack (whether from within the Gulf or outside); and the protection of the sea-lanes leading from the Gulf to the rest of the world (primarily through the Indian Ocean). The contention of the writer is that China has no interest in engaging with the first two elements, and that its interest in the third is in working cooperatively with other powers in ensuring the safety of the sea-lanes (much as it is doing already in the anti-piracy operations in the Eastern Indian Ocean).

Three key dimensions sustain this argument. First, **the Gulf is not defined as a Chinese "core interest"**. The term "core interest" has been of key importance to the Chinese government in defining its foreign policy interests in recent years, especially within the context of China's "new type of great power relations" with the United States. The concept is used to identify the interests which arc of key concern to China. The intention is to identify areas which are of key concern to China. The intention is that the United States will similarly identify its own core interests – and each side will then take care not to threaten the core interests of the other. Although the United States has not been eager to follow this line (seeing its own interests as much wider and less amenable to arbitrary limitation than China's), the joint statement which followed the 2009 China-US summit meeting did, nonetheless, use the term - recognising the need to respect core interests. The 2010 summit did not use the term, but made reference to the 2009 document. China originally used the term in relation to Chinese national interests in Tibet, Xinjiang and Taiwan, but the 2011 White Paper on China's Peaceful Development (a key document of Chinese foreign policy) defined China's core interests as comprising:

i. State sovereignty, national security, territorial integrity and national reunification.

ii. The Chinese political system established by the Constitution and overall social stability.

iii. The basic safeguards for ensuring sustainable economic and social development.[30]

There has never been any suggestion that any of these "core interests" might impinge on Chinese relations with Gulf countries. In fact the opposite is true. China, meeting with some reluctance on the US side for the US to define its own core interests, has for its own part recognised a number of US core interests (as China perceives them). One of these is "the prevention of nuclear proliferation in Iran". In practice the Iranian nuclear issue is linked into a variety of other aspects of US Gulf relations, so the Chinese concession of US "core interests" in this regard could be regarded as covering the Gulf region in general. It should be noted, moreover, that US engagement in the Gulf can be regarded as serving a Chinese interest, in so far as it distracts the US from focusing on East Asia – where China's core interests are located.

Second, **China has nothing to gain from engagement in security issues in the Gulf.** Present security arrangements in the Gulf are in fact much to China's advantage, although this perhaps can not be openly acknowledged. China's access to Gulf oil is, effectively, safeguarded by the US navy, at considerable expense to the US and no expense to China. China gains considerably, moreover, from being able to trade with and invest in all of the 8 countries of the Gulf. Engagement in regional security issues, in current conditions, would inevitably bring this to an end, requiring China to side with one Gulf state (or group of Gulf states) against another. China's interests lie in it being able to project itself as a friend of all states in the region, and a dispassionate partner to all – based on the mutual benefits which are drawn from the relationships. The Chinese position is also influenced by the rather negative view which Chinese policy-makers have of the Middle Eastern region and especially of the record of external engagement there. They tend to see the Middle East (not inaccurately) as a treacherous morass into which great powers are drawn, and where security engagement has led these powers into heavy expenditure and considerable damage to their global credibility. Nor should one discount the importance of China's ideological (and security-driven) adhesion to the principle of national sovereignty and its aversion to policies which could compromise this principle. China's own "hundred years of humiliation" reminds policy-makers that an external strategic presence and external interference in the domestic political scene often go together.

Third, **China has limited capacity for a potentially-combative role in the Indian Ocean**. While the acquisition of an aircraft carrier, and the planned construction of others, may be sufficient to enable China to pursue a maritime strategy, the naval strength is not significant when compared with that of the United States. While China currently has one aircraft carrier in operation, the US has 11. The USS George Washington by itself, moreover, can carry three times as many fighter-planes as the Liaoning (the existing aircraft carrier). Even if China does have three aircraft carriers in operation by 2020, the overall naval capacity of all three together may not exceed that of one US aircraft carrier. China's concerns, moreover, are primarily with the East and South Asia Seas, where the country's most pressing security interests are located. It is not likely to be distracted from this.

It follows from these three points that China will not see its interests in terms of a direct security engagement in the Gulf. It does have an interest in maintaining a naval presence in the Indian Ocean, but the emphasis here is on cooperating with other great powers in maintaining the safety and security of the shipping lanes – not in seeking to displace other great powers from the region (which would, in any case, be a highly unrealistic objective). The Blue Book on the Indian Ocean, published in June 2013, defines China's objectives in the Indian Ocean as being commercial and not military.[31] There is no reason to doubt this. The model being followed is that of the anti-piracy operations in the Western Indian Ocean, where the Chinese navy works closely with other navies – and in particular coordinates its activities closely with Japan, India and South Korea. The deep water port facilities which China has been helping develop along its "Maritime Silk Route", in Myanmar, Bangladesh, Sri Lanka, and Pakistan would be able to house and service People's Liberation Army Navy (PLAN) ships and submarines, but they would be of little use in the case of a regional conflict. All are within the range of the Indian Air Force – among other regional armed forces. Their primary purpose is to act as commercial bridgeheads for Chinese companies.

It is important to bear in mind, furthermore, that India is better placed than China to engage with the Gulf in security terms. India tends to regard the Indian Ocean, with the access into the Gulf, as an area where India does or should have "natural pre-eminence". While this would not be acceptable to China or to some other powers, India does have a substantial naval presence there, and the support lines from India are not hard to maintain. Nonetheless, India shares with China many of the same interests and principles which lead China away from seeking a direct security presence in the Gulf. An Indian security role in the Gulf, moreover, would raise sensitivities in the Gulf countries. With 6 million Indians currently present in the Gulf region, the addition of a security role might raise concern over the extent of Indian influence in and on the region.

6. Conclusion

The changing economic orientation of Gulf states is significant, especially as the predominance of Asian countries in Gulf trade, contracting and increasingly investment, is likely to intensify over the coming years. The economic interests which have led the United States and other Western countries to adopt security roles in the Gulf will not constitute so strong a motivating force as they have done in the past – although wider questions of global strategy may still provide the rationale for a strategic presence in the region. Any lessening of Western interest in maintaining a security presence in the Gulf, however, is unlikely to be substituted by a Chinese (or any other Asian) security presence. It is not in the interest of Asian powers to play such a role. Nor is it in the interests of Gulf countries themselves, which stand most to gain from terminating their reliance on external powers for security, and instead finding ways to handle their security by resolving intra-Gulf conflicts and creating collective security institutions for the Gulf region. They would, in the latter context, then be able to cooperate with other powers in securing the safety of the shipping lanes in the wider Indian Ocean area.

Notes

1   Official statements (at least on the Chinese side) did on occasion refer to "strategic cooperation", such as in the course of President Hu Jintao's visit to Saudi Arabia in April 2006. The Xinhua General News Service reported on 24 April that the Chinese president had talked of his enthusiasm for "advancing strategic cooperation" with Saudi Arabia. The context of the president's speech, however, made it clear that it was the economic and cultural dimensions of "strategic cooperation" in which China was interested, and in fact the Chinese government had already assured the United States at this stage that it was not "creating a new alliance with Riyadh against US vital interests" (E.T.C. Cheow, "China's Emerging Role in the Middle East", *Pacnet*, no. 7, 23 February 2006). Accessed at http://csis.org/files/media/csis/pubs/pac0607.pdf.

2   See Tim Niblock, "China's Growing Involvement in the Gulf", in Simon Chen and Jean-Marc Blanchard, *Multidimensional Diplomacy of Contemporary China* (New York: Lexington Books, p. 216).

3   See, for example, Schmidt, Anne, "Strategic Partnerships – a Contested Concept", SWP Working Papers, Berlin, December 2010.

4   For example Grevi, Giovanni, "The Rise of Strategic Partnerships: between Interdependence and Power Politics", in G.Grevi and A.Vasconcellos, eds, *Partnerships for Effective Multilateralism: EU Relations with Brazil, China, India and Russia.* Chaillot Paper 109 (Paris: IIUSS, 2008).

5   It may seem surprising that there could be an Asian concept of strategic relationship, given that the governments of the region espouse very different ideologies and approaches to international relations. In practice, the clearest adherence to this definition of strategic relationship is that espoused by the Chinese government. Nonetheless, it does figure in the foreign policies of most other Asian countries besides China. India's strategic partners do seem to be geared more to defence/political cooperation, but

6   there also the defence/political dimension is not necessarily inherent in the relationship. In the 2010 statement by the Indian and Saudi governments on the establishment of a strategic partnership between them the emphasis is almost entirely on the economic fields.

6   There are, admittedly, some exceptions to this. The EU-China Comprehensive Strategic Partnership, created in 2003, does cover defence as well as economic issues, even though in practice it has been the economic and diplomatic-political aspects of the relationship which have been the main focus of cooperation.

7   See, Niblock, Tim, "The Role of East Asian Countries in the Evolving Security Dynamics and Architecture of the Gulf Region" in Tim Niblock and Yang Guang, eds, *Security Dynamics of East Asia in the Gulf Region* (Berlin and London: Gerlach, 2014).

8   It is important to note that the base year taken here is 2005. By that year China and India had already established themselves as major Gulf trade partners – ranking 5th and 6th. If the year 2000 had been taken as the base year the rates of increase would have been significantly larger, but that would have reflected mainly the low base from which the trade of these two countries started.

9   The figures given by BP in its 2014 report are that non-OPEC oil supply will increase by 2035 by 3.6 mbd in the US, 3.4 mbd in Canada, and 2.4 mbd in Brazil. BP, *BP Energy Outlook 2035* (London: BP, January 2014), 25.

10   "Liquids" refers to both oil from conventional sources (crude oil, natural gas liquids and condensate liquids) and unconventional sources (oil from oil sands, extra heavy oil, gas liquids etc).

11   BP, *BP Energy Outlook 2035* (London: BP, January 2014), p. 25.

12   BP, *BP Energy Outlook 2035* (London: BP, January 2014), p. 39.

13   The slowing down of the Chinese economy, which has been apparent in late 2104 and early 2015, may lead to a lesser growth in China's oil demand than that which is predicted here. There is little doubt, however, that – unless there is a major breakdown of the Chinese economy – there will still be a significant increase in China's demand for oil. Paradoxically, the hydrocarbons link between China and the Gulf is likely to be strengthened as a result of ongoing developments. It seems likely, as is evident in the falling price of oil, that global oil is entering a "buyers' market" phase, and that Asian states will be the main buyers of Gulf oil. Gulf oil exporters may need to be more pro-active in fostering good relations with China so as to ensure that the Chinese market looks favourably on them.

14   BP, *BP Energy Outlook 2035* (London: BP, January 2014), p. 27.

15   There are some European-Gulf strategic partnerships which do appear to be mainly economic. One example of this is the Germany-UAE strategic partnership, concluded in April 2004. The latter does, however, have some clauses in it related to political cooperation. Accessed June 2014 at http://www.auswaertiges-amt.de/EN/Aussenpolitik/Laender/Laenderinfos/01-Nodes/VAE_node.html.

16   Presidential address to Congress, 31 January 2006.

17   See Norafidah Ismail, "The Political and Economic Relations of the People's Republic of China and the Kingdom of Saudi Arabia, 1949-2010" (University of Exeter: Unpublished PhD, 2011), section 4.4.3.

18   Reported in a China government press release entitled "Third Round of China-Gulf Cooperation Council Strategic Dialogue Held in Beijing, on 17 January 2014". Accessed June 2014 at http://www.chinese-embassy.org.uk/eng/zgyw/t1121625.htm

19   "GCC China to Set up Strategic Partnership", 17 January 2014. Accessed April 2014 at http://in.news.yahoo.com/gcc-china-set_strategic_partnership-120806711.html.

20   It is, in fact, difficult to discern precisely what the South Korea-UAE strategic partnership consists of. There is no published text which is available, but both sides frequently make mention of their strategic partnership (See, for example, UAEinteract, "Abdullah bin Zayed Stresses the Importance of Strategic Partnership between UAE and South Korea", 26 February 2014. Accessed April 2014 at http://www.uaeinteract.com/docs/Abdullah_bin_Zayed_stresses_the_importance_of_strategic_partnership_between_UAE_and_South_Korea/53719.htm. See also Joachim Kolb, "Small is

Beautiful: South Korean-Gulf Relations as an Example of Strategic Engagement by Players in Different Areas", in *Asia-Gulf Economic Relations in the 21st Century: the Local to Global Transformation*, ed. Tim Niblock, with Monica Malik (Berlin and London, Gerlach Press, 2013), 289-319; Jeongmin Seo, "Changing Gulf-South Korea Strategic Interests: Nuclear to Military Cooperation", in *Security Dynamics of East Asia in the Gulf Region*, ed. Tim Niblock, with Yang Guang (Berlin and London, Gerlach, 2014).

21 This appears to consist of a variety of different agreements in a variety of fields. See Bahrain News Agency, "Bahrain-Japanese Relations: A Solid Partnership and Fruitful", 21 March 2013. Accessed April 2014 at http://www.bna.bh/portal/en/news/552588. Most of the agreements are simply economic, cultural or technological, but there is also one on defence exchanges between the Ministries of Defence on both sides.

22 India's foreign relations are sometimes described as characterised by an absence of foreign alliances and a multiplicity of strategic partnerships. The latter, therefore, inevitably comprise military-, defence- and politics-related elements, enabling India to balance between a variety of powers in safeguarding its security-related interests. India's main strategic partnerships are with leading world powers rather than with less powerful countries.

23 See South Asia Analysis Group, "India Jettisons Strategic Partnership with Iran under United States Pressure: a Perceptional Analysis", 25 March 2013. Accessed April 2014 at http://www.southasiaanalysis. org/node/1213.

24 Bodeen, C., 'China aligns with India, Japan on piracy patrols', *The Guardian*, 3 July 2012, accessed June 2014 at: http://www.guardian.co.uk.; and 'Anti-piracy bid: South Korea joins India, Japan, China', *The Times of India*, 13 June 2012, accessed June 2014 at: http://timesofindia.indiatimes.com.

25 See, for example, Marhoun, Abd al-Jalil, "A New Paradigm for Gulf Security: Regional Security System Based on Local Structures Necessary to Confront Future Crises". Accessed June 2014at: http://www. aljazeera.com/focus/2010/07/201072013104813376.html. Iran has, of course, consistently advocated a regional security system, where external powers would be excluded. For this position see Mazaheri, Mohammad Mehdi,"A Framework for Persian Gulf Security", *Iran Review*, March 2012. Accessed June 2014 at http://www.iranreview.org/content/Documents/A_Framework_for_Persian_Gulf_ Security.htm.

26 Indian currently has two carrier groups in the Indian Ocean, and a further one is expected to be operational from 2018. Recently Rear Admiral Atul Kumar Jain of the Eastern Naval Command stated that it was India's intention to have a 200-ship navy within the next 10 years. Whether this is attainable is questionable, but the current heavy investment in the Indian navy makes it clear that serious attempts are being made to reach the objective. See "India: Budding Blue-Water Capabilities", in *The Daily Signal*, 10 December 2013. Accessed June 2014 at http://daily.signal.com/print/?post_ id=133251.

27 The announcement that China sought to become a maritime power was made by President Hu Jintao in his address to the 18th Congress of the Chinese Communist Party, on 7 November 2013. See http:// www.ft.com/cms/s/0/ebd9b4ae-296f-11e2-a604-00144feabdc0.html#axzz35l9ENIUw, accessed June 2014. The Blue Book on the Indian Ocean, formally entitled "Development Report on the Indian Ocean", was published by the Chinese Academy of Social Sciences in June 2013. See http://www. dailymirror.lk/business/features/31520-chinas-new-blue-book-for-the-indian-ocean.html, accessed June 2014.

28 Xinhuanet, "China Pursues Peaceful Development, Active International Role", accessed February 2015 at http://news.xinhuanet.com/english/special/2014-03/08/c_133170742.htm.

29 "Development Report on the Indian Ocean", *op.cit.*

30 Government of the People's Republic of China, "The Path of China's Peaceful Development", accessed February 2015 at http://www.china.org.cn/government/whitepaper/2011-09/06/content_23362449. htm.

31 "Development Report on the Indian Ocean", *op.cit.*

Bibliography

Bodeen, C., 'China aligns with India, Japan on piracy patrols', *The Guardian*, 3 July 2012. Accessed June 2014 at: http://www.guardian.co.uk.

BP, *BP Energy Outlook 2035* (London: BP, January 2014).

Cheow, E., "China's Emerging Role in the Middle East", *Pacnet*, no. 7, 23 February 2006). Accessed at http://csis.org/files/media/csis/pubs/pac0607.pdf.

China government press release entitled "Third Round of China-Gulf Cooperation Council Strategic Dialogue Held in Beijing, on 17 January 2014". Accessed June 2014 at http://www.chinese-embassy. org.uk/eng/zgyw/t1121625.htm.

Government of the People's Republic of China, "The Path of China's Peaceful Development". Accessed February 2015 at http://www.china.org.cn/government/whitepaper/2011-09/06/content_23362449. htm.

Grevi, Giovanni, "The Rise of Strategic Partnerships: between Interdependence and Power Politics", in G.Grevi and A.Vasconcellos, eds, *Partnerships for Effective Multilateralism: EU Relations with Brazil, China, India and Russia*. Chaillot Paper 109 (Paris: IIUSS, 2008).

"India: Budding Blue-Water Capabilities", in *The Daily Signal*, 10 December 2013. Accessed June 2014 at http://daily.signal.com/print/?post_id=133251.

Ismail, Norafidah, "The Political and Economic Relations of the People's Republic of China and the Kingdom of Saudi Arabia, 1949-2010" (University of Exeter: Unpublished PhD, 2011).

Kolb, Joachim, "Small is Beautiful: South Korean-Gulf Relations as an Example of Strategic Engagement by Players in Different Areas", in *Asia-Gulf Economic Relations in the 21ˢᵗ Century: the Local to Global Transformation*, ed. Tim Niblock, with Monica Malik (Berlin and London: Gerlach Press, 2013), 289-319.

Marhoun, Abd al-Jalil, "A New Paradigm for Gulf Security: Regional Security System Based on Local Structures Necessary to Confront Future Crises". Accessed June 2014 at: http://www.aljazeera.com/ focus/2010/07/201072013104813376.html.

Mazaheri, Mohammad Mehdi, "A Framework for Persian Gulf Security", *Iran Review*, March 2012. Accessed June 2014 at http://www.iranreview.org/content/Documents/A_Framework_for_Persian_ Gulf_Security.htm.

Niblock, Tim, "China's Growing Involvement in the Gulf", in Simon Chen and Jean-Marc Blanchard, *Multidimensional Diplomacy of Contemporary China* (New York: Lexington Books, p. 216).

Niblock, Tim, "The Role of East Asian Countries in the Evolving Security Dynamics and Architecture of the Gulf Region" in Tim Niblock and Yang Guang, eds, *Security Dynamics of East Asia in the Gulf Region* (Berlin and London: Gerlach, 2014).

Schmidt, Anne, "Strategic Partnerships – a Contested Concept", SWP Working Papers, Berlin, December 2010.

Seo, Jeongmin, "Changing Gulf-South Korea Strategic Interests: Nuclear to Military Cooperation", in *Security Dynamics of East Asia in the Gulf Region*, ed. Tim Niblock, with Yang Guang (Berlin and London: Gerlach, 2014).

South Asia Analysis Group, "India Jettisons Strategic Partnership with Iran under United States Pressure: a Perceptional Analysis", 25 March 2013. Accessed April 2014 at http://www.southasiaanalysis.org/ node/1213.

2

Hegemonic Stability and American Power

Steven W. Hook

1. Introduction

The defining feature of the global balance of power since World War II has been the predominance of the United States in the global balance of power. In contrast to other great powers, the United States emerged from the war stronger militarily and economically. With economic output in 1946 greater than all other countries combined, American leaders adopted a grand strategy of sustained primacy whose aim was to extend the unipolar era far into the future.

This strategy was directly linked to three broad tactics of US foreign policy. The first focused on rebuilding Western economies and creating the foundations of a market-based trading regime. The second tactic focused on promoting democratic governance and creating international institutions and laws that would discourage militarized violence while protecting citizens' political and human rights. The third tactic of sustained primacy involved the Cold War containment strategy that provided a stable and relatively benign basis for bilateral relations with the Soviet Union and its proxies.

A common term describing America's stature during this period is *hegemony*, a concentration of power that provides the preponderant state a sphere of influence over weaker nation-states at the regional or global levels.[1] Hegemony may be considered oppressive if it submits weaker states to coercive control.[2] A more cooperative model produces "win-win" outcomes as the hegemon provides material and public goods that benefit weaker states while preserving the hegemon's stature. Such an arrangement confers a degree of legitimacy on the hegemon that must ultimately gain "a status bestowed by others... in the exploitation of asymmetries for collective advantage."[3] It is this latter form of hegemony that characterizes the American role in the global power balance since World War II.

Early in the 1970s, analysts of world politics became interested in the growing interdependence of nation-states, due in large measure to technological advances, the recognition of transnational problems, and the accelerating globalization of the world economy.[4] Such interdependence, particularly in the economic domain, complicated existing assumptions about hegemony, as it became clear that asymmetric power balances must be moderated through the provision of public goods that were not affordable to weaker states but were also vital for the maintenance of a stable economic system and world order in general. As the political economist Charles Kindleberger demonstrated, such a tacit contract provided for the adoption of America's hegemonic stability.[5] This arrangement was embraced by many liberal theorists, particularly those from the international society tradition who sensed an opening for shared values and new forms of global governance.[6]

Theorists from the neo-Marxists tradition, however, were skeptical of the presumed positive-sum gains to be realized under hegemonic stability. Their doubts were based upon the notion of Gramscian "historical blocs" that, far from sharing universal values, served instead as instruments of co-optation.[7] To theorist Richard Saull, "hegemony rests on *consensual acceptance of socioeconomic and political hierarchy* through a network of social, ideational, cultural, and institutional means" (italics in original).[8] Critical theorists also argued that hegemonic stability, far from locking in cooperative ties between rich and poor states, instead locked impoverished states in the Global South into permanent positions of economic dependence.

Neo-realists also expressed doubts about hegemonic stability, although from a different perspective. Robert Gilpin argued that the provision of public goods such as political, military, and economic security could not be sustained indefinitely as hegemons inevitably faced rising costs and commitments.[9] Such erosion in the hegemon's ability to maintain a stable world order, Gilpin observed, would favor rising states that had benefited from the hegemon's provision of public goods. The intersection of the declining hegemon and the rising great-power challenger would likely trigger systematic conflict and a changing of the hegemonic guard. Despite these critiques, the logic of hegemonic stability continues to inform popular assumptions and expectations of world politics. A systemic shift toward bipolarity or multipolarity, it is feared, would reduce the incentives of major powers to provide weaker states essential public goods.

This chapter examines US primacy in the context of hegemonic stability theory. We begin by recalling the historical experience of the United States as a rising, then preponderant hegemonic power. The chapter then examines the hard and soft power assets that have enabled the persistence of the nation's primacy for seven decades. In the third section, we place these assets in the context of geopolitical shifts in the balance of power. We then outline a series of challenges to sustained US primacy that stem from historic and domestic experience. The fifth section considers transnational regimes as barometers of hegemonic influence, focusing specifically on the development aid regime that the United States and European powers have overseen for the past fifty years. Finally, we consider US actions in the Middle East that reveal weakening US hegemonic influence in the region.

2. The Roots of American Primacy

Maintaining a "predominance of power" has been a central goal of US foreign policy since World War II.[10] The Cold War strategy of communist containment advanced this overriding goal of sustained primacy. Following the Cold War, the George H.W. Bush administration devised a strategy to convince "potential competitors that they need not aspire to a greater role."[11] To Bill Clinton, who served as president from 1993 to 2001, the United States must remain the "indispensable nation." His successor, George W. Bush, vowed after the 9/11 terrorist attacks that US military forces "will be strong enough to dissuade potential adversaries from pursuing a military build-up in hopes of surpassing, or equaling, the power of the United States."[12] Most recently, while recognizing the domestic limitations of America's world power, the Obama administration proclaimed that the nation "will continue to underwrite global security."[13]

History provides no case of such pervasive aspirations of hegemony. Indeed, studies of hegemony suffer from a "small-n" problem due to the lack of modern hegemonic contracts. The Concert of Europe performed some of the functions of hegemonic rule, particularly with its emphasis on maintaining regional stability and respect for sovereign authority. The era of *Pax Britannica* was founded upon an economic basis, conferring material benefits to peripheral states that participated in a market-driven trade regime that preceded the US Revolutionary War.[14] A purer system of hegemonic rule was created by the US government just four decades after its independence, as the Monroe Doctrine established a sphere of influence from the southern border to the furthest reaches of Latin America. The hegemonic mission was largely defensive – discouraging re-colonization of the region – but US leaders established diplomatic ties designed to foster economic integration and trade. While the United States later exploited asymmetric power relations along the Pacific Rim later in the nineteenth century, gaining favorable terms of trade in China and Japan, US leaders adopted the colonial model in assuming control of the Philippines from 1902 until 1946.

The post-World War II broadened the scope of hegemonic influence to include Western Europe, whose governments accepted the US provision of military security through the North Atlantic Treaty Organization (NATO). The United States conferred the same benefits upon its Pacific Rim allies in Japan, South Korea, and the Philippines. The postwar regional hegemony of the United States later encouraged its leaders to pursue dozens of state-building missions in the developing world. This effort took on a new urgency in the early 1960s with the decolonization of Africa and growing concerns about poverty in Latin America. President John Kennedy's Peace Corps, Alliance for Progress, and foreign aid programs supported political reform as well as economic development in these areas.

With the end of the Cold War the global balance of power shifted from bipolarity to a unipolar structure dominated by the United States. Realist theories of world politics generally frown upon such a power balance for three reasons.[15] First, they presume that the dominant power will exploit its stature by taking advantage of weaker states. Second, a unipolar balance of power can only be temporary, as the costs of maintaining its control will inevitably exhaust the global hegemon.[16] Finally, second-tier powers in a unipolar world will be dissatisfied with this arrangement and would seek to bring down the hegemon. A return to bipolarity or a multipolar world of many great powers will create a true balance of power.

While realists draw upon modern history in making these claims, they fail to account for the unique nature of American primacy. As one scholar observed, "the current world would be very different if it had been the US and Western Europe rather than the USSR that had collapsed."[17] For the United States, whose foreign policy served as an extension of its values as well as hard power, global primacy would be best preserved through the creation of a liberal world order. In such a system, smaller states would be drawn into a network of global governance that established rules of cooperative behavior and imposed sanctions on governments that broke those rules. For its part, the United States would underwrite the costs of this liberal order and abide by the same rules set out for weaker states. In sum, the United States would assume the rule of a "liberal leviathan" whose unrivaled power would be directed toward constructive ends.[18]

Washington's construction of this liberal world order had a life of its own and related only indirectly to the onset of the Cold War. The creation of the United Nations provided "voice opportunities" for all states in the General Assembly and opportunities for the five permanent members of the Security Council to pursue collective security. The same motivations prompted US leaders to ensure that newly created multilateral bodies such as the United Nations and World Bank "locked in" US advantages after World War II while providing tangible benefits for less powerful countries.[19] After the Cold War, the network of multilateral institutions and agreements led to the creation of the World Trade Organization and International Criminal Court. While member states retained their sovereignty, most were careful to follow the rules of the liberal order in order to maintain profitable trade and other ties with more powerful governments.

As noted earlier, however, modern hegemons are expected to adhere to the tacit contract they entered into with weaker states. To many analysts, foreign leaders, and public-interest advocates, recent actions by the US government have turned away from this hegemonic bargain. The George W. Bush's preemptive war against Iraq and documented reports of torture against suspected terrorists, were widely condemned by foreign governments. Also deeply troubling was the US-based financial crisis of 2007 and 2008 that sparked a globalized economic slowdown. More recently, President Barack Obama's escalation of drone warfare drew widespread concern and revelations of espionage by the US National Security Agency targeting US allies further eroded the international community's trust in American power.

This array of grievances, combined with the deepening erosion of US financial security, has made it "questionable whether the United States retains the credibility and legitimacy to spearhead the revamping of the international order."[20]

3. The Metrics of American Primacy

The concentration of America's world power detailed is notable given that the United States is home to less than 5 percent of the world's population. Much of the nation's advantage derives from the global scale of its economy, which produced $16.8 trillion in goods and services, or about 19 percent of the world's total in 2013. America's economic production exceeded that of China ($9.1 billion in 2013) and is roughly the volume of all the countries of Europe, whose regional economy has been battered in recent years by weaknesses in its monetary union. Russia, the heart of the former Soviet Union, has produced less than 10 percent annually since the Cold War. Of the top twenty multinational corporations in the world in terms of 2013 revenues, six are based in the United States.

The United States holds the additional distinction of being the world's foremost trading state, exporting more than all other nations since World War II while displaying a voracious appetite for overseas goods and services. American firms exported more than $1.6 trillion in merchandise in 2011 while providing more than $600 billion in services overseas. The nation's imports were even larger in absolute terms (more than $2.3 trillion in 2013) and as a share of world imports. The United States has also served as the world's leading source and destination of foreign direct investment (FDI) in recent years. In 2011, US firms spent $419 billion on foreign operations, about one-quarter of the global total. Foreign firms, meanwhile, invested more in the United States ($234 billion) than in any other country (OECD 2012).

The degree of US predominance is even greater in the military realm. The United States, the only country that has divided the world into regional military commands, also maintains "command of the commons—command of the sea, space, and air."[21] This is a major geopolitical asset in an age in which holding physical territory, while vital, does not ensure national security. In recent years the US government has averaged about nearly $650 billion on military defense, almost 40 percent of the global total (see Table 1). This edge in military spending is compounded by the superior technology of US weapons systems and the dominant position of the United States in its military alliances. In addition to its unrivaled defense forces, the United States annually provides the largest volume of weaponry to other countries, with American defense contractors representing seven of the top ten worldwide in terms of defense revenues in 2013. In 2011, American arms merchants signed sales agreements with foreign governments amounting to $66 billion, or 78 percent of all weapons sales worldwide.[22] At the same time, the United States annually provides more than 100 foreign governments with military training and education, further solidifying its projection of world power.

American primacy also derives from its soft power, the expression of its political and cultural values that other societies and governments find appealing.[23] The United States is often regarded as an "idea" rather than an ordinary nation-state as defined by physical boundaries, common ethnic or religious identities, and material interests. This "idea" combines several features of US government and society: limited government, individual liberties, free markets, and vibrant forms of cultural expression. The soft power of the United States is reflected in many ways. A recent study found that thirteen of the world's top twenty universities—ideal centers for the sharing of ideas, knowledge, and culture—are located in the United States. American fashions, popular music, movies, and television programs are so pervasive overseas that they provoke charges of cultural imperialism. These charges aside, US inventors are widely credited for bringing the world personal computers, the Internet, Facebook, YouTube, instant messaging, and Tweets – not to mention baseball.

4. Geographic Shifts and Continuities

This unmatched combination of hard and soft power allows the US government to maintain its primacy in a unipolar balance of world power. This primacy, in turn, enables the United States to cover the costs of collective (or public) goods that weaker states rely on in return for their acquiescence to US hegemony. This deference, in turn, fosters the multilateral cooperation that is needed to empower international law, build problem-solving regimes, and engender trust in ways that discourage the use of military force.

These presumed benefits of hegemonic stability, however, may at risk given widespread expectations that the People's Republic of China (PRC) will begin surpassing the United States on a variety of power metrics in the next decade or two. According to the National Intelligence Council,[24] China is likely to have the largest volume of global power by 2042, as measured by a formula derived from a variety of economic, military, and social indicators. The same forecast envisions the PRC surpassing the European Union in 2035. Longer-term projections expect India to catch up with the United States and EU between 2050 and 2060, although its trajectory runs parallel to that of China, albeit at a much lower level of aggregate power.

For decades, the prospect of China "rising" has preoccupied strategic analysts in the United States. Debates continue as to whether China poses a threat to US primacy and hegemonic influence. According to Aaron Friedberg,[25] a prominent China expert, the United States and China have "strategic objectives that threaten the fundamental interests of the others side." Other analysts adopt a more optimistic view of the bilateral relationship. "The main task of Chinese foreign policy are defensive and have not changed much since the Cold War," Nathan and Scobell[26] observed, "to blunt destabilizing influences from abroad, to avoid territorial losses, to reduce its neighbors' suspicions, and to sustain economic growth." As these debates continue today, in the midst of heightened regional disputes over territorial waters, perhaps the best source of guidance comes from Deng Xiaoping, China's premier from 1978 to 1992 who opened the PRC to global commerce. According to his 24-Character Strategy, "observe calmly, secure our position, cope with affairs calmly, hide our capabilities and bide our time, be good at managing a low profile, and never claim leadership."

The medium-term prospect is a return to bipolarity, which characterized the balance of power during most of the Cold War. As in the Cold War, however, Sino-American bipolar parity is not likely to displace US hegemonic influence, its provision of public goods, and the "constitutional" world order that was forged in the aftermath of World War II. Whereas the Soviet Union's basis for parity with the United States was founded on the Kremlin's military strength and nuclear deterrence, China's equalizing asset will on rest on economic grounds.

The Obama administration clearly recognized this shift by initiating a geopolitical "pivot" from the trans-Atlantic region to East Asia.

Three features of the PRC and its regional alignments mitigate its geo-economic parity with the United States. First, China lacks the US soft-power assets due its authoritarian government, its denial of political and human rights, and the lack of a dynamic civil society that both reflects and propagates social, political, and cultural values that are attractive to other states and societies. Second, China's economy remains dependent on the manufacturing and assembly of consumer goods, largely for export. While providing jobs for the PRC's vast population, this production model comes at the expense of technological innovation and the development of world-class educational institutions.

The third constraint on Chinese hegemonic parity involves the PRC's regional relations. Unlike the Soviet Union, which maintained "hard" hegemony through its satellites in Eastern Europe, China is surrounded by nation-states that are neither controlled by Beijing nor drawn to the PRC as a potential bloc partner. To the contrary, the governments of Japan, South Korea, Taiwan, the Philippines, Indonesia, and other regional states have drawn closer to the United States through a variety of bilateral alliances and regional economic and security arrangements. In this context, the United States "pivot" to East Asia can be seen as a means to maintain rather than establish hegemonic influences in the region.

This final factor is additionally relevant when broader intra-regional suspicions and historical resentments are considered. It is important to recall that, early in the post-World War II era, the Western European powers were socialized to accept political integration as a means to ensure regional cooperation and peace. This hub-and-spoke model of cooperation, underwritten by the NATO alliance, did not apply to East Asia, where the intra-regional divisions forced the United States to recruit allies and partners on a piecemeal basis. Once could argue, however, that this multilateral model favors US-driven hegemonic stability by limiting the likelihood that East Asian states will, in the distant future, form their own regional sphere of influence.

5. Challenges to US Hegemony

Aside its strengths in hard and soft power, the United States faces a variety of challenges to maintaining its current stature in a unipolar balance of power. As this section describes, these challenges come from several sources. They also reflect widespread societal perceptions of the nation's trajectory in this power balance. Perceptions of US decline are informed by empirical claims as well as normative concerns regarding US foreign-policy actions, which have raised doubts about the American government's adherence to the "consensual" relationship with lesser governments. Historical experience suggests that the conduct of any dominant state determines the extent to which lesser powers align, or "bandwagon," with that state, or seek to balance against it by forming opposing blocs. When the most powerful state is "unalterably aggressive," observed political scientist Stephen M. Walt,[27] "other states are unlikely to bandwagon."

Beyond the many unpopular episodes of US foreign policy in recent years noted elsewhere in this study, more subtle forces threaten the persistence of the nation's hegemonic stature. These challenges can be grouped into three categories:

Cycles in the Balance of Power. The first challenge to sustained US hegemony is based upon historical cycles in the global balance of power. Historian Paul Kennedy traced *The Rise and Fall of the Great Powers* to a pattern of imperial overstretch by which the Roman, Dutch, Ottoman, Spanish, British, and Russian empires bit off more than they could chew, and then succumbed to uprisings in their far-flung provinces and to political infighting at home.[28] World history has revealed the "increasing costs of dominance" that accompany global primacy.[29] According to long cycle theory,[30] the dominant power's strength in relation to others inevitably peaks and then erodes as smaller powers benefit from the leader's technological advances, economic aid, and military protection. Major wars and a restructuring of the global power balance result from this cycle of hegemonic boom and bust.

Shadows of the Past. A second challenge, unique to US foreign policy, stems from past actions of the United States that have provoked resentments abroad that linger today and inspire anti-American social movements, hostile regimes, and potential threats to the nation's citizens or government.[31] Frequent interventions in Latin America revealed that for all its rhetoric about freedom and justice, the US government frequently observed the Darwinian logic of the survival of the fittest. This pattern continued during the Cold War, when US leaders turned to the Central Intelligence Agency (CIA) to overthrow elected regimes in Guatemala (1954) and Chile (1973). Elsewhere, the United States supported dictators such as Ferdinand Marcos of the Philippines and Mobutu Sese Seko of Zaire.

More recently, resistance to US hegemony persisted as the White House and Congress took a "unilateral turn" during George W. Bush's presidency, rejecting major global treaties, international laws, and the authority of the UN. The Bush Doctrine, which called for preventive attacks on state sponsors of terrorism, raised fears of open-ended military operations around the world. The invasion of Iraq, which lacked support from the UN Security Council, left the United States and Great Britain virtually alone in the "coalition of the willing." Anti-Americanism took many forms around the world during this period, ranging from general discontent over the US government's violations of its own democratic principles to "radical" efforts to transform the US-led international system.[32]

Resistance to Economic Globalization. Another challenge to US hegemony stems from the process of globalization.[33] According to the Washington Consensus, a prosperous world economy should resemble that of the United States, with few internal barriers to the movement of goods, services, labor, and capital. Trade, not political or military competition, is the primary arena of foreign policy, as "trading states" have strong interests in a stable international system and are reluctant to wage wars against each other. This neo-liberal model, however, has not produced greater economic growth in many developing states. China's system of state capitalism, meanwhile, fuels economic growth at the expense of the political freedoms of its citizens. As scholars Steven Weber and Bruce W. Jentleson observed,[34] "Those winners outside the West who have in some degree benefited (from globalization) largely attribute their good fortune not to liberal internationalism or American ideals, but rather to state-directed capitalism run by illiberal governments."

The quickening pace of economic globalization has brought improved living standards to many nations, but others have fallen behind, unable to attract foreign investment or find new markets for their goods. The growing gap between the world's rich and poor impose new strains on the international system. Critics believe globalization produces a variety of other problems: the triumph of consumerism over cultural diversity, heightened pollution and deforestation, and the exploitation of "sweatshop" laborers by MNCs. Because many of these MNCs are based in the United States, and that the US government played such a vital role in the globalization boom, the United States bears the brunt of these protests. From this perspective, globalization "aggravates anti-Americanism and appears to further isolate the United States in the world."[35] This lesson gained greater weight as a result of the financial crisis of 2007 and 2008, which was sparked by reckless US lending and banking practices.

For those who claim that the United States is in decline, the downward trend in US economic output as a percentage of world output is revealing. According to the Maddison Project, which tracks this statistic dating back to the early nineteenth century, the US share of global economic output reached a peak of about 27 percent in 1950 and has since fallen to less than 19 percent in 2013 (see Table 5).

6. Regimes as Hegemonic Barometers

Among other public goods provided by hegemons (and other highly affluent industrialized states), support for issue-based regimes that address transnational problems are vital to global governance. Hegemonic states have the financial resources to pay a disproportionate share of the regimes' costs, and they commonly take a strong role in articulating the regimes' values, ideas, and institutional forms. Like hegemonic stability theory, regime theory emerged in the 1970s with a primary goal to explain a pattern of behavior already established. In both areas, scholars of international relations (IR) have sought to explain growing evidence of inter-state cooperation in the context of a structurally anarchic world order (see Nye and Kehone 1971, Ruggie 1975 and Haas 1980).[36] Regimes are "implicit or explicit principles, norms, rules and decision-making procedures around which actors' expectations converge in a given area of international relations."[37] This language laid out a conceptual framework for regime analysis that would shape theory building for decades to come.

The development aid regime casts light on the ability of a hegemon, namely the United States with the support of like-minded industrialized states, to maintain leadership in a vital issue area. The transfer of Official Development Assistance (ODA) by the 26 member states reached record levels of ODA in recent years, peaking at $134 billion in 2011. Disbursements from the United States, by far the largest source of ODA in absolute terms, surged from $12.5 billion in 2000 to $31 billion in 2011 (OECD 2012, 268) and have remained close to that level in subsequent years.

Although aid donors retain sovereign control over their aid allocations, regime members have agreed upon a set of principles, norms, rules, and decision-making procedures roughly in keeping with the standard s regime definition. Aid donors, for example, are expected to spend at least 0.7 percent of their economic output on development aid; they are also expected to send aid as grants rather than loans and to commit a significant part of their aid to the world's poorest states. These governments, however, repeatedly voice a variety of long-standing concerns about donor ODA policies.[38] Among these complaints: the terms and functions of aid flows are dictated by elites in donor countries; conditions for aid reflect a neo-liberal bias and fail to account for regional and cultural diversity; aid flows commonly support repressive governments and/or strategic allies of donors; and too much aid is spent on overhead and on donor-based goods and services. Aid recipients also complain that most donors fall far short of the 0.7 percent threshold for aid spending.

Meanwhile, emerging donors such as China and Saudi Arabia continue to step up aid programs outside the boundaries of the current regime. In 2010 alone, these donors transferred an estimated $22 billion to developing countries while continuing to write off debts owed by impoverished states.[39] This rise in "South-South" aid transfers has challenged many of the ODA regime's norms, particularly the requirement that the volume and terms of aid transfers should be fully reported. These non-regime donors also link aid packages to trade agreements, the provision of mineral resources, and foreign direct investments, also violations of the aid regime's institutional norms. In pursuing their aid policies outside the aid regime, these donors have established an alternate and competing model of North-South development cooperation that will have long-term consequences. "It is becoming evident that the traditional focus, concepts, and approaches in the study of development and political economy are not sufficient for understanding the dynamics that are associated with the rising states as aid providers."[40] If this alternative narrative becomes embedded in rival institutions, the aid regime will weaken significantly. More generally, this trend may further signal the eroding hegemony of the United States and its reduced capacity to advance its policy goals on important global issues.

Other signs of weakening regimes reinforce this pattern. The lack of Washington's support for the Kyoto Protocol on climate change, due largely to domestic self-interests, greatly weakened prospects for meaningful reductions in fossil fuel emissions. More recently, the US government proved unable to persuade the Nuclear, Biological, and Chemical Weapons (NBC) regime to support military action against the Syrian government, whose use of chemical weapons against civilian populations violated international norms and human rights. Obama anticipated, but did not gain, support from the NBC regime and its key Western European members, providing another example of weakening US hegemonic influence.

7. "Leading from Behind" after the Arab Spring

The unexpected democratic uprisings that became known as the Arab Spring altered the political and strategic landscape of the Middle East and North Africa (MENA) region. By 2010, nearly one-half of the world's population lived in "free" governments, according to Freedom House, a prominent human rights group. The MENA region, however, stood apart from the rest of the world in its resistance to fair elections, freedom of speech, minority rights, freedom of belief, and gender inequality. The pattern was especially acute in North Africa, home to some of the world's most entrenched authoritarian rulers, including Libya's Muammar el-Qaddafi (41 years) and Hosni Mubarak of Egypt (29 years).

In August 2010, President Obama foreshadowed the Arab Spring in a five-page memorandum to his top advisers entitled "Political Reform in the Middle East and North Africa." He cited "evidence of growing citizen discontent with the region's regimes" and predicted that "if present trends continue" the targeted governments would "opt for repression rather than reform to manage domestic dissent." Further, Obama predicted that US government's "regional and international credibility will be undermined if we are seen or perceived to be backing repressive regimes and ignoring the rights and aspirations of citizens."

The appropriate role of the United States in influencing this expected uprising was unclear given its controversial history and reputation in the Arab world. Aside from providing moral and rhetorical support for the pro-democracy movements, a more active response risked familiar allegations of American imperialism. Recognizing this problem, Obama ordered his advisers to develop a "country-by-country" plan in the case of pro-democracy uprisings. No single strategy, he concluded, would adequately serve American interests. As the dominos of repression fell eastward from Tunisia, the White House found itself trying to manage a historic transformation that was largely out of its control. This confusion was revealed as the US government clung to the Mubarak regime during Egypt's uprising, then called for his resignation in the face of mounting public unrest.

The lack of US leverage was also evident in the Syrian crisis. American leaders had long considered Syria a Russian client and pariah state that abused its citizens while funding Islamist groups such as Hezbollah and Hamas in their ongoing conflicts with Israel. Unlike Mubarak's regime in Egypt, however, Syria did not rely on massive volumes of US foreign aid to stay in power. Unilateral military action against Syria had dubious chances of success while posing multiple risks, including anti-American reprisals by Islamists across the Arab world. Furthermore, the United States could not rely on support from the UN Security Council, especially after China and Russia vetoed a resolution calling for collective action against Syria in February 2012. Faced with these constraints on American power, Obama could only "lead from behind" in Syria, providing the freedom fighters with encouragement and covert economic aid while otherwise keeping the conflict at arm's length.

The United States remains able to secure its interests through regional leaders that share American policy preferences, affirming the realist principle that "the enemy of my enemy is my friend." Rather than through hegemonic pressure, the US government found common ground with Saudi Arabia and the United Arab Emirates (UAE) on issues relating to al Qaeda, the Islamic State, and Iran's nuclear program. Lacking common values and cultural traditions, the United States and its regional "partners" rely on expedience as the basis for cooperation. In Saudi Arabia, this accounts for the $87 billion in military hardware sold to the kingdom between 2011 and 2014. The UAE meanwhile, benefits from the same military pipeline along with the security provided by US military operations in the emirate. As these arrangements are not a part of a hegemonic bargain, there is no need for consensus on normative issues or the provision of public goods to oil-rich regimes that are largely self-sufficient.

As for Qatar, the US government continues to rely on its government as a critical strategic outpost. The use of Qatar as a base of the regional command CENTCOM will continue to tie the two countries together until 2023, if not longer. This infrastructure will be vital to the United States as it organizes a regional coalition to "degrade and destroy" the Islam State of Iraq and Syria (ISIS). The US government, however, recognizes and respects Qatar's independent foreign policies, many of which are not consistent with US objectives. The Obama administration, represented by former Defense Secretary Chuck Hagel, reached out to Emir Tamin for greater defense cooperation in the future.

The United States, in conjunction with the United Nations and EU member states, has been more successful in placing pressure on Iran through economic sanctions that have greatly weakened the nation's economic base. For the Obama administration, US credibility depends on the successful outcome of the Joint Plan of Action that was approved in November 2013. Conversely, the failure of these talks would encourage critics of the US government to claim the nation's clout as the world's self-proclaimed "indispensable nation" has run its course. The same can be said for negotiations between Israel and its Palestinian population, which were suspended after the West Bank and Gaza enclaves chose to negotiate with a united front. As did his predecessors, Obama vowed to mediate a two-state solution with security guarantees to both parties, only to see the proposal break down despite intense US pressure. The United States was more successful, however, in urging Israel to avoid large-scale military intervention on its two borders that were entangled in domestic upheavals, Syria and Egypt. As with the Persian Gulf region, however, these outcomes had less to do with concerns for hegemonic stability than the exploitation of common security interests.

Unilateral actions by the United States aside, its grand strategy of sustained primacy depends on multilateral institutions that provide forums that facilitate coordination of economic and security policies of member states. To the extent that such outlets, including the Gulf Cooperation Council and the Arab League in the Mideast, share US policy interests, "they correlate well with US goals of stability and the maintenance of alliance relationships in the region."[41] The same can be said for the dense network of intergovernmental organizations in East Asia, including the Association of Southeast Nations (ASEAN) a relic of the Cold War designed by the United States to contain the PRC. Today, ASEAN consists of several forums, most of which include China. The United States participates in most of these forums, including the Asia-Pacific Economic Cooperation group that has established norms, standards, and methods for conflict resolution on trade matters that affect East Asia and the Western Hemisphere. The East Asian Summit, created in 2005 among the ASEAN+3 countries along with Australia, New Zealand, and India, excluded the United States. Several other benefits can result from institutionalized cooperation, as these agents of global governance take on a permanence that can mitigate conflicts and produce agreements on issues that are not currently apparent.

8. Conclusion

As we have seen, the logic of hegemonic stability has been widely applied to contemporary world politics, which since World War II has witnesses an unprecedented degree of influence of a single world power, the United States. In the parlance of social science, if the dependent variable is relative global stability, the key independent variable is the presence of hegemony and its provision of public goods. "Unipolarity favors the absence of war among the great powers and comparatively low levels of competition for prestige or security for two reasons: the leading power's advantage removes the problem of hegemonic rivalry from world politics, and it reduces the salience and stakes of balance of power politics among the major states."[42] Recent data supports these claims. The Global Peace Index, produced by the Institute for Economics and Peace, reported decreases of political violence in all regions of the world except the Middle East and North Africa.[43] The same pattern has been demonstrated in cases of regional hegemony, which are historically less likely to suffer from violent conflict.[44]

If the current system of hegemonic stability, girded by a "constitutional bargain" that materially benefits and empowers weaker states, can be considered a collective good, the critical question turns to how sustainable such a balance of world power can be. This chapter has highlighted both the hard- and soft-power assets of the US government as well as the many challenges to its hegemonic future. These include factors that may be out of Washington's control, including the historically recurring "rise and fall of the great powers" caused by growing costs and decreasing benefits to the hegemon.[45] From this view, the presumed compatibility of hegemonic control and the collective interests of weaker states may not be sustainable due to "the uneven logic of capitalist development, which tends to develop new forms of production, new logics of accumulation, and social relations that, ultimately, undermine the existing order."[46]

Other factors, however, are within the US government's capacity to manage. These factors would include a shift in policy emphasis from military might to economic solvency. To Daniel Drezner, a well-known American scholar, "The United States needs to focus primarily on policies that will rejuvenate economic growth, accelerate job creation, and promote greater innovation and productivity."[47] These reforms would undoubtedly strengthen the foundation of US hegemony. They would not, however, directly resolve the problems noted earlier regarding recent US foreign policies which have alienated many foreign governments, including US allies. These actions, such as waging war against of Iraq without a UN mandate and, more recently, evidence of pervasive US espionage targeting friends and foes, undermine the "consensual" relationship that provides essential legitimacy to hegemonic power.

In this context, leadership becomes an important factor in the development of a secure and just world order. Considered as a key element of democratic government, leadership is not inherently transactional but is instead "characterized by the pursuit of common objectives and, therefore, a commonality of interests beyond leaders and followers."[48] According to an earlier conception of the term, leadership effectively occurs when "one actor gives something of value to another without condition, without any stipulated payment, now or later."[49] When nations form a custom union, for example, they do so without coercion and with collective benefits in mind. In many such cases, both the leader and her followers may benefit equally, as when accommodations are made for transnational regimes to coordinate environmental policies.

The United States, therefore, may reserve for itself a position of leadership even after its unipolar stature has lapsed. President Obama made this connection when he spoke to West Point cadets in May 2014. "Because of American leadership," President Obama observed in regard to the crisis in Ukraine, "the world immediately condemned Russian actions, Europe and the G-7 joined with us to impose sanctions, NATO reinforced our commitment to Eastern European allies, the IMF is helping to stabilize Ukraine's economy, and OSCE monitors brought the eyes of the world to unstable parts of Ukraine." From this standpoint, the legitimacy of state actions rests upon the nature of authority that leaders provide. Authority in a consensual and legitimate order is not law, but a contract.

Despite its many faults and domestic problems, the United States retains its predominant position in world politics, and it continues, along with associated subordinate states, to benefit from the dynamics of hegemonic stability. The nation, however cannot expect to maintain this status forever. In its place, American leaders will have many opportunities to remain the "indispensable nation" in a world that exists after hegemony.

Table 1 Global Military Balance of Power

Country	Military spending, 2011 (billions of US dollars)	Armed forces (total active military), 2013 (thousands of active personnel)	Military aircraft, 2013	Total navy ships, 2013	Total land-based weapons, 2013	Nuclear warheads, 2013
United States	$640	2,285	13,683	473	39,162	7,315
China	188	1,430	2,788	520	23,664	250
Russia	87.8	766	3,082	352	57,503	8,000
Saudi Arabia	67.0	234	652	55		0
France	61.2	229	1,203	120	8.672	300
United Kingdom	57.9	205	908	66	6,935	225
Germany	48.8	183	710	82	5,124	0
Japan	48.6	248	1,595	131	4,611	0
India	47.4	1,325	1,785	184	15,681	90-110
South Korea	33.9	640	1,393	166	13,078	0
Italy	32.7	320	795	174	10,360	0
Brazil	31.5	328	748	109	2,657	0
Australia	24.0	58	395	53	2,228	0
Turkey	19.1	411	989	115	15,948	0
UAE	19.0	65	444	75	3,806	0

Source: Stockholm International Peace Research Institute, 2013.

Notes

1   In this respect hegemony is very different from colonization, which denies its subjects statehood.

2   Immanuel Wallerstein, *The Capitalist World-Economy* (Cambridge, UK: Cambridge University Press, 1979).

3   Ian Clark, "Bringing Hegemony Back In: The United States and International Order," *International Affairs* 85 (2009): 23-36.

4   Joseph S. Nye, Jr., and Robert O. Keohane, "Transnational Relations and World Politics: An Introduction." *International Organization* 25 (1971): 329-349.

5   Charles P. Kindleberger, *The World in Depression, 1929-1939*. Berkeley, CA: University of California Press, 2013. See also Stephen D. Krasner, "State Power and the Structure of International Trade," *World Politics* 28 (1976): 317-347.

6   Oran R. Young, *International Cooperation: Building Regimes for Natural Resources and the Environment* (Ithaca, N.Y.: Cornell University Press, 1989).

7   Robert Cox, *Production, Power, and World Order: Social Forces in the Making of History* (New York: Columbia University Press, 1987).

8   Richard Saull, "Rethinking Hegemony: Uneven Development, Historical Blocs, and the World Economic Crisis," *International Studies Quarterly* 56 (2012): 328-338.

9   Robert Gilpin, *War and Change in World Politics* (Princeton, N.J.: Princeton University Press, 1981).

10 Melvyn Leffler, *A Preponderance of Power: National Security, the Truman Administration, and the Cold War* (Stanford: Stanford University Press, 1992); see also Steven W. Hook and John Spanier, *American Foreign Policy since World War II, 19th ed.* (Washington, D.C.: CQ Press, 2013).

11 Patrick E. Tyler, "U.S. Strategy Plan Calls for Insuring No Rivals Develop: A One-Superpower World," *New York Times*, March 8, 1992.

12 White House. *The National Security Strategy of the United States of America*. Washington, D.C.: White House, 2002 (September), 30.

13 White House. *The National Security Strategy of the United States of America*. Washington, D.C.: White House, 2010 (May), 1.

14 James A. Morrison, "Before Hegemony: Adam Smith, American Independence, and the Origins of the First Era of Globalization," *International Organization* 66 (2012): 395-428.

15 Waltz, Kenneth. Theory of International Politics. Boston: McGraw-Hill, 1979.

16 Robert Gilpin, ibid.

17 Robert Jervis. "Unipolarity: A Structural Perspective," *World Politics* 61 (2009), 204.

18 G. John Ikenberry, *Liberal Leviathan: The Origins, Crisis, and Transformation of the American World Order* (Princeton, N.J.: Princeton University Press, 2011).

19 G. John Ikenberry, *After Victory: Institutions, Strategic Restraint, and the Rebuilding of Order after Major Wars* (Princeton, N.J.: Princeton University Press, 2001); see also Skidmore, David. "Understanding the Unilateralist Turn in U.S. Foreign Policy." *Foreign Policy Analysis* 1 (2005): 207–228.

20 Christopher Layne, "This Time it's Real: The End of Unipolarity and the Pax Americana." *International Studies Quarterly* 56 (2012): 203-213.

21 Barry Posen, "Command of the Commons: The Military Foundation of U.S. Hegemony." *International Security* 28 (2003): 5–46.

22 Richard Grimmett, Richard F., and Paul K. Kerr, *Conventional Arms Transfers to Developing Nations, 2004-2011* (Washington, D.C.: Congressional Research Service, September 22, 2012).

23 Joseph S. Nye, Jr. *Soft Power: The Means to Success in World Politics* (New York: Public Affairs, 2004).

24 National Intelligence Council, *Global Trends: 2030* (Washington, D.C.: National Intelligence Council, 2012).

25 Aaron Friedberg, *A Contest for Supremacy: China, America, and the Struggle for Mastery in Asia* (New York: Norton, 2012).

26 Andrew Nathan and Andrew Scobell, "How China Sees America: The Sum of Beijing's Fears," *Foreign Affairs* (2012): 32-47.

27 Stephen Walt, *Taming American Power: The Global Response to U.S. Primacy* (New York: W.W. Norton, 2005).

28 Paul Kennedy, *The Rise and Fall of the Great Powers* (New York: Random House, 1987).

29 Gilpin, 1981.

30 George Modelski, *Long Cycles in World Politics* (Seattle: University of Washington Press, 1985).

31 Julia E. Sweig, *Friendly Fire: Losing Friends and Making Enemies in the Anti-American Century* (New York: Public Affairs, 2006).

32 Peter J. Katzenstein and Robert O. Keohane, eds. *Anti-Americanisms in World Politics* (Ithaca, N.Y.: Cornell University Press, 2007).

33 Joseph E. Stiglitz, *Globalization and its Discontents* (New York: Norton, 2002).

34 Steven Weber and Bruce W. Jentleson, *The End of Arrogance: America in the Global Competition of Ideas* (Cambridge, Mass.: Harvard University Press, 2010).

35 Andrew Kohut and Bruce Stokes, *America against the World: How We Are Different and Why We Are Disliked* (New York: Times Books, 2006): 13.

36 John G. Ruggie, "International Responses to Technology: Concepts and Trends," *International Organization* 29 (1975): 557-583. See also Ernst B. Haas, "Why Collaborate? Issue Linkage and International Regimes," *World Politics* 32 (1980): 357-405.

37 Stephen D. Krasner, "Structural Causes and Regime Consequences: Regimes as Intervening Variables." *International Organization* 36 (1982): 186.

38 William Easterly and Claudia R. Williamson, *Rhetoric vs. Reality: The Best and Worst Aid Agencies Practices*. May 4, 2012. Singapore: Social Science Research Network.

39 United Nations, *Toward Human Resilience: Sustaining MDG Progress in an Age of Uncertainty*. New York: United Nations, 2011: 150.

40 Gregory Chin and Fahimul Quadir. "Introduction: Rising States, Rising Donors and the Global Aid Regime." *Cambridge Review of International Affairs* 25 (2012): 493-506.

41 Dick Nanto, *East Asian Architecture: New Economic and Security Arrangements and U.S. Policy* (Washington, D.C.: Congressional Research Service), January 4, 2008.

42 William Wohlforth, "The Stability of a Unipolar World." *International Security* 24 (1999): 4-41.

43 Institute for Economics and Peace. *Global Peace Index*. Sydney: Institute for Economic and Peace, 2012. See also Steven Pinker, *The Better Angels of our Nature* (New York: Viking, 2011); and Joshua Goldstein, *Winning the War on War: The Decline of Armed Conflict Worldwide* (New York: Dutton).

44 Daniel Geller, "Explaining War: Empirical Patterns and Theoretical Mechanisms," in Manus I. Midlarsky, ed., *Handbook of War Studies II* (Ann Arbor, University of Michigan Press, 2000).

45 Recall Gilpin 1981 and Kennedy 1987.

46 Saull, 329.

47 Daniel Drezner, "Military Primacy Doesn't Pay (Nearly as Much as You Think)." *International Security* 38 (2013), 79.

48 Sandra Destradi, "Regional Powers and their Strategies: Empire, Hegemony, and Leadership," *Review of International Studies* 36 (2010): 903-930.

49 Klaus Knorr, *The Power of Nations: The Political Economy of International Relations* (New York: Basic Books, 1975).

Bibliography

Friedberg, Aaron, *A Contest for Supremacy: China, America, and the Struggle for Mastery in Asia*. New York: Norton, 2012.

Gilpin, Robert. *War and Change in World Politics*. Princeton, N.J.: Princeton University Press, 1981.

Hook, Steven W., and John Spanier, *American Foreign Policy since World War II, 19th ed*. Washington, D.C.: CQ Press, 2013.

Ikenberry, G. John, *Liberal Leviathan: The Origins, Crisis, and Transformation of the American World Order*. Princeton, N.J.: Princeton University Press, 2011.

Kennedy, Paul. *The Rise and Fall of the Great Powers*. New York: Random House, 1987.

Kindleberger, Charles P. *The World in Depression, 1929-1939*. Berkeley, CA: University of California Press, 2013.

Nye, Joseph, S., Jr. *Soft Power: The Means to Success in World Politics*. New York: Public Affairs, 2004.

Wallerstein, Immanuel. *The Capitalist World-Economy*. Cambridge, UK: Cambridge University Press, 1979.

Walt, Stephen. *Taming American Power: The Global Response to U.S. Primacy*. New York: W.W. Norton, 2005.

White House. *The National Security Strategy of the United States of America*. Washington, D.C.: White House, May 1, 2010.

3

Arabia to Asia:
The Myths and Merits of an American "Pivot"

John Duke Anthony

1. Introduction

That the foreign policies of various governments often appear to be contradictory is because they frequently are. Certainly of late, this seems to characterize aspects of America's relations with the six Gulf Cooperation Council (GCC) countries: Bahrain, Kuwait, Oman, Qatar, Saudi Arabia, and the United Arab Emirates. This ambiguity and the confusion and uncertainty that accompany it are among the things that President Barack Obama sought to dispel and clarify in the course of his March 2014 visit to Saudi Arabia. As this chapter seeks to demonstrate, what he had to contend with in terms of background, context, and perspective was not easy of resolution, amelioration, or even abatement.

Despite the many largely unreported positives, there were numerous negatives that needed to be addressed when the president visited Riyadh. Had this not been done, the situation seen then and subsequently by many within this globally vital region as increasingly tendentious and quarrelsome would likely have become the more so, for no good reason. Both before and since the president's visit, Washington had strengthened and extended its overall position and influence in the GCC region through the GCC-US Strategic Dialogue. Former Defense Secretary Chuck Hagel, along with John Kerry, the Secretary of State, came with ten millions of dollars in U.S.-manufactured defense and security structures, systems, technology, and arms to GCC countries; and long-term munitions and maintenance contracts.[1]

Yet, simultaneously, signals from Washington and the mainstream US media before and since the president's March visit have continuously indicated that the Obama administration is recalibrating the strategic focus of its international priorities to emphasize the Asia-Pacific regions in the period ahead. Affecting the need for the recalibration have been major budget reductions and their impact on strategic concepts, forces, and operational dynamics. At issue and under examination in this regard, according to the Secretary of Defense in advance of the Quadrennial Defense Review (QDR), are, and for the foreseeable future will continue to be, America's assumptions, ambitions, and abilities. Understandably, the GCC region's reaction to these trends and indications has been mixed.

2. Positives and Negatives of US Policies

On the positive side, many among the region's strategic analysts and policymakers have been and remain pleased with the continuing high-level of military, security, and intelligence cooperation between the United States and the GCC countries.[2] Others continue to appreciate that America's forward-deployed land, air, and naval forces have ensured the ongoing safety of the region's oil exports and preserved the member-states' national sovereignty, political independence, and territorial integrity, and, in these ways and others, contributed substantially to the region's overall security and governmental stability.[3]

Member states have also been relieved that, so far, a robust US diplomacy has averted an American and/or Israeli armed attack against Iran's nuclear facilities. They appreciate, more than words could convey, how such efforts have thus far prevented an international conflict that such an attack could provoke.[4] America, its worldwide allies, and, most important, the Gulf countries have grown weary of wars in this region.

Indicative of this reality is a palpable malaise among a budding core of US strategic analysts. Among them are those who have come to perceive the Arab and Islamic countries in general as a perennially exhausting enterprise that is unceasingly difficult to manage and sustain.[5] Others echo such sentiments. They maintain that, economically, financially, politically, and otherwise, the United States is less and less in a condition or mood to prolong what, in the eyes of many, have been associated with the violent attacks against the United States on September 11, 2001, by Arabs and Muslims.

In this regard, growing numbers of Americans believe it unnecessary, if not reckless and foolhardy, for the United States to be expected to continue, as it were, with business as before. More specifically, they are no longer as inclined to expend the extraordinary amount of time, effort, and resources, unaided by others, to protect American and allied interests in these regions to anywhere near the extent of protection that went largely unquestioned in years past.

On the negative side, many chafe and remain disappointed at the continued unwillingness of the United States, in concert with Saudi Arabia and other GCC countries, to do whatever is necessary to bring down the Syrian regime.[6] Only thus, many contend, could one expect to weaken Iran's ability to foment and sustain the civil strife in Iraq and the domestic dissension in Bahrain, other GCC countries, and beyond and to continue to support the Lebanese Hizbollah.

In these regards, no one should doubt the pan-GCC opposition to the Islamic Republic's longstanding designs on and history of intrusion into the domestic affairs of Bahrain.[7] Though small in size and population, Bahrain, owing to its having hosted an American naval presence nonstop since the late 1940s, has long played and would likely seem destined to continue to play an outsize role in the safe flow of Gulf energy sources through the Hormuz Strait. Less well known, but equally if not more important from the perspective of GCC nationals, is the other side of the coin. The reference is to the similarly key role that the Bahrain-based US naval presence has long played in assuring the region's vast supply of unfettered imports reaching local markets through the same waterway. The American land-based naval forces centered on Bahrain therefore remain vital to the economic, social, political, and governmental security and stability of the Gulf as a whole as well as the entire eastern Arabian littoral from Kuwait to Oman.

As for Hizbollah, the concerns of GCC observers have been accurately rooted. Members of the party's worldwide networks have been and remain organized, trained, disciplined and capable, with some ready at a moment's notice to strike anywhere to create crises and wreak havoc the world can ill afford to suffer.[8] Additional GCC dismay has been rooted in the Obama administration's change of plans as to whether to bomb Syria and its perceived backtracking and flip-flopping of American actions towards Egypt, given that the Mubarak regime had been a stalwart American ally for thirty years.[9]

3. Embedded Echoes of an Earlier Error

Members of the GCC continue to resent the fact that the P5+1 (the five UN Security Council members plus Germany) excluded them from the US-led negotiations with Iran, their largest, far more populous, militarily stronger, meddlesome, and threatening neighbor.[10] The content of conversations that practically anyone has had on this subject with political analysts in the GCC region should be illustrative. None with whom I have discussed the matter, whose names I promised not to reveal and whom in any event arguably ought to be irrelevant, could conceive of the United States being expected to accept and accommodate a comparable *fait accompli* were China or Russia to enter into sensitive strategic security- or defense-related negotiations with Canada or Mexico.

In GCC eyes, particularly irksome in this regard have been Washington's attitudes and behavior regarding this matter. If measured by the need for policymakers to be careful with what they say or imply, what the United States did was unconscionable. In what appears to have been with little thought to the consequences, the United States, by all accounts, seemingly almost off-handedly opted to appease and accommodate Iran.[11] It did so in response to the latter expressing its opposition to representatives of the GCC countries being allowed to be present in the meetings or even attend as non-participant auditors.

Together with regional analysts and representatives of private-sector communities, these and other slights have caused some in the GCC region to wonder whether their governments might be next on the list of America's partners whose leaders – in the manner of the Shah of Iran, the Philippines' Ferdinand Marcos, and others – end up becoming disregarded and, ultimately, deemed dispensable. Those analysts and others who have wondered can perhaps be forgiven for their further reactions. That is, some have indicated they cannot help but ask whether America will stand by its longtime friends and strategic allies. If so, they wonder whether such help as Washington officialdom might extend will prove to be effective or, as in other instances, too little and too late.

Not least among numerous developments that have fueled such concerns were reports in late June 2014 of how the United States and Iran might collude in matters of strategic import sooner rather than later. An example, in ways at once previously unthinkable, was in how GCC analysts have come to imagine the lengths to which Washington's and Tehran's diplomats might go to mend their fences *vis-à-vis* matters of joint concern. The matter in question was hardly trivial. It was whether Washington and Tehran might agree to coordinate their efforts (which in short order they did) on a matter of great sensitivity not just to Iraqis but, also, Iraq's neighbors. The issue was whether the United States and Iran would try to thwart the fall of the Shiite-led Iraqi government in Baghdad, which the United States and the Islamic Republic had helped to install, lest it fall to Sunnis led by former Ba'athists and extremist insurgent offshoots of al-Qaeda bent on its ouster.[12]

In the eyes of GCC leaders, whatever the strategic basis for Washington's and Tehran's connivance, the effect of the perceived US-Iranian unity of objectives in this instance was more than troublesome; in the eyes of some, it smacked of American policymakers' callousness. To others, it betrayed yet another instance of Washington, however inadvertent its intention, lending a *de facto* boost to Tehran's regional standing and clout regarding a matter of grave importance to GCC country relations with Iraq and Iran.

Added to the negative interpretations and anxieties that resulted was something else that, perceptually, seemed of related importance. This was the ongoing suspicion among GCC analysts of an untimely and inordinate American intention to pivot from the GCC region towards not just Europe and Latin America, but, especially, Asia.[13] However much they would have wished it were otherwise, more and more GCC intelligence and policy analysts came to view the purported American geopolitical strategic shift as being, at a minimum, at least partially true.

3.1. *Faits Accomplis* Run Amok?

Underscoring their consternation was the view that the US decision had apparently been arrived at unilaterally. This alone left many among the more ardent pro-American elites within the GCC region taken aback. In the interplay of action, reaction, and interaction of diplomacy, *faits accompli* regarding a matter as serious as this one would be are ordinarily unacceptable. On either side of a special relationship and an unofficial, informal alliance, which is what the GCC-US relationship has been since the day the GCC was established, such acts are supposed to be off-limits.

It was not just the way in which the United States went about arriving at its decision. And it was not only the manner in which Washington issued the announcement and tried to explain it that so many in the GCC found upsetting. More profoundly, it was the substantive dimension of Washington's decision that especially riled GCC policy commentators who endeavored to fathom its implications.

Even the most clinical, objective, and dispassionate GCC analysts failed to reach a positive conclusion about the potential consequences. Instead, they perceived the matter in many ways with the same disbelief they had perceived the American determination to invade Iraq, which occurred despite strong and repeated opposition by most of the GCC region's most astute and seasoned experts and policy practitioners. As with the George W. Bush administration's decision to effect regime change in Baghdad in 2003, more recent US actions seemed at once not only inopportune and unwarranted to GCC analysts. Worse, US foreign policies seemed likely to embolden an adventurist streak that was known to have long existed among Iran's leaders.[14] Still, none among the GCC's foreign policy elites take issue with the reality that there are moments in any country's history that mandate a reassessment and realignment of its strategic international relationships, resource allocations, and foreign policy priorities.

3.2. Propellant Factors and Forces

Four phenomena, each one fueling the others, have fed such apprehensions among GCC members. One is a consequence of the severe US government budget cutbacks. A second is a growing concern expressed unofficially by a prominent member of the New York-based National Resources Defense Council. In mid-August, 2014, a senior longtime strategic adviser to the Council informed me of members' apprehensions regarding China who, he emphasized, are certain that it is determined to position itself in such a way so as to be able eventually to mount a serious challenge to the United States' hyper-power status globally, if only, to begin with, in Asia, China's near-abroad.

A third phenomenon is the lure of Asia's vastly greater consumer markets for US exporters. With this, it is believed, would come the accompanying prospects for generating thousands of American jobs, vastly greater flows of revenue into the US Treasury, and perceptually a correspondingly enhanced capacity, if not to reduce, then slow the increase in the American taxpayers' levels of dependence upon China and other nations that own American national debt instruments.[15]

A fourth phenomenon is the impact on strategic thinking that derives from a looming specter of China, along with Russia, becoming world-class blue water oceanic powers to a far greater extent than previously.[16] Already, both countries are increasingly well positioned to expand their maritime trading routes, potentially, in the eyes of those who think in zero-sum terms, at America's and other countries' expense. In so doing, they are validating the adage that time – and ideas perceived as potentially beneficial – wait for no one. Indeed, both countries are already proceeding to expand their naval capacities and involvement not only in and through the Indian Ocean. They are doing so also via a heretofore inadequately charted area in a distant and different direction, one that is laced with innumerable strategic uncertainties. The region in question is the Arctic Circle, whose waters have become navigable to a greater extent than any previous time in recorded history.

Reflecting the push and pull of these four phenomena has been a steady progression of high-level Obama administration visits to countries in the Asia-Pacific region.[17] Not surprisingly, the visits have been accompanied by declarations of ongoing US support for key American and Asian foreign policy objectives. Such declarations have been linked to two domestically rooted phenomena that are increasingly receiving serious and favorable consideration.

The first of these domestic factors involves America's oil and gas sectors achieving record-high production levels. The second phenomenon, linked to the first, has to do with a greatly lessened likelihood of America remaining as dependent upon hydrocarbon fuels from the Middle East to anywhere near the same extent as in the past. The two phenomena combined are being likened in the minds of domestic components of the US body politic to a welcomed strategic opportunity not previously present. While envisioned as likely to transpire at some indeterminate time in the future, the opportunity has come at a much earlier moment than most expected. For energy independence advocates, in the event these trends remain linked and become operational, America may no longer feel any urgency to assign as much importance to Arabia and the Gulf as before.[18]

4. Strategic Signalling

The Asia-centric visits and declarations of American leaders have been exercises in strategic messaging. The Obama administration has sought not only to dispel any notion that America may have lessened the overall level of its appreciation for its Asian partners. It has also sought to leave no doubt about its intentions. The administration seeks, first, to strengthen and expand its presence in the region. Second, it has sought to reconfirm that America has important interests in Asia that it is determined to protect and, if necessary, defend.[19]

China, however, has viewed such matters differently. Indeed, even without regard to whether the West in general is or is not as committed to its interests and involvement in Arabia and the Gulf, the Chinese leadership clearly is in a revisionist mode. To the extent that America is nowadays perceived to evince less of an appetite for intervention in foreign affairs than in days of yore, and for it to have such diminished economic resources for being able to do so were it inclined, China's leaders would only naturally seek to advance their country's interests in nearby areas.[20] Certainly there is no reason to wonder why or even whether this is happening. A similar phenomenon occurred after World War Two when British imperial power proceeded to be diminished considerably, rapidly, and, in the end, irreversibly.

In the wake of Britain's imperial demise, the Americans stepped into the Gulf breach for two overarching reasons. First, it was an extraordinary opportunity for the world's largest consumer and importer of hydrocarbon fuels to strengthen and expand its political, technological, economic, and financial footholds and influence. Second, there was a belief that the United States had no choice but to proceed in this direction. Otherwise, Moscow would be tempted in ways that America's Cold War containment stalwarts were determined never to encourage.[21]

With bountiful historical examples buttressing their analyses and perceptions of potential threat scenarios, US policymakers believed that the Soviet Union, like Tsarist Russia before it, would try to fill the vacuum that Britain had created.

In taking steps to preclude such an eventuality, Washington's foreign affairs establishment cannot be accused, metaphorically, of having been asleep at the wheel. Rather, it behaved in the exact opposite manner: it opted to succeed and continue the essence of what the British had long been doing. This took the form of the United States crafting and emulating a tailored version of Britain's previous extended, unfettered, and low-key but nonetheless activist and overall effective role in the foreign relations and *de facto* defense of the countries that, ten years later, would come to comprise the GCC.[22]

5. Some Common Themes

In Arabia and the Gulf, the recent narrative of an America suspected of intending to pivot from the world's most vital region to one that is arguably of considerably less strategic importance is and remains a legitimate cause for pan-GCC concern and incredulity. This is so because in the past three decades the United States has *thrice* sent hundreds of thousands of its armed forces to Arabia with the purported aim of establishing or restoring a degree of security and stability that had been shattered, threatened, or looked as though their certainty or the prospects for their prolongation might be thrown open to question.

The United States was the lead country in the internationally concerted action that ended the 1980-1988 Iran-Iraq War. It was the foremost in-region Great Power working in concert with its mainly Western European allies and key GCC country leaders that helped to prevent the Iranian Revolution from expanding to the GCC countries.[23] In tandem with the assistance of several GCC countries' governments, America's armed forces did more than any other country's military to help drive the final nail into the casket of the Red Army and, hence, the so-called Soviet Bloc if not international communism itself. And, of course, the United States was without a peer in leading the internationally choreographed actions in 1990-1991 that restored safety and freedom to Kuwait.[24]

5.1. America's Undoing and Waning

What vitiated all the earlier pan-GCC goodwill towards the United States was not only that the United States attacked Iraq despite the fact that Iraq had not attacked the United States. Neither was it limited to the added factor of revulsion at the totally unnecessary and morally repugnant slaughter and maiming of lives. Nor was it merely the external and domestic displacement of fully a quarter of Iraq's 24 million people; and it was not solely the devastation of such vast swaths of the country's infrastructure. And it was not simply the increase in the spread of anti-Americanism on a scale without precedent in the history of American-Arab and American-Muslim relations.

All of these tragic developments ensued as a direct consequence of what the United States did to Iraq. It was the individual and combined impact of the horrors mentioned – inflicted not only upon the country but its people and their resources, not to mention the citizenry's physical security and the government's political stability.[25]

Not to put too fine a gloss on it, the angst in Arab hearts and minds against US policies as a result of what the United States did to Iraq was perhaps best capsulized by two quite different, but coupled, analyses and assessments, each in turn rooted in two linked sentiments and statements. One effect took the form of a comment by a former GCC Secretary-General, who remarked to me that, "Whatever else America did *in* and *to* Iraq, it killed a country and an extraordinary array of people." He added, "And not just any country or people but, rather, Iraq and the Iraqis – who, in the hearts of the more than 300 million Arabs and the world's 1.6 billion Muslims, are the heirs of what was long the center of Arab and Islamic civilization at their zenith."[26]

The second set of analyses and assessments brings the focus back to square one. It echoes the earlier account of GCC analysts having taken umbrage at Washington's approach to the still relatively recent strategic discussions with Tehran that excluded participation by the GCC countries – despite the record of Iran's extensive interference in the domestic affairs of most of the GCC countries.

Participants at the annual GCC ministerial and heads of state summits that I attended were heard trying hard but finding it difficult to make light of an observation agreed to by practically everyone.[27] Paraphrased, the observation was the following: "Try this one on for credibility or incredulity. The United States invaded Iraq and Iran won. And Iran did so without firing a single shot or shedding a drop of blood." Along these lines, one may ask: "Given the longstanding animosity between Tehran and Washington, when before has a power massively more powerful than an adversary presented the latter a strategic gift of even remotely comparable magnitude as the United States did in this case?" Perhaps against this additional background and perspective as context, it becomes easier to comprehend much of what otherwise might seem inexplicable.

5.2. Bewilderment's Grounds and Blowback's Consequences

Certainly what this account has endeavored to do is indicate, with as much relevant specificity of reference and detail as possible, the grounds for the sustained pan-GCC bewilderment towards Washington officialdom's most recent decision to pivot from Arabia to Asia. More specifically, the objective of this chapter is to underscore the roots of GCC country disenchantment regarding American foreign policies, actions, and attitudes of late. The reference is to issues that, in the eyes of GCC analysts, are of overriding importance to their legitimate needs, concerns, interests, and major objectives *vis-à-vis* Iran, Iraq, and the United States.

What has been the impact of the US-led invasion and occupation of Iraq in 2003? One among numerous answers to this timely and relevant question is the following. Washington's national security elites rode roughshod over most of the GCC country leaders' strong and impassioned advice for the United States not to invade Iraq.[28] The consequences have hardly been marginal. Indeed, a maelstrom of disastrous effects followed in the wake of Washington overriding its GCC allies' advice. In so doing, by its attitudes, actions, and policies, the United States has effectively pulled the rug out from beneath what had for some time been the extraordinarily positive pan-GCC impact of some of its earlier positive achievements.

The blowback to failed US policies, which can be pegged to the 2003 American invasion of Iraq, ushered in a range of nemeses that unleashed previously contained forces. The ensuing chaos, destruction, violence, looting, and corruption resulted in the killing and disabling for life of hundreds of thousands of Iraqis over and beyond the untold numbers affected by the US-led sanctions against Iraq throughout the 1990s and continuing through the 2003 invasion.

Regarding its decision to "pivot" to Asia, an American foreign policy establishment seen as partly credible and partly incredible simultaneously in an area such as the GCC region would be humorous were the matters at issue not so serious. For starters, one need only ponder the potential implications that an actual American pivot could have on Tehran-GCC, US-GCC, and US-Iranian relations. The fallout would likely have a worldwide negative impact on stock markets and financial investment institutions, threaten global security and stability, and encourage Iranian assertiveness, and possibly aggression, among other things.[29]

iewed in this light, many wonder whether Washington is certain of the efficacy of the direction in which its foreign policies are headed. This much is clear: the United States is indeed doing two seemingly contradictory things at once. Already, the consequence has been partly disheartening, partly frustrating, and partly a growing source of greater anger, disbelief, and disappointment with regard to US foreign policies than already existed.

6. The Provenance of Strategic Ideas and Concepts

Making sense of this confusion requires focusing in this instance not so much in Asia but on the GCC region, which is where the uncertainty lies. Doing so begs several questions. Does America have a strategy towards this region? If so, for how long has it had such a strategy? What is its nature and extent? And what are its conceptual origins and parameters?

Many in the GCC region believe what the United States is doing in Arabia and the Gulf is without a strategy. Others conclude that instead of a strategy, Washington, for the most part, has been inclined to offer *ad hoc* reactions and improvised responses to a disparate array of regional challenges.[30] There are some who claim that the focus and behavior of the Obama administration are, at best, tactically, not strategically, driven. Within this view, the consensus is that the most important issues that are arguably at once strategic and tactical include (1) maintaining an adequately produced, manageably priced, and effectively administered flow of oil from the region to international markets, (2) keeping the Hormuz Strait open to unfettered maritime commerce, and (3) stemming the influence and spread of Al-Qaeda and other extremist and violent ideologies.

Added to these matters are myriad other issues having to do with Afghanistan, Egypt, Iran, Iraq, Libya, Syria, Tunisia, Yemen, and Israel-Palestine. What is one to make of all this?

As to the numerous and widespread allegations that the sum description of America's approaches to Arabia, the Gulf, and much of the region beyond have been tactical only, this writer disagrees. I contend instead that Washington's policies, positions, actions, and attitudes towards Arabia and the Gulf have all along been and to this day remain grounded, in general, in strategic concepts relating to, and emanating from, the immediate post-WWII era, Great Britain's withdrawal from the Gulf in 1971, the 1973-74 oil embargo, the Carter Doctrine, the Camp David Accords, the Soviet invasion of Afghanistan, the American hostage crisis in Iran, the Iran-Iraq war, the Kuwait liberation, the collapse of the Soviet Union, and others.

6.1. The Asymmetry of Empathy and Understanding

The challenge of comprehending the roots of these considerations is admittedly not easy. But neither is it overly difficult. What is required is viewing the matter through the eyes of the strategy formulation's participants and asking difficult and, certainly for some, controversial questions. Some examples follow.

Has the United States sought to advance American interests and policy objectives in Arabia within the context of a strategic perspective? Has Washington's approach to the GCC countries been anchored in a strategic appreciation and net assessment of the GCC region? Unfortunately, any attempt to answer such questions from the US side of the equation is hampered by the greater *inability* of the American side to understand the Arab side than the reverse. What is sure, however, is that the framework for America's overall strategic analysis of Arabia and the Gulf was not established in the context of a vacuum. Rather, it was hammered out on the anvil of analytical prisms at given points in time. Importantly, three strategic developments set the American agenda: (1) the 1989-1990 implosion of the Soviet Union, (2) the fall of the so-called Eastern Bloc, and (3) the accompanying end of the decades-old international communist threat.[31]

In retrospect, it is easy to forget what, for the Washington political establishment, were the heady days of the late 1980s and early 1990s. Yet the strategic implications of the communist coffin being slammed shut spread quickly and reverberated far and wide. No less significant, the vertical consequences of interring the unrelenting effort led by Moscow to "bury" capitalism tunneled deeply into the dynamics of the surviving international systems of governments and politics. To Washington policy analysts in search of a more congenial strategic environment within which to pursue American national interests from then onwards, the result could hardly have been more favorable: the United States, for the first time in its history, had indisputably become the world's preeminent power.[32] The implications of the new reality were not lost on American officials tasked with charting the way forward.

America's policy planners and decision makers were acutely aware that such an unparalleled moment could not possibly endure indefinitely. They recognized that the ensuing geopolitical advantages and economic gains, together with the privileges and benefits associated with what had been termed "the American Century," could not be sustained for long. The only way they could have a chance to prolong the unipolar moment would be through the formulation and implementation of a sound, long-term, strategic vision. The strategic analysts of the day were confident that this extraordinarily auspicious juncture in America's history could be extended only if it were based on four conditions. One was the availability of and access to adequately produced amounts of manageably priced hydrocarbon fuels. A second was the assurance of sound planning and preparation. A third was the availability of the requisite human and financial resources. And, above all, a fourth was, or rather in this case as in the other three, would inevitably and unavoidably be, the steady presence of a visionary, decisive, and strategically focused leadership.[33]

From a related perspective, just as vital would be the effective aid of working partners who would of course have economic clout, financial wealth, and/or geopolitical weight – and preferably all three. More important would be for such actors to attempt to translate whatever influence they might have and be willing to exert on issues and interests of importance to key foreign policy objectives within regional circles and major international organizations.

6.2. "Yankee, Don't Go Home!"

Whatever new or elevated priority America may have assigned to its strategic relations and involvement with Asia at the time that the so-called coming pivot in America's strategic orientation was proclaimed, the following was and remains of over-arching importance. One should not expect to see any significant diminution in the overall strategic importance America has assigned and will continue to assign to the GCC countries and the Gulf as a whole in comparison to the Asia-Pacific region. If there were any doubt among strategic planners that this was, will, and/or would for some time remain America's moment in Arabia, the Gulf, and the GCC region, the reasons would soon enough come into focus.

Dispelling any doubt about America's resilience and resolve to take seriously its Gulf defense responsibilities was the extraordinary effectiveness, as previously indicated, of the US-led internationally concerted action in 1990-91 that reversed Iraq's aggression against Kuwait. No other country could have led such a global assemblage of effective power to help restore to Kuwait what was noted earlier as vitally important to each of the GCC countries, namely their national sovereignty, political independence, territorial integrity, security, and stability.[34]

To American planners then in search of a recalibrated vision and mission, the plaintive pleas scrawled on the walls of the US Embassy in Kuwait after the country's liberation said everything: "Yankee, don't go home." This was the context during the final months of the Bush 41 administration when then-US Secretary of Defense Dick Cheney tasked Under-Secretary of Defense for Policy Paul Wolfowitz with drafting a long-term strategic plan that would ensure the United States in 2020 A.D. would still retain its position as the world's only super power.[35]

Not long after the plan's drafting was underway in the spring and summer of 1992, a Department of Defense representative asked me to visit and brief him and his foreign policy colleagues on what we agreed were then the most pressing challenges to America's interests and policies in the GCC region. An additional goal was for me to critique the direction in which the "20-20" strategic plan – subsequently referred to as the Defense Policy Guidance – which he and his colleagues were then involved in conceptualizing and writing was headed. I was also informed that the analysts and writers of the Guidance had already reached a preliminary consensus that the United States could meet its strategic objectives.

7. Five Contextual Criteria

For the United States to remain the uncontested globally preeminent power that it had unquestionably become, it had no choice but to remain preeminent in *five* separate but interrelated fields of power: economy, finance, technology, military, and industry. It was understood that regardless of the cost and toll on the American economy, the United States would have no choice but to maintain superiority in the five categories that all agreed would remain paramount to maintaining its international position, power, influence, and role.

7.1. Energy the Key

Asked whether I thought any one single factor might be essential to all five categories, I said that *energy* was and would continue to be such a factor. Energy is the one commodity, more than any other, over which human beings have control or influence that not only fuels humanity's health, defense, security, and material wellbeing but also drives the engines of the world's economies. More than that, energy directly affects the three commodities upon which all humanity are dependent in order to live and survive, namely air, water, and food. The question of whether "Our energy or someone else's" seemed trickier and more difficult. However, after taking some time to ponder the implications of how I might respond, I answered "someone else's." In so doing, I added a caveat: "But only if, at all, possible and feasible – by which I mean not immorally, manipulatively, exploitatively, and/or at the expense of others' legitimate needs and rights."

Regarding supplies, it is instructive that the GCC countries are the equivalent of energy behemoths. The latest figures produced by the American Petroleum Institute and the US Department of Energy make no pretense disguising the reality. The member states account for thirty per cent of the world's proven hydrocarbon energy reserves. Iran and Iraq combined account for an additional twenty percent.[36] Add to this, for context and perspective, the following four realities. One, the production costs of America's oil supplies continue to be much more expensive than the production costs of the GCC oil-producing countries. Two, the per unit production levels of GCC member-states' oil wells are substantially higher than the production level of American wells.

Three, the vast majority of the oil wells in the GCC region flow without the need of an additional energy cost associated with pumps – instead, natural pressure pushes the oil to the earth's surface. In contrast, America's oil wells require additional energy, lubricant, and maintenance expenses just to operate the pumps. Four, the average production of an American well was, and has remained at, around 14 barrels a day. In contrast, the average production of numerous Saudi Arabian (and Kuwaiti) wells has remained relatively constant at around 12,000 barrels per day.[37]

7.2. Facts are Stubborn Things

These figures are geological constants and facts. And as others have noted, facts are stubborn things – they have implications for policies. As is the case with other realities, the implications for policymakers worldwide in this instance – and in conjunction with any American serious intent to re-balance its priorities away from Arabia and towards Asia – are, or ought to be, obvious, and the more so given that the world's most adequately produced, manageably priced, and prodigious energy exports are located primarily not in Asia but in Arabia and the Gulf.

Also clear, and hardly the least important among considerations for American strategic analysts and policymakers to ponder, is what could prevent the United States from reaching 2020 A.D. with its preeminent 1992 status intact. The answer: America's competitors. There is every reason to believe that Washington's rivals for global prominence in 2020 are in agreement regarding the importance of the same five identical fields of activity. These fields are the ones in which other countries, too, would have little choice but to perform well. Arguably in no other way would they likely have any chance of mounting an effective challenge to America's preeminently powerful global position in terms of overall power and influence. The foremost competitors of the United States then as now have been China and Russia. Others possibly able to mount a credible challenge over time include the heavily populated developing countries. Among these are Brazil, India, and South Africa, which even then had rapidly growing and increasingly energy-hungry economies.

8. A Look at the Score Card

Where is the United States in terms of the strategic objectives it set out to achieve in 1992? Without a doubt, the United States has remained the world's most militarily powerful country. In addition, with an annual GDP of nearly $18 trillion in 2014, America's economy remains the world's largest, still several trillion dollars ahead of the production of China, its foremost economic rival. In addition, the global financial system, with the preeminence of the US banking system, is still intact.[38] Moreover, as Americans continue to recover from the US-induced 2008 global financial crisis, the American dollar, at least for the immediately foreseeable future, seems likely to continue to reign dominant as the principal monetary instrument of exchange for most international business transactions.

But for how much longer, given China-influenced musings in recent years about the need for an alternative international reserve currency, no one can say for sure. Further, the US strategic telecommunications, information, cyber, and transportation infrastructure within America's industrial base has remained in place. What is more, the ongoing prowess of American technology – and the extent to which the United States continues to invest in technological research and development and in efforts to prevent or counter infringements upon intellectual property rights and patented inventions – is still supreme worldwide.

Thus, the strategic planners of 1992 have helped to ensure that the United States is well on its way to meeting the goals that were set for 2020. More particularly, up to this point in time, they have met the objectives they set with regard to the specific roles they expected Arabia and the Gulf to play in helping to prolong the unparalleled array of benefits associated with "the American Century."

As positive as this may sound, America's achievements in the five categories of measurable might and associated influence have not been free of cost. The road along the way has been bumpy. Here and there, it has also been synonymous with disasters.

With regard to the latter, some were unforeseen. For others, the disasters were foreseen but with a degree of seeming American inaction and indifference in the face of the tragically unjust results. By any standard, the consequences – read Iraq; read Palestine; read Egypt; read Syria – have been and continue to be unconscionable. The positive accomplishments, moreover, did not occur in a vacuum. They often transpired in association with the contentious, heavy-handed, and at times brutal, often accountable, and internationally illegal means employed by the United States. If one can put to the side the allegations of America's "unethical," "hypocritical," "opaque," "double standard," and "morally audacious" actions, together with its "violations of international law and the norms of international legitimacy," it is difficult not to conclude candidly other than that Washington has thus far succeeded in meeting the overall goals of the 1992 plan.

Analysts within the GCC region readily acknowledge not only that America's strategic achievements and goals pertaining to this region remain largely intact. They are quick to note that the achievement has not been cheap. The achievement was accompanied not only by the expenditure of *trillions* of dollars. And, as noted earlier, it was directly linked to the horrific scale of sheer destruction in human lives, limbs, and minds. Overall, however, the consequences had been occasioned by the American-led invasion and occupation of Iraq combined with the earlier ruinous regime of international sanctions imposed by the United States and the entire United Nations membership upon that country.

An additional self-inflicted wound is the United States's ongoing tacit and overwhelming domestic support for Israel's ongoing fulfillment of its quests for territorial and resource acquisition – for *Lebensraum* – at the expense of the Palestinian Arab Christians and Muslims. That much of this American support has been and continues to be domestically rooted politically, diplomatically buttressed, militarily expressed, financially underwritten, authorized by the Executive Branch and the Congress, and supported generally by the US mainstream media is a reality that only the most hardened GCC political realist and strategic analyst can find the means to accommodate.

That such an accommodation has proceeded nonetheless is not by accident or coincidence. It is due as much as anything else to the pan-GCC view that – certainly on-and-over the horizon – thus far there is no viable alternative to the United States as the region's ultimate protector. Nor do most GCC policymakers envision an effective replacement in the immediately foreseeable future for myriad other things that they and their constituents seek to obtain from the United States – if not for themselves then for their progeny and succeeding generations as yet unborn.

9. Why Pivot from "Success"?

Leaving aside the negative aspects associated with America achieving thus far what it set out to accomplish in 1992, and with six years remaining to reach the end game envisioned for 2020, there is a nagging question. Why switch the focus to Asia, where the vicissitudes of international forces and variables are as yet unclear and the prospects for a level of success comparable to that achieved in Arabia and the Gulf would seem uncertain and questionable? Why, indeed, when the dynamics of the new and profoundly different region in terms of America's necessities, apprehensions, and interests are nowhere nearly as in alignment as they have long been between the United States and the GCC countries? And why, given that Asia arguably can hardly compare to the GCC region in terms of globally strategic energy and economic relevance and benefit?

None of this is meant to imply that the forces and factors propelling the reported shift in American strategic analysis and priorities are not understandable. They are. However, what is not being said or written about are the masked and questionable motives and the intended end games of those promoting the pivot policy.

9.1. So Many Questions

Looking at possible motives and endgames for the "pivot mongers" brings up a host of additional questions. Is there in play even a hint of inter-service rivalry among America's uniformed armed forces? Does the rationale for turning from Arabia to Asia have anything to do with the corporate bottom lines of the defense and aerospace sectors, on one hand, and future Congressional budgetary outlays, on the other, for the country's costly high-ticket navy and air force? Is it not at all the case that the acute competition for the dramatically shrunken defense budgets affecting the various military branches is completely absent from the root of what is prompting the shift in strategic focus from the GCC region to Asia?

In short, is the mammoth arms manufacturing sector of the U.S industrial base and its important role in the American economy not a major albeit largely unspoken factor fueling at least a portion of this debate? If so, might the road to maintaining massive infusions of American taxpayers' dollars into this particular sector of the preeminent superpower's economy possibly be underpinned by routes to, through, and around Asia? If the answer is yes, could it be that some see the paving of such routes being potentially enhanced by hyping a largely non-existent challenge in a part of the planet that many at present do not view as threatening?

Finally, if the market for exporting arms to the GCC countries' defense sectors is believed to be satiated for the foreseeable future, can one understand the logic of those whose livelihoods are dependent upon this sector doing what they can to devise seemingly plausible reasons for generating sales elsewhere?

9.2. Anyone for Conspiracies?

Shifting the focus and search for causal factors and forces in a different direction produces additionally possible credible insights. For example, to what extent, if any, are Israel and its American supporters' perennial strategy of deflecting negative international focus from the Jewish state in play here? Does one need to be a died-in-the-wool-conspiracy theorist to give any credence to Israel's understandable support for a different kind of pivot, namely one away from the world's attention to the Eastern Mediterranean, Israel's increased settlement of the Occupied Palestinian and Syrian territories, and that Israel's innumerable violations of international law and a record number of United Nations Security Council resolutions?

If one lends any credibility to this possibility-cum-probability, does it not follow that an American pivot from Arabia to Asia has particular relevance for Israeli strategists and leaders? If so, is "By way of deception" – literally the motto of Mossad, the country's foreign intelligence agency – lacking in relevance here? Is the Obama administration's failed effort to conclude an Israeli-Palestinian peace agreement in the near term, with the implication that Israel would have been required to grant concessions it wishes to avoid having to make, lacking in relevance in this regard? Is it not in Israel's strategic interests to silently and indirectly hype the allegedly growing greater global strategic importance of the India Ocean – one of the world's main maritime routes – to and from the Asia-Pacific region, knowing that doing so logically and inevitably downplays the importance of Arabia, the Gulf, and the GCC region?

In the same line of reasoning, does not what is in play resemble previous Israeli governments' effective efforts periodically to single out Lebanon, Syria, Iran, and/or Iraq, and, from time to time, even Saudi Arabia, Egypt, Sudan, or Yemen for international attention – but seldom if ever the need to reach a peaceful, negotiated, enduring, and comprehensive political settlement over Occupied East Jerusalem, the West Bank, the settlements, water, and the Palestinian refugees?

9.3. Suspicion Mongering?

Another question is why would America appear determined to embark upon a different, strategic, regional emphasis when doing so would appear to risk arousing deep and widespread suspicions of its true intentions in Asia? And why do so where, among friends at least if not also adversaries, the grounds for such suspicions were not present before? Would the reason be solely to be able to strengthen US capabilities to observe and, if need be, respond to future developments in the region? If so, would the United States be willing to reciprocate were Asian countries to seek to do the same *vis-à-vis* the United States in the Western hemisphere? In keeping with this line of reasoning, is it in US interests to awaken in America's leaders and elites, let alone the broader American public, an unwarranted impending fear of Asia? Alternately, does the United States want to implant in Asia the perception of an American threat?

Does a US government responsible for nearly 320 million Americans want to provoke the more than 1.3 billion Chinese, who would understandably not look kindly upon a country or people that, in the view of, say, the Chinese leadership, needlessly antagonizes and provokes them? Are America's Asian allies really in such dire straits of external threat from *any* regional or global challenge or challenger? Or, if not, might America be providing grounds for such challenges, would-be challengers, or even mere competitors to be perceived as threats? Are the possibly coming trends and indications in the Asia-Pacific region likely to be of such a threatening nature and extent as various American fear-mongers and powerful interest groups would have the US government, media, and general public believe? And are the alleged threats likely to be used in support of arguments in favor of a coming greater intrusion of America's armed forces into a region where, in the eyes of its inhabitants, larger numbers than already exist are neither in all of the region's countries either wanted or perceived as necessary?

Most importantly: Would it not be the height of strategic folly for the United States to even pretend to be looking at imaginary greener pastures? And why do so in light of the possible additional taxpayers' expenditure in troops and treasure that will likely be required to make the envisioned pivot? Even if one's analyses and assessments are confined to the realm of strategic thinking as opposed to acting, why would one contemplate acting thusly so openly at the expense of disappointing and frustrating one's longstanding strategic partners and allies? Why do so, given the countless Iraqis, Americans and others killed, wounded, and maimed for life in the wake of the still relatively recent US-led invasion, occupation, and subsequent war in Iraq? And why do so amid the clouds of uncertainty in Afghanistan and attendant anxieties associated with the rising fortunes of anti-American and anti-American allies' insurgents in the sweep of land from Iraq to the Mediterranean? In all of this, where is the strategic merit in America's reasoning?

10. Conclusion

A final question concerns the news media's heavy dependence upon private sector advertisers, who are known to have strong emotionally, ideologically, and politically opinionated views, and may stand to gain economically from a shift toward Asia. If such pressures prevail, would this create a source of otherwise inexplicable editorial influence and pressure in the pivot-to-Asia narrative that is being fed to the American public? The fact that American mainstream media have largely failed to examine and explain the questions, concerns, and issues raised and addressed herein should be a matter worthy of investigation. Absent such an investigation, the alleged validity versus the myths of the efficacy envisioned in the proposed pivot to Asia away from the GCC region would seem to stand unchallenged.

The transition of a country's strategic and foreign policy approach from one region to another under any circumstances is neither easy nor cost-free. Such things seldom are. Certainly, this would be the case when considering a pivot from an existing overall successful approach to one region toward another region where the alleged merits are questionable and debatable, the prospects dubious, and the potential implications and repercussions with regard to costs, rationale, efficiency, and necessity are serious and far-reaching. In this particular instance, it is difficult to make sense of the "Pivot to Asia School" when compared with the merits of the "Stand by One's Friends School." It is also difficult to imagine how it would be necessary or wise for the United States to imply it is pivoting from an area that is far more strategically vital globally than the Asian countries are or could realistically hope to become in the immediately foreseeable future.

And why contemplate doing so at the expense of one's strategic partners and in-region allies when doing so would certainly make no sense at all to America's strategic friends? Lastly, why do so when it would not make sense, either, to America's foes, whose leaders would trade places with the United States in a second were it seriously to contemplate pivoting from the GCC region to Asia, let alone actually do so?

Notes

1   The Third Ministerial Meeting of the GCC-US Strategic Dialogue was held on September 26, 2013, in New York. See *Media Note*, Office of the Spokesperson, U.S. Department of State, Washington, D.C., September 26, 2013, at http://www.state.gov/r/pa/prs/ps/2013/09/214834.htm.

2   Former Secretary of Defense Chuck Hagel stated at the US-GCC Defense Dialogue, May 14, 2014: "In recent years, the United States' defense cooperation with the nations of [the GCC] region has dramatically expanded…This has been demonstrated by the United States Central Command's continued, forward military presence, which includes 35,000 personnel; our Navy's 5th Fleet; our most advanced fighter aircraft; our most sophisticated intelligence, surveillance, and reconnaissance assets; and a wide array of missile defense capabilities. It has also been demonstrated by recent defense sales agreements, including some of the largest in American history." See *Secretary of Defense Speech* (U.S. Department of Defense, Washington D.C. May 14, 2014). http://www.defense.gov/Speeches/Speech.aspx?SpeechID=1847.

3   Frank A. Rose, Deputy Assistant Secretary, Bureau of Arms Control, Verification and Compliance, discussed the importance of US-GCC cooperation for political and economy security. See *Gulf*

Cooperation Council and Ballistic Missile Defense U.S. Department of State, Washington, D.C., May 14, 2014). http://www.state.gov/t/avc/rls/2014/226073.htm.

4   George Perkovich, Brian Radzinsky, and Jaclyn Tandler contend that GCC countries have worked with the US in power-balancing in the region to prevent potential nuclear escalation with Iran. See "The Iranian Nuclear Challenge and the GCC," Carnegie Endowment for International Peace, May 31, 2012. http://carnegieendowment.org/2012/05/31/iranian-nuclear-challenge-and-gcc.

5   Philip Seib, for example, suggested that "in the United States and elsewhere in the West there is a decided "Arab fatigue."See Philip Seib,"Arab Fatigue and Today's Middle East," *The Huffington Post*, June 30, 2014 at http://www.huffingtonpost.com/philip-seib/arab-fatigue-and-todays-m_b_5415259. html.

6   Nabeel Khoury, "GCC Wrath, Talk of Unity, and Beyond," The Chicago Council on Global Affairs, Chicago, December 12, 2013, at http://middleeastcorner.org/2013/12/12/gcc-wrath-talk-of-unity-and-beyond/.

7   Brandon Friedman, "Battle for Bahrain: What one Uprising Meant for the Gulf States and Iran," *World Affairs Journal*, April 2012.

8   For the regional and global threat Hizbollah poses, see Thomas Donilon,"Hezbollah Unmasked," *The New York Times*, February 17, 2013.

9   On U.S. and GCC views regarding US policy in Syria and Egypt, see "Despite Tensions, US-GCC Relations Strong," *Defense News,* November 10, 2013.

10   Prince Turki Al-Faisal discusses the importance of the GCC joining talks with Iran in "GCC 'Must join P5+1 Iran talks,'" *Gulf News*, December 8, 2013.

11   "POMED Notes-Changing Dynamics in the Gulf, GCC, Iran, and the U.S." Project on Middle East Democracy, Stimson Center conference on "Changing Dynamics,"Washington, DC. July 2 2014.

12   Kelly McEvers, "Support for Iraq's Maliki Puts U.S., Iran in the Same Camp." *National Public Radio,* September 20, 2010.

13   President Barack Obama announced at the beginning of January, 2012, a new Defense Strategic Guidance that, among other things, emphasized a strategic geographical shift of priorities to East Asia and the Pacific, while maintaining current interest in the Middle East. On the DSG, see, Catherine Dale and Pat Towell, "In Brief: Assessing the January 2012 Defense Strategic Guidance (DSG)," Congressional Research Service, R42146, Washington, DC. August 13, 2013. http://fas.org/sgp/crs/natsec/R42146.pdf. Many in the Gulf feared that this `pivot' to Asia was the beginning of America's withdrawal from the Middle East.)

14   Abdullah al-Shayji, "Overhauling the GCC-US partnership." *Gulf News*, May 4, 2014.

15   "Letters from America: Selling US Exports to Asia's Middle Class Consumers," *China Briefing,* October 22, 2012.

16   "Washington's Nightmare Comes True: The Russian-Chinese Strategic Partnership Goes Global." *Global Research,* August 23, 2014.

17   Trevor Moss, "Obama's Visit Signals Progress for Asia `Pivot'," *Wall Street Journal*, May 2, 2014.

18   See the discussion by Loren Thompson, "What Happens When America No Longer Needs Middle East Oil?" *Forbes*, December 3, 2012.

19   The expanding relationship between the US and Asia is described in "Asia Task Force: US-East Asia Relations: A Strategy for Multi-Lateral Engagement," *Council on Foreign Relations*, Washington, D.C. November 2011.

20   On the other hand, Beauchamp argues that China is in no condition to replace the United States as world leading superpower. See Zack Beauchamp, "China has not replaced America – and it never will," *The Week,* February 13, 2013.

21   See an outline of the motivations and interactions of the United States in the Middle East following World War in Mike Shuster, "The Middle East and the West: The US Role Grows." *NPR*, August 23, 2004.

22   Julie Finnin Day outlines the history of American political action in the region in "50 Years of US Policy in the Middle East," *The Christian Science Monitor*, September 27, 2001.

23 See James Russell, "Searching for a Post-Saddam Regional Architecture," in Brian Loveman, Ed., *Strategy for Empire: U.S. Regional Security Policy in the Post-Cold War Era, Vol. 2*, (Lanham, MD: Roman and Littlefield, 2004), pp. 101-121.

24 See, *inter alia*, "From the Archive: 28 February, 1991: The Liberation of Kuwait," *The Guardian*.

25 The Global Policy Forum details the timeline and effects of American and international economic sanctions on Iraq in "Sanctions Against Iraq," *Global Policy Forum*.

26 Author's interview with a former GCC Secretary General, March 2009. Name of source and venue withheld for reasons that the source was not authorized to speak for the public record.

27 GCC Heads of State Summit, specifically in 2003, 2004, and 2005.

28 Christian Koch explores the involvement of the US in Iraq in the 2000's in the context of GCC security and expectations of American support (and subsequent tensions with the US upon its decision to invade) in *The GCC as a Regional Security Organization*, KAS International Reports. November 2011.

29 See, *inter alia*, Naofumi Hashimoto, "The US 'Pivot' to the Asia-Pacific and US Middle East Policy: Towards an Integrated Approach," *Middle East Institute*, March 15, 2013.

30 Anthony Cordesman, "US Strategy in the Gulf: Shaping and communicating US Plans for the Future in a Time of Region-Wide Change and Instability." *Center for Strategic and International Studies*, Washington DC, April 14, 2011.

31 Rashid Khalidi and Lynn Neary, "Tracking the Cold War's Legacy in the Middle East," Lynn Neary, *National Public Radio*, March 24, 2009.

32 Michael Lind, "Beyond American Hegemony," *The New America Foundation*, Washington DC, May/June 2007.

33 Kenneth N. Waltz, *Structural Realism after the Cold War* (New York: Columbia University Press, 2000).

34 Louis Kriesberg, "The Political Psychology of the Gulf War: Leaders, Publics, and the Process of Conflict." *American Political Science Review*, September 1994. http://journals.cambridge.org/action/displayAbstract?fromPage=online&aid=8761322&fileId=S0003055400094430.

35 Bernard Weiner, "A PNC Primer: How We Got Into this Mess." *Counter Punch*. May 27, 2003.

36 Jassim Hussein, "The Oil Resources of the GCC States." *The Middle East Monitor*, June 23, 2014.

37 Christopher Helman, "The World's Biggest Oil Companies." *Forbes*. July 2013.

38 Harold James, "Which Country Will Dominate the World?" December 4, 2013. http://forumblog.org/2013/12/which-country-will-dominate-the-world-economy/.

Bibliography

Cordesman, Anthony. "US Strategy in the Gulf: Shaping and communicating US Plans for the Future in a Time of Region-Wide Change and Instability." *Center for Strategic and International Studies*, Washington DC, April 14, 2011.

Kriesberg, Louis. "The Political Psychology of the Gulf War: Leaders, Publics, and the Process of Conflict." *American Political Science Review*, September 1994.

"POMED Notes-Changing Dynamics in the Gulf, GCC, Iran, and the U.S." Project on Middle East Democracy, Stimson Center conference on "Changing Dynamics," Washington, DC. July 2 2014.

Russell, James. "Searching for a Post-Saddam Regional Architecture," pp. 101-121 in Brian Loveman, ed., *Strategy for Empire: U.S. Regional Security Policy in the Post-Cold War Era, Vol. 2*. Lanham, MD: Roman and Littlefield, 2004.

Waltz, Kenneth N. Waltz, *Structural Realism after the Cold War*. New York: Columbia University Press, 2000.

4

The Evolving American Security Role in the Gulf

David B. Des Roches

1. Introduction

The American role in the Gulf region is easily misinterpreted. The strategic interests of the United States in the region remain constant, but its operational presence will inevitably decrease. It would be a mistake, however, to assume that a decrease in physical presence indicates a correlating decrease in strategic relevance. An examination of the US military posture will show that there is no strategic decrease in the US ability to achieve its security goals in the Gulf. Indeed, one can make a strong case that the decrease in American day-to-day military presence increases the possibility of extraordinary American military actions as Washington policy makers have to deal with greater margins of uncertainty.

This emerging American posture, shaped by the parallel drawdown of US forces in Afghanistan and Iraq as well as by the climate of austerity at home, is nothing new. Indeed, it is a return to the historical American presence in the Gulf, which tends to stress reliance on allies and partner-capacity building efforts, such as arms sales and joint training exercises. The period of American build-up to confront Saddam Hussein and deal with other post-9/11 contingencies should be viewed as a departure from the norm, not the norm itself. This old strategy has a new name, "Building Partner Capacity," and was first formalized as a Department of Defense (DoD) mission in the 2006 Quadrennial Defense Review. The new posture is generated by political and technical developments in the United States, as well as by partner states' increased willingness to collaborate on defense issues. The main foci of this effort will be missile defense and the buildup of central Gulf Cooperation Council (GCC) capabilities along the lines of the North Atlantic Treaty Organization (NATO).

Moving forward, the United States will seek to expand an independent Gulf military capability that will remain dependent upon American weapons and a limited military presence, and will seek to move the GCC towards a more integrated military command structure, particularly for missile defense. There has been quite a bit of energy and thought expended over the evolving role of the United States in the Persian Gulf.[1] America's allies in the GCC are concerned that the United States is leaving the region, that it is blind to the threat posed by Iran and is generally an unreliable ally. As American military forces draw down globally, GCC fears of a new US policy are exacerbated by the decrease of forces in the region. Gulf leaders look at the decrease in US forces on the ground in GCC countries as well as at the decrease in aircraft carrier days in the Gulf and worry they are being left to their own devices by a fickle USA. An examination of the historical record, as well as the general pattern of American activity in the gulf, will prove these fears to be overstated. Rather than abandoning the Gulf, the American military is instead reverting to the norm, maintaining a small but scalable military presence while at the same time encouraging the development of indigenous GCC military capabilities.

This chapter examines the concerns the GCC states have voiced over American defense policy in the region and looks at the proposed American force structure as well as the evolving nature of the military threat in the Gulf. I will argue that, rather than representing an abandonment of the GCC states, the American presence is reverting to the normal, pre-9/11 force presence. Additionally, such large-scale visible military capabilities such as aircraft carriers may actually be overall liabilities for the defense of GCC nations, as they are increasingly vulnerable. In this context, the American public would likely not support prolonged military operations in the Gulf if such an asset were to be lost.

2. The Airing of Grievances

Decision-making in the GCC countries is highly centralized.[2] Issues of national security are rarely discussed in public, and criticism of security partners such as the United States had been extremely rare and is still somewhat uncommon. The general GCC dissatisfaction with the perceived drift of recent American defense policy adheres to this formula. There has not been overt criticism by the GCC governments, but several figures close to government, in particular to the Saudi government, have been outspoken in their criticism of the United States. The Saudis appear to have entrusted former ambassadors who do not hold current posts within the government but are known to be close to the Saudi leadership. This use of non-governmental emissaries allows for a level of candor that is rare in Saudi diplomatic discussions and creates an opportunity for the Saudi government to not be bound by the public pronouncements of these emissaries.

The two most prominent of these emissaries have been Prince Turki al-Faisal and Prince Muhammad bin Nayef. Turki al-Faisal, in his November 2013 address before the National Council on US-Arab Relations, was outspoken in his criticism of American defense policy. This speech, which followed Prince Muhammad Bin Nayef's *New York Times* editorial, reads as a detailed airing of grievances.[3]

The first grievance involves the proclaimed US "pivot" to the Asia-Pacific region. First introduced as a DoD concept in the Defense Strategic Guidance of 2012, the pivot referred to a shift in the emphasis of US forces from Europe, which was regarded as relatively secure, towards Asia, where the growth in American trade and security interests were perceived to lay.[4] Member states of the GCC felt the pivot was also away from the Gulf. While the Europeans had grounds for concern, and forced the Obama administration to backtrack on the "pivot" during the Chicago NATO summit, the GCC member states had less cause for concern.

The pivot did not by itself indicate a lessening of GCC importance to the United States. Indeed, it actually enhanced the GCC, since the US has limited bases in the Indian Ocean littoral, and most of those are in the Gulf. The strategic assets associated with the pivot are all in Europe; for example, there are no longer any American tanks stationed on European soil as of early 2014.[5] Two years after the pivot was announced, the only concrete increase in American presence in Asia is a rotational force of about 2,500 Marines in northern Australia and the movement of a few ships that could easily be moved elsewhere.[6] There has not been an increase in shipbuilding or long-range aircraft construction needed to adopt a policy of power projection in Asia. In the absence of these steps, the pivot remains primarily a European concern. As far as the Persian Gulf is concerned, a dispassionate analysis shows the pivot to be irrelevant.

The second area of concern was the general decrease in American forces. The overall fielded strength of the US military was declining globally due to fiscal austerity measures as well as the winding down of the American presence in Afghanistan.[7] Among other consequences of this congressionally mandated cutback in DoD spending, there would be fewer days that an American carrier would be present in the Gulf or nearby in the Gulf of Oman. Once again, this did not reflect a lack of strategic concern by the US government, which remained poised to respond to any crisis in the vital region.

The third area of concern voiced by GCC officials was the haphazard American response to the Arab Spring. Clearly, US intelligence sources failed to anticipate the outburst and had no immediate response. Arab leaders found this lack of the American government's foresight irresponsible, particularly its lack of long-term vision regarding the possible adverse consequences of a democratic revolution in the Middle East and North Africa. These governments predictably resisted the rapid changes, fearing for their own political and personal security. In this narrative, the GCC countries perceived a long-standing Iranian-directed plan of Shi'i encirclement of the GCC. This alleged plan would be carried out both by the Iranian armed forces and intelligence services as well as by Hezbollah, seen as an Iranian proxy. Adherents of this view point to the following manifestations of an Iranian plan,

- the Shi'i state-within-a-state in Lebanon,
- the pro-Iran Bashar al-Assad regime in Syria,
- the pro-Iranian Nouri al-Maliki regime in Iraq,

- the chronic Shiʻi unrest in Bahrain and the eastern province of Saudi Arabia, and
- the Huthi uprising in Yemen.

There were other sources of Arab anxiety about this perceived challenge to the GCC and its strategic interests. The first was the speed with which the United States renounced a decades-long relationship with Egyptian President Hosni Mubarak, who for decades had served as a model ally of the United States. Gulf countries had seen Egypt, with its large army, as the Arab bulwark against the Iranian strategy of encirclement.[8] Mubarak had contributed a large contingent of forces to Operation Desert Storm and had enforced the Camp David peace accords to the letter of the agreement. He had participated in the isolation of Gaza following the Hamas takeover there, hosted an extremely large US military training mission, and armed his nation with one of the largest concentrations of US military equipment in the region.

Objectively, there was no doubt that Mubarak was one of America's strongest and most reliable partners. The low level of protest which brought a hasty American denunciation of Mubarak truly frightened the GCC members. Interestingly, this view was virtually identical to that of the Israelis, who were extremely concerned by the possibility of a transition from a reliable partner in Mubarak to the uncertainty of a Muslim Brotherhood-influenced Egyptian government, which later emerged.[9]

From the standpoint of the GCC and its member states, a group of relatively unorganized protestors were seen to persuade America to renounce a long-standing and loyal ally, one who stood by some of America's most controversial policies and ruled with a similar or greater degree of democratic accountability than most GCC countries. To many in the GCC, the United States overreacted in calling for regime change in Egypt. Many hard-liners were fearful that a precedent was being set. To many analysts, it was this fear that the United States would precipitously call for regime change in a variety of settings that led to the unannounced Saudi and Emirati deployment of security forces to Bahrain.[10] Even though this deployment was mostly political –there were no reports of Saudis coming into direct contact with protesters, for example – the preemptive action was carried out without notifying the US or other Western powers, who learned of it on television like everyone else. In sum, Mubarak was seen by GCC members as a potent and loyal Sunni ally who could be relied upon in extremis to defend GCC interests against any and all outside aggressors.

Perhaps most disturbingly, however, was the fear of a new precedent in American foreign policy, the idea that American support for a friendly regime could be summarily withdrawn in the face of popular protests. This was, to the GCC, a violation of the "Pact of 1979," an unwritten commitment by the United States to defend the Gulf against any form of outside aggression. The United States at the time was extremely concerned by the southward spread of the Soviet Union, most notably the Soviet invasion of Afghanistan and the potential for the Soviets to move into the chaos of post-revolution Iran and then achieve the "dream of Peter the Great" by gaining access to the Indian Ocean. The pact was a typical Cold War marriage of convenience, an informal but strong alliance between a group of absolute monarchies and a representational democracy to cooperate against a dyad of perceived Communist and Shi'a fundamentalist expansion. The American commitment was more fully articulated by US President Jimmy Carter in his 1980 State of the Union address:

> Let our position be absolutely clear: An attempt by any outside force to gain control of the Persian Gulf region will be regarded as an assault on the vital interests of the United States of America, and such an assault will be repelled by any means necessary, including military force.[11]

Over time, the GCC states saw this pact as less of a situational security agreement and more of a Westphalian-like recognition of their regime legitimacy. The abrupt US renunciation of Mubarak in the face of spontaneous demonstrations was a rude and abrupt shattering of this misconception. For the Emirs and Shaykhs of the Gulf, the sight of the United States aligning itself with a mass of Twittering students and protesters of various stripes rather than the established ruler of long-standing was an abomination. Instead of an American reassertion of the Wilsonian values of self-determination, the GCC rulers saw a direct criticism of their rule, and the establishment of a dangerous precedent that would haunt the region for decades to come.

Such suspicions of American disloyalty intensified when the Syrian uprising exploded into a full-blown civil war. The Obama administration's call for military action in response to a Syrian use of chemical weapons – the famous "red line" – turned out to lack support both among a war-weary American population as well as among key American allies, most notably the United Kingdom.[12] What analysts in the West saw as an American domestic political issue was understood by hardliners in the GCC as further proof of American unreliability – the degree to which on any given day ranged along a narrow spectrum from feebleness to treachery.[13]

These conflicting world views extend to the region's cartography. While American leaders are likely to interpret Syria's civil war as the inevitable dynamics of a Sykes-Picot-created artificial state, GCC officials construe the crisis as a Manichean struggle between an Iranian proxy and the West.[14] These critics of US foreign policy winced when they saw the nation and its closest allies back down on the chemical red line. They also could not countenance the sight of Hezbollah, yet another Iranian agent, bolstering Assad in key battles and acquiring valuable experience for military forces that may someday fight in the Arabian peninsula.

Further compounding the perception of willful US military inaction in Syria was the almost simultaneous revelation that the United States and Iran had been holding secret discussions on the Iranian nuclear program. This development was distressing for several reasons. The first was the perception that the Arab Gulf was being used as a bargaining chip by American strategists. The second, more disturbing but less quantifiable concern, was an unsettling fear that the United States was on the verge of a "grand bargain" that would see the US swapping its Arab allies for Persian ones.[15] The Saudi fears of an American grand bargain with Iran, which later included a tacit alliance in opposing the Islamic State, went to the heart of their suspicion that the American interest in the Gulf is conditional. These concerns remained as the P5+1 talks continued in the second half of 2015.

There was a second-order effect of the US-Iran nuclear negotiations which is of more immediate concern: by focusing on the nuclear issue, the West had effectively given a blank check for continued Iranian meddling in conflicts such as Syria, Bahrain and Yemen. Saudi Arabia, the UAE and Bahrain in particular were concerned by what they saw as Iran's role among dissatisfied Shi'i populations in their countries.[16] These hard-line states see Iran's role as directing and controlling various Shi'i protest movements, and discount the legitimacy of Shi'i grievances or concerns. In this telling, Shi'i protest movements (most notably in Bahrain) are not inspired by domestic inequities but rather are created, directed and controlled by Iran and her proxy arm of Hezbollah.

Despite the many concerns and suspicions at play in US-GCC relations, the two sides are well aware of their interdependence in the highly volatile and dangerous strategic environment they share. Stability in the Gulf region remains a vital interest of the United States and its allies. For their part, pragmatic GCC rulers consider a state of complete self-reliance to be a by-product of wishful thinking. They are well aware that any possibility of building, let alone maintaining, a collective security system that excludes the United States is out of the question.

3. The US Military Drawdown

As noted above, the turbulence in US-GCC relations coincided with deep cutbacks in the nation's military budget. This fiscal drawdown had two sources. The first involved the withdrawal of the vast amount of American troops from Iraq and Afghanistan by the end of 2011 and 2014, respectively. The second, and related, impetus for military cutbacks were mandated by Congress, which required all federal agencies to reduce their spending by 10 percent in 2013. This "sequestration" of federal spending did not spare the DoD, by far the largest discretionary budget expense. The combined effects of these two actions led to a reduction in military spending from approximately $700 billion in fiscal year 2009 to about $550 billion in fiscal year 2015. As these expenses fell, so did the US military presence in the gulf region.

With the GCC countries already concerned about the political reliability of the United States, the reduction in American forces in the Gulf was problematic, if not entirely unsuspected news. American forces had not been present in large numbers in the Gulf prior to the Iran-Iraq war, and (aside from various training and equipping missions) had not established much of a significant presence in the Gulf. Prior to the Tanker War of the 1980s, the American military presence was mostly token. America preferred to rely on its strong regional partners (Iran and Saudi Arabia) and generally used the region only as a port call or to project power into other regions.

From the GCC perspective, this was a historic norm. It is generally forgotten today, but the American security presence in the Gulf in World War II was entirely in support of other policy priorities. The first American request for a military base in the region, at Dhahran, was not for defense of the region but rather as an aircraft refueling spot on the route between Cairo and Karachi in 1944. The US military did not have a dedicated joint command for the Middle East until events of the late 1970s made the need essential. Until then, the Middle East was either the responsibility of a joint command whose primary mission was readiness and training of US-based military forces or the ward of US Navy forces in Europe.[17] The increase in American forces in the region was first to stabilize it and preserve freedom of navigation during the Iran-Iraq war, and second, to confront Saddam Hussein in the aftermath of the invasion of Kuwait and during the interminable and expensive operations to contain Saddam after the war.

Under current conditions, the resource-constrained US military will have a smaller presence in the Gulf. This is not, as commonly thought, an implication of the much-discussed "rebalancing" to Asia-Pacific. When one reads into the strategic guidance, it becomes readily apparent that the pivot is away from Europe and toward the Indian Ocean and Middle East. Indeed, the Gulf is more likely to gain American military assets as a result of the pivot than it is to lose them, due both to the paucity of military bases in East Asia and to the financial benefits of operating in the Gulf, where GCC partners often subsidize fuel and other expenses for US forces.[18]

As noted earlier, there has only been one major increase in U.S force projections in East Asia: the establishment of a bare-bones base for a rotational Marine force in northern Australia. There has been no major increase in the numbers of ships, carriers, long-range bombers or other assets that would be required to project additional power in East Asia. There has been no significant increase in military construction at any power projection base in the Pacific since the debut of the pivot. American forces that operate in the Indian Ocean will, of necessity, continue to stage out of the Gulf.

Fiscal constraints in the United States may modify the nature of the continuing military presence in the Gulf. The large number of aerial tankers and other power projection assets currently stationed in the Gulf in order to facilitate continuing operations in Afghanistan will, of necessity, decrease. As the number of US forces in Afghanistan drew down, the requirement to maintain an aircraft carrier group in the Indian Ocean to provide close air support also drew down. And the fiscal crunch in the United States will likely lead to the mothballing of the *USS George Washington*, bringing the carrier fleet down to ten and thus leading to gaps in carrier coverage in and close to the Persian Gulf.

4. The Silver Lining

These spending and force reductions, however, were not entirely negative. Instead, they could increase the security of the GCC states. Developments in missile technology are negating the utility of large naval ships at just the time America is developing an increased aversion to overseas military action. The recent advent of domestic energy independence, furthermore, reinforces the Pentagon's primary security functions. These trends favor a smaller but more agile US military presence in the region.

Missile guidance systems, along with all other solid state electronics, are becoming more accurate, cheaper, and more widespread every year. At the same time, nations are developing better fuel systems for their missile-propulsion systems. As missile-based firepower improves, their cost has been reduced. In sum, the math is not in favor of carriers. As military analysts have argued, carriers are both increasingly vulnerable and prohibitively expensive as force-projection platforms.[19]

These technological developments extend beyond the United States. Consider that, in 2001, Iran's Fateh 110 missile was thought to have a circular error probability of about 100 meters. Even assuming that there have been no increases in terminal guidance or innate targeting accuracy, these relatively low-cost missiles could have the capacity to overwhelm a carrier's close-in weapons systems and disable an aircraft carrier which costs billions of dollars. If such a carrier were sunk with its full crew, the casualty count would exceed 4,000 sailors. The Fateh 110 is not the only Iranian missile under development, and Iran has also invested in high speed torpedo technology. These developments, coupled with recent advances in naval mines and silent diesel submarines, mean that the extraordinary era of aircraft carrier dominance is coming to an end.

Figure 1 Estimates of Iran's Ballistic Missiles

Iranian SRBMs

	2000	2001	2002	2003	2004	2005	2006	2007	2008	2009	2010	2011	2012
Jane's Strategic Weapon Systems													
Shahab1 and Shahab 2(Scud B and Scud c)			some number have been acquired, assembled, produced and used to date				300 – 00 missiles				around 50 launchers; 200 – 300 missiles	around 50 launchers; 200 – 300 missiles	around 50 launchers; 200 – 300 missiles
Tondar 69 (CSS-8)			some number exported from China in 1992							up to 30 launchers: up to 200 missiles	around 20 launchers; less than 100 missiles	around 20 launchers; less than 100 missiles	around 20 launchers; 200 missiles
Fateh A-110		tested	low-rate production		Initial operational capability					3 versions may be in service	3 versions may be in service	3 versions may be in service	
The Military Balance (The International Institute for Strategic Studies)													
scud B / scud C	est 10 launchers;	est 17 launchers;	est 17 launchers:	est 17 launchers:	12-18 launchers:	12-18 launchers:	12-18 launchers:	12-18 launchers	12-18 launchers	12-18 launchers:	12-18 launchers;	12-18 launchers;	12-18 launchers;
Shahab - 1/2	300 missiles	300 missiles	300 missiles	300 missiles	300 missiles	300 missiles	300 missiles	300 missiles	300 missiles	300 missiles	300 missiles	300 missiles	300 missiles

	2000	2001	2002	2003	2004	2005	2006	2007	2008	2009	2010	2011	2012
CSS-8	esc, 25 launchers; 150 missiles	est, 30 launchers; 175 missiles	est. 30 launcher; 175 missiles	est. 30 launcher; 175 missiles	est. 30 launcher; 175 missiles	est. 30 launcher; 175 missiles	est. 30 launcher; 175 missiles	est. 30 launcher; 175 missiles	Est. 30 launcher; 175 missiles	Est. 30 launcher; 175 missiles	Est. 30 launcher; 175 missiles	Est. 30 launcher; 175 missiles	Est. 30 launcher; 175 missiles
Shahcen-1 Hatf-4/ Shaheen-2						some	some	some	some	some		some	some

Iranian MRBMs

	2000	2001	2002	2003	2004	2005	2006	2007	2008	2009	2010	2011	2012
Jane's Strategic Weapon Systems													
Shahab 3 and variants			Production underway	Production underway					< 20 TELs				25
Sejil / Ashura									testing	testing		IOC	
Shahab-¾ (Ghadr-1)				IOC	~20		30 50						
The Military Balance (The International Institute for Strategic Studies)													
Shahab-3	some	some (20 missiles)	some	at least 3	at least 6 launchers (Shahib 3 /Zelial-3)	6 launchers; each with est- 4 missiles	est. 6 launchers: each with est 4 missiles	est. 6 launchers: each with est 4 missiles	est. 6 launchers: each with est 4 missiles	est. 6 launchers: each with est 4 missiles	up to 12 launchers, some Ghadr (or Kadr)	6 launchers, some Ghadr	12+ Shahab 3/ Ghadr
Sajil													
Sajil-2												in development	some (in development)

Source: As noted. Missale designations as used by the source.
Notes: Where launcher numbers onty are noted, actual missile inventory may be larger because launchers can be reused to fire additional missiles.

Source: http://www.iranintelligence.com/arsenal (accessed May 26, 2014).

The silver lining in this trend is that smaller, more nimble ships, such as mine countermeasure vessels, are more appropriate for countering the military threat posed by Iran to the GCC. Iran's capabilities are generally disruptive rather than overwhelming. Their conventional forces are not a match for the combined GCC forces, and it is clear by their reliance on missiles, torpedoes, fast-attack craft, and mines that they do not seek to control the sea lanes in the Gulf, but rather to disrupt shipping there.

The smaller ships required to counter this threat are less likely to disrupt the American commitment to the GCC partnership. Recall that there was little or no debate over the United States quitting the 1980s oil tanker reflagging mission when 37 sailors were killed in an Iraqi missile attack aboard the *USS Stark*. Similarly, the loss of life on the *USS Cole* in Aden harbor was not large enough to lead America to reassess its fundamental position in the Middle East. The smaller, more flexible force that America has deployed in the Gulf region is prudent both militarily as well as politically.

A second silver lining relates to declining American support of military intervention, particularly when American national interests are not seen to be at stake. Nearly two decades ago, the Rand Corporation studied American public opinion of overseas military intervention since World War II. These studies detail the general trend that the American public is willing to accept overseas American military action only if a significant national interest is at stake or so long as there are not significant casualties. For example, American support for operations in Somalia, where there were no perceived national interests at stake, plummeted in the wake of the Ranger attack memorialized in the film *Black Hawk Down*. At the same time, there was support for military operations to liberate Kuwait in 1991, because Americans felt the global energy market was at stake.[20] These conclusions validate what many Americans feel intuitively, that military action is worthy of support only if it is relatively cost-free or vital to American national interests. If there were a major casualty incident in the Middle East, such as large-scale attacks by a rapidly expansionist Islamic State, the costs of intervention would be more than Americans would be willing to accept.

Yet another silver lining stems from American cultural values. While there remains an American commitment to support long-standing defense partners such as the GCC against outside aggression, the GCC's autocratic regimes are not compatible with the general tenor of America's historic normative approach to foreign policy. Appeals from the GCC, therefore, would probably not generate the same public and governmental responsiveness as seen for the "alliance of democracies" in World War II.

The American commitment to the Gulf is one that is somewhat at odd with the traditional American philosophy of foreign involvement. None of America's allies in the Gulf are democracies by any reasonable definition. Some of these states have a degree of democratic participation or institutions, but this is license granted by the state rather than a manifestation of inherent citizen rights. The US military presence in the Gulf has never been an affirmative positive value, but rather has been rationalized as a necessary compromise of

American democratic principles in order to preserve American security interests against an even greater enemy – at first, to prevent expansion of the Soviet Union, and later, to prevent the spread of first Shi'a religious fundamentalism and later a radical Salafi strain of Sunni Islam which threatens regional economic and political interests.

5. What is to be Done?

The American defense presence in the Gulf will remain robust, but less so than in the past. The guidepost to these intentions are the remarks of Secretary of Defense Chuck Hagel at the Manama Dialogue in December 2013 and at the US-GCC Defense Ministerial in Riyadh in May 2014.[21] In his Manama remarks, Hagel laid out what he sees as the enduring US military footprint in the region, allocated among the domains of land, air and sea:

> As we have withdrawn US forces from Iraq, are drawing down our forces in Afghanistan, and rebalancing toward the Asia Pacific, we have honored our commitment to Gulf security by enhancing our military capabilities in the region. We have a ground, air and naval presence of more than 35,000 military personnel in and immediately around the Gulf. Two years after our drawdown from Iraq, the US Army continues to maintain more than 10,000 forward-deployed soldiers in the region, along with heavy armor, artillery, and attack helicopters to serve as a theater reserve and a bulwark against aggression.

The United States is reverting to form in the Gulf. There will continue to be a persistent expeditionary capability, focused on maritime and air forces, which is scalable in response to Iranian provocations and other incidents. At the same time, the land forces presence will remain at relatively small but significant levels, with US Army forces continuing to man Patriot batteries in some GCC states and with a rotational Armor brigade in Kuwait. The emphasis of US security forces in the Gulf will continue to be to develop Arab capacity through foreign military sales and ongoing training relationships.

The replacement of Hagel as Secretary of Defense by Ashton Carter will not alter this trend. Nor, indeed would any likely change in the White House in 2016: the American presence in the Gulf in recent years has not been affected by changes of Presidential administrations. The American ground forces footprint in Kuwait, for example, will continue to resemble that during the Clinton Administration. Carter's limited amount of time as Secretary of Defense, together with the internal problems the Department faces as it restructures itself for peacetime, will not allow for a major restructuring of the US military footprint in the Gulf absent a crisis.

The emphasis on building partner capacity will continue under Secretary of Defense Carter, who has served as the Pentagon's chief of weapons procurement and development. He can be expected to have a keen understanding for the importance of developing GCC military forces which are capable of operating alongside American forces[22]. The trend will be towards stronger US-GCC military ties.

The largest customers for US military weapons and training in the world are the GCC states. The Saudi F-15 upgrade, together with the Saudi National Guard Apache helicopter purchase, could total as much as $60 billion.[23] The UAE, Oman and Bahrain all fly the F-16 fighter, and the UAE F-16s are actually more advanced than those flown by the United States Air Force.[24] The Saudis will eventually purchase the THAAD missile defense system, and are rumored to be on the verge of making a major US purchase for their naval modernization program. Qatar has been offered Patriots, two batteries of THAAD and an advanced early warning radar, which would total $6.5 billion if all options are exercised.[25]

In addition to the large and established programs with the Saudi Armed Forces and the Saudi National Guard, recent years have seen the launch of a major training case with the Saudi Ministry of Interior Facility Security Forces.[26] There has also been the establishment of a new US Marine Corps training effort with the UAE Presidential Guard[27]. The future generals of the UAE and Saudi armed forces are taught by American instructors at their National Defense Courses[28], and the Saudi military's demand for English instruction in the United States has overwhelmed the US military education system.

At Riyadh, Hagel laid out several new directions for US – GCC security cooperation. In addition to conventional arms sales and train-and-equip activities, Hagel's priorities included:

- A GCC-US integrated air defense command,
- The GCC taking command of the Combined Maritime Force's Gulf operations,
- A US-GCC cyber defense cooperation,
- A GCC Foreign Military Sales case, which would enhance GCC interoperability.[29]

The truly new innovation mentioned by Hagel was the offer of US support to the GCC as an institution. This proposal would help the GCC develop effective multinational institutions -- along the lines of NATO – to simplify cooperation and streamline alliance military actions. It is uncertain how effective the GCC states want the GCC to be, however, and progress may be held hostage to the current contretemps between Qatar and some other GCC members.

A significant area of cooperation will be missile defense. US missile defense systems (Patriots and/or THAAD) have been purchased by or offered for sale to all the GCC states. The US rather hastily accepted the UAE's offer to establish an International Air and Missile Defense Center of Excellence in Abu Dhabi, and has officers assigned there, developing and conducting exercises with GCC and other partners on a regular basis.[30] The capstone US missile defense exercise, *Nimble Titan*, has had GCC participation in the past and will continue to in the future. The engineering requirements of missile defense call for cooperation and collaboration among GCC partners and the US, and this engineering imperative is likely to lead to political agreement in the future.

The robust GCC reaction to the rise of the Islamic State in Syria and Iraq seems to have validated the American emphasis on building partner capacity. Fighter aircraft from the UAE, Saudi Arabia and Bahrain (US-built F-16s and F-15s) have participated in the attacks on Islamic State positions in Syria – a development which lends credence to the theory that political will can follow the development of military capacity. These multinational air operations were made possible by the decades of American train and equip efforts in the GCC. The rise of a common threat together with the existence of a force that is militarily interoperable with American forces made these operations possible.[31]

The recent removal of Nouri al-Maliki from the Iraqi government leadership was also seen by the GCC as a positive, albeit a small, step towards moving Iraq out of the orbit of Iran. The rise of the Islamic State in Iraq has shown that the Sunnis of Iraq cannot be ignored or repressed without consequence – this conclusion is certainly welcome in Riyadh and other capitols.

6. Summary and Conclusion

The US military presence in the Gulf is reverting to form – that which stresses a smaller, mobile force in place which can be enhanced if the need arises. The main factors driving this change are the downsizing of the support structure in the Gulf needed for US operations in Iraq and Afghanistan as well as the overall decrease in the US government budget.

America's GCC partners are extremely concerned about America's declining presence, about America's differing view of the Iranian threat, and about America's lack of support for long-time partners such as Mubarak during the Arab Spring. In spite of this, however, the American building partner capacity effort with GCC states continues to be among the largest in the world in terms of both weapons sales as well as numbers of military training and education programs. The United States will continue to press for GCC military integration, particularly in the field of missile defense. This smaller American footprint, together with a continuing building partner capacity effort is actually more in keeping with America's interest in the Gulf. The large numbers of forces America had in the Gulf from the mid-1980s until relatively recently were a departure from the norm.

Ironically, developments in missile technology and other area denial weapons mean that the smaller platforms the United States will have in the Gulf will actually be much more survivable in the event of a conflict. This bolsters the possibility that America will support its GCC partners in the event of a conflict: American public opinion will probably only support military action in support of a GCC regime if the possibility of American casualties is relatively low. American political leaders, most notably former Secretary of Defense Chuck Hagel, have publicly laid out American security goals for the region. These goals are likely to be unaffected by personnel or political party changes either at Defense or in the White House.

In spite of recent statements of GCC dissatisfaction with American actions in the Gulf, the recent GCC participation in airstrikes against the Islamic State in Syria shows that GCC partners have developed the military capability to conduct combat operations in conjunction with American and other coalition forces at some distance from their bases – a truly revolutionary change in GCC military capabilities, albeit one that builds on the experiences of combat in Libya. At the same time, the September 2014 air strikes also show that, in spite of GCC concerns about American motives and policy, the GCC states will be willing to take part in military actions with the United States against a perceived common threat.

Regardless of how the ongoing Iranian negotiations play out, America will continue to be the indispensable security partner of the GCC states. If a nuclear deal is reached, GCC states can be expected to request additional American security assurances, at least some of which will be in the form of increased American forces and platforms on their territory. One hopes that the negotiations with Iran produce results which everyone can live with. However, the GCC member states have clearly decided to plan for the worst while hoping for the best. The surprisingly strong GCC reaction to the rise of the Islamic State has shown that, if there is a common threat, the GCC will act militarily alongside the United States and its allies. America's defense contribution to the GCC will revert to that of an enabling partner on a regular basis, a key military force provider in a crisis, but one whose strategic interests may diverge from those of the GCC member states. To the extent that GCC interests support American interests, and GCC states pursue reforms and political modernization that makes this security partnership palatable to the average American, this security arrangement can continue to be productive and effective indefinitely.

Notes

1   For a dispassionate analysis of the "pivot" and its military implications, see Mark Manyin et al, *Pivot to the Pacific? The Obama Administration's "Rebalancing" Toward Asia* (Washington, D.C.: Congressional Research Service, 2012).

2   A readable accounting of the development and driving forces behind GCC defense dynamics is Matteo Legrenzi, *The GCC and the International Relations of the Gulf* (London: I.B. Tauris, 2011, Ch. 7).

3   Mohammed Bin Nawaf bin Abdulaziz al Saud, "Saudi Arabia Will Go It Alone," *New York Times* (December 17, 2013) http://www.nytimes.com/2013/12/18/opinion/saudi-arabia-will-go-it-alone.html?_r=0, (accessed December 16, 2014).

4   The document which laid out this shift can be found in DoD, *Sustaining Global Leadership: Priorities for 21st Century Defense* (http://www.defense.gov/news/Defense_Strategic_Guidance.pdf, accessed May 26, 2014). The term "pivot" was coined by Secretary of State Hillary Clinton in the lead-up to the release of the document. See Hillary Clinton, "America's Pacific Century." *Foreign Policy*, October 11, 2011: http://foreignpolicy.com/2011/10/11/americas-pacific-century/ (accessed December 16, 2014).

5   A concise analysis of the Defense Strategic Guidance is found in Ty Cobb, "The Defense Strategic Guidance: What's New? What is the Focus? Is it Realistic?" *Harvard Law School National Security Journal*, January 8, 2012, http://harvardnsj.org/2012/01/the-defense-strategic-guidance-whats-new-what-is-the-focus-is-it-realistic/ (accessed December 16, 2014).

6   A senior Department of Defense official noted to a Navy trade group that the pivot was not possible with current DoD resources. See Zachary Fryer-Biggs, "DoD Official: 'Asia Pivot' Can't Happen Due

to Budget Pressures" *Defense News,* March 4, 2014, http://archive.defensenews.com/article/20140304/DEFREG02/303040022/DoD-Official-Asia-Pivot-Can-t-Happen-Due-Budget-Pressures (accessed December 16, 2014).

7   For a discussion of the U.S. Department of Defense budget cuts, see Nick Simeone, "Hagel Outlines Budget Reducing Troop Strength, Force Structure" *American Forces Press Service,* February 24, 2014, http://www.defense.gov/news/newsarticle.aspx?id=121703 (accessed December 16, 2014).

8   Juan Cole had discussed the GCC fears of a "Shiite Crescent," albeit in the context of the United States clearing the way for a pro-Iran government in Iraq. See Juan Cole, "A "Shiite Crescent": The Regional Impact of the Iran War," *Current History* (January 2006, pp 20-26).

9   See Douglas Hamilton, "Israel Shocked by Obama"s ""Betrayal" of Mubarak" *Reuters,* January 31, 2011, http://www.reuters.com/article/2011/01/31/us-egypt-israel-usa-idUSTRE70U53720110131 (accessed December 16, 2014).

10 See Shadi Hamid, "Old Friends, New Neighborhood: The United States, The GCC and its Response to the Arab Spring," in *The GCC in the Mediterranean in Light of the of the Arab Spring* (Washington, D.C.: German Marshall Fund, December 2012, pp. 30-35).

11 Video of the State of the Union address is at http://www.c-span.org/video/?124054-1/1980-state-union-address (accessed May 26, 2014).

12 For a typical critique, see Taimur Khan, "Obama Aims to Reassure Arabian Gulf Leaders over Policy Shift" *The National,* March 24, 2014, http://www.thenational.ae/world/middle-east/obama-aims-to-reassure-arabian-gulf-leaders-over-policy-shift (accessed December 16, 2014).

13 See, for example, Martin Chulov "Is America"s Relationship with Saudi Arabia Broken beyond Repair?" *The Guardian,* March 28, 2014, http://www.theguardian.com/world/2014/mar/28/barack-obama-saudi-arabia-syria-iran (accessed December 16, 2014).

14 The Sykes-Picot agreement, reached in 1916 among British and French diplomats, established the map of much of the Middle East upon the collapse of the Ottoman Empire.

15 Gregory Gause, "Why the Iran Deal Scares Saudi Arabia" *The New Yorker,* November 16, 2013, http://www.newyorker.com/news/news-desk/why-the-iran-deal-scares-saudi-arabia (accessed December 16, 2014).

16 See, for example Kenneth Katzman, *Bahrain: Reform, Security and U.S. Policy* (Washington, D.C.: Congressional Research Service, March 24, 2014, pp. 30-31).

17 See Ronald Cole et al., *History of the Unified Command Plan 1946-1993* (Washington, D.C.: Joint History Office, Office of the Chairman of the Joint Chiefs of Staff, 1995: pp 29-30 and 74-78).

18 The Congressional Research Service's experts felt that the document called for "a focus on the Middle East," in direct contrast to a commonly expressed view in the region that the "pivot" was to be at the expense of the American presence in the Middle East. See Catherine Dale and Pat Towell, *In Brief: Assessing the January 2012 Defense Strategic Guidance* (Washington, D.C.: Congressional Research Service, August 13, 2013: p 2).

19 Henry J. Hendrix, *At What Cost A Carrier?* (Washington, D.C.: Center for a New American Security, 2013).

20 Eric Larson, *Casualties and Consensus: The Historical Role of Casualties in Domestic Support for U.S. Military Operations* (Santa Monica, CA: Rand Corporation, 1996).

21 Summarized by Claudette Roulo, "Hagel Urges Expanded Cooperation in Gulf Region," May 14, 2014, http://www.defense.gov/news/newsarticle.aspx?id=122247 (accessed May 26, 2014).

22 Department of Defense, "Ashton Carter Biography," http://www.defense.gov/bios/biographydetail.aspx?biographyid=186 (accessed December 16, 2014).

23 The sales notice was widely misreported at the time the U.S. Government offered the aircraft as an offer of F-15s totaling $60 billion. In fact, the offer included F-15s, Apache helicopters and a considerable amount of other defense equipment and services. The deal which was actually concluded for F-15s was worth $29.5 Billion. See the White House, "Statement by Principal Deputy Press Secretary Joshua Earnest on U.S. Sale of Defense Equipment to Saudi Arabia," December 29, 2011, http://www.whitehouse.gov/the-press-office/2011/12/29/statement-principal-deputy-press-secretary-joshua-earnest-us-sale-defens (accessed May 26, 2014).

24 An excellent technical reference to the capabilities of the UAE F-16 (and those capabilities which were denied the UAE, such as the ability to launch the Black Shahine cruise missile) is found at the Defense Industry Daily website, which conveniently lists associated weapons and services and links to formal Congressional notifications of sales. "Top Falcons: The UAE"s F-16 Block 60/61 Fighters," http://www.defenseindustrydaily.com/the-uaes-f-16-block-60-desert-falcon-fleet-04538/ (accessed May 26, 2014).

25 Aaron Mehta, "Qatar, UAE Request THAAD Purchases," Defense News, November 5, 2012, http://www.defensenews.com/article/20121105/DEFREG04/311050010/Qatar-UAE-Request-THAAD-Purchases (accessed 26 May, 2014).

26 The Saudi Ministry of Interior case was notified to Congress on April 17, 2014, and would initially be worth $80 Million over three years. This case does not include any provision of equipment to the Saudi forces – it is only concerned with the provision of trainers and their life support. See Defense Security Cooperation Agency, "Kingdom of Saudi Arabia – Support Services," April 21, 2014 http://www.dsca.mil/sites/default/files/mas/saudi_arabia_14-02.pdf (accessed May 26, 2014).

27 For a discussion of the commercial Emirati program, see Mark Mazetti, "Secret Desert Force Set Up By Blackwater"s Founder," *The New York Times*, May 15, 2011, page A1. For a (rather vague) description of the U.S. Marine Corps UAE training case, see Defense Security Cooperation Agency, "United Arab Emirates (UAE) – Blanket Order Training," January 8, 2014, http://www.dsca.mil/sites/default/files/mas/uae_13-46.pdf (accessed May 26, 2014).

28 "NESA Hosts Saudi War Course in Washington," http://nesa-center.org/news/2014/05/14/nesa-hosts-saudi-war-course-washington-dc (accessed 26 May, 2014). See also Robert Sharp, "Greater Critical Thinking Following the 'Arab Spring,'" *International Policy Digest*, which includes a discussion of U.S. professional military education in the UAE and other Middle East countries http://www.internationalpolicydigest.org/2014/01/22/greater-critical-thinking-following-arab-spring/ (accessed May 26, 2014).

29 Roulin, op cit.

30 See Daniel Karber, "Fires Mud to Space: An Assessment of Opportunities for the US Army Air Defense Artillery," *Fires*, May-June 2012, pp. 8-13.

31 Jessica Schulberg, "Five Arab Countries Are Supporting Obama's Strikes in Syria. What's Their Strategy?" *The New Republic*, September 23, 2014, http://www.newrepublic.com/article/119552/five-arab-countries-support-obamas-airstrikes-syria-heres-why (accessed December 16, 2014).

Bibliography

Cobb, Ty. "The Defense Strategic Guidance: What's New? What is the Focus? Is it Realistic?" *Harvard Law School National Security Journal*, January 8, 2012.

Cole, Juan. "A 'Shiite Crescent:' The Regional Impact of the Iran War," *Current History*, January 2006.

Gause, Gregory. "Why the Iran Deal Scares Saudi Arabia" *The New Yorker*, November 16, 2013.

Shadi Hamid, "Old Friends, New Neighborhood: The United States, The GCC and its Response to the Arab Spring," in *The GCC in the Mediterranean in Light of the of the Arab Spring*. Washington, D.C.: German Marshall Fund, December 2012.

Larson, Eric. *Casualties and Consensus: The Historical Role of Casualties in Domestic Support for U.S. Military Operations*. Santa Monica, CA: Rand Corporation, 1996.

Legrenzi, Matteo, *The GCC and the International Relations of the Gulf*. London: I.B. Tauris, 2011.

Manyin, Mark, *Pivot to the Pacific? The Obama Administration's "Rebalancing" Toward Asia*. Washington, D.C.: Congressional Research Service, 2012.

Schulberg, Jessica. "Five Arab Countries Are Supporting Obama's Strikes in Syria. What's Their Strategy?" *The New Republic*, September 23, 2014.

5

The Eagle's Nest in the Gulf:
Analysis of US Military Deployment in
the GCC Countries (1991-2014)[1]

Degang Sun and Yahia H. Zoubir

1. Introduction

After the end of the Gulf War in 1991, US military deployments in the GCC states were transformed from aiming solely at the containment of Iran to the dual containment of both Iran and Iraq.[2] In the light of the 9/11 2001 terrorist attacks, the US further readjusted its military presence in the GCC states in two respects. First, the task of the bases evolved from dual containment to the more complex and enduring tasks of safeguarding Gulf security, countering terrorists, and containing Iran. Second, the major military base distribution shifted from Saudi Arabia and Kuwait to Qatar, Bahrain and the UAE. Thus, a multifaceted security mechanism under US leadership took shape to counter Iran's proposal for a "collective Gulf security initiative". On the morrow of the Arab uprisings of 2010/2011 and the rise of the Islamic State of Iraq and Syria (ISIS), US military deployments in the GCC states, enunciated in the Obama Doctrine which shifts US strategic focus to the Asia-Pacific regions, has revealed five distinct features: these are that the bases are spreading geographically, diminishing in size in the form of "lily-pads", becoming stronger in mobility, developing multi-dimensional functions, and gradually being interlinked with other US bases in Central Asia, Turkey, and Djibouti in the Horn of Africa.

To put this in historical perspective, foreign military presences have been a continuing phenomenon since ancient times. The Roman Empire, Portugal, Spain, the Netherlands, the United Kingdom, the Soviet Union and the United States have all relied on such presences to project power, establish spheres of influence, grab regional resources and politically exclude other powers from seeking hegemony.[3] Foreign military presences can generally be classified into three types: main operating bases (MOBs) that boast command, control and communication systems; forward operation sites (FOSs) that are smaller and more flexible than MOBs; and cooperative security locations (CSLs) that are small-sized, austere and less visible (hence sometimes referred to as "lily pads") for prepositioning weapons, munitions, and modest numbers of troops.[4]

Following the UK, the US is the second empire that has built a global military presence, and foreign military bases remain the bridgeheads of US global power projection. After the consolidation of continental dominance, there were three periods of expansive global ambition in US history, beginning in 1898 with the American-Spanish War, then in the period following WWII, and finally post-2001 with the Global War on Terrorism.[5] Since the end of WWII, the United States has been a global hegemon with unparalleled power projection capabilities. As former CIA analyst Chalmers Johnson put it:

> most Americans do not recognize — or do not want to recognize — that the United States dominates the world through its military power. Due to government secrecy, our citizens are often ignorant of the fact that our garrisons encircle the planet. This vast network of American bases on every continent except Antarctica actually constitutes a new form of empire — an empire of bases with its own geography. Without grasping the dimensions of this globe-girdling base world, one can't begin to understand the size and nature of our imperial aspirations or the degree to which a new kind of militarism is undermining our constitutional order.[6]

Since the end of the Cold War, the Gulf region has been one of the key strategic areas for the US to build its military bases. As noted above, the United States military bases in the Gulf, acting as "beachheads", have gone through three historical stages since the demise of the Soviet Union, marked by the Gulf War in 1991, the 9/11 terrorist attacks in 2001, and the Arab uprisings since 2010. In the past two-and-a-half decades, both Democrats and Republicans have reached a consensus on the deployment of military bases in the region: conservatives highlight the US's need to deploy military might to deter regional threats, while liberals underscore US responsibility to (allegedly) provide regional order for the peace, stability and prosperity of the Gulf region.

2. A Historical Review of US Military Deployment in the Gulf Region: A Perspective on Military Doctrines

Located in the Western Hemisphere, the United States is geographically disadvantaged with regard to participating in Eurasian affairs. However, Washington has overcome this handicap and steadily intensified its intervention in the affairs of peripheral Eurasia through overseas military deployments since the end of World War Two.[7] The United States has, on this basis, projected its military power, exhibited political resolve to contain potential enemies, and acted to defend its allies. Since the 1990s, the United States has undoubtedly established naval preponderance in the world and is the only, unrivalled, power with global basing presence, a presence which enables it to project power in areas in which US access and freedom to operate are challenged.[8]

The US foreign military deployments have focused on five strategic zones: the Middle East, Europe, the West Pacific, North America, and the Caribbean Sea. The military bases in the GCC countries are part of its grand deployments under the leadership of the US Central Command. The latter's area of responsibility covers 20 countries: Afghanistan, Bahrain, Egypt, Iran, Iraq, Jordan, Kazakhstan, Kuwait, Kyrgyzstan, Lebanon, Oman, Pakistan, Qatar, Saudi Arabia, Syria, Tajikistan, Turkmenistan, United Arab Emirates, Uzbekistan, and Yemen.[9] Such military deployments should not be seen simply in terms of direct military ends, but are also used to promote economic and political interests as well. One example of such interests would be the geopolitics of energy, where the bases in the Gulf can serve US energy interests and at the same time facilitate US exports of arms and other products.[10] In recent times, the bases in the Gulf have played quite a dynamic role, in the light of the evolution of US military doctrine and the US's diplomatic agenda and changing economic pursuits. The last two decades can be divided into the three periods underlined earlier.

Compared to the former colonial powers, such as Great Britain and France, the United States is a relatively newcomer to the Gulf. In the 1950s and 1960s, the United Kingdom was still the dominant power in the Gulf region, enjoying supreme military presence, with US influence limited to sporadic and temporary port visits.[11] In 1968, in line with its declining power and influence, Britain declared that it would withdraw all military forces east of the Suez Canal and terminate its mandate in the Gulf which had lasted for over two centuries.[12] Although the United States was ready to fill the vacuum of power in the region, President Richard Nixon hesitated to do so due to the rise of Arab nationalism after the 1967 War. Therefore, following Britain's final withdrawal in 1971, the United States did not seek large-scale military presence in the region. The military presence in the Gulf mainly relied on aircraft carriers afloat in nearby waters. The number of permanent military facilities was quite small (mainly in Bahrain), and the base facilities had more political symbolism than military significance. The aircraft carriers were interlinked with the Sixth Fleet in the Mediterranean Sea, with a view to preventing the former Soviet Union from interfering in Gulf affairs.

The collapse of the Soviet Union and the end of the Cold War offered the George Bush administration a great opportunity to expand military influence in the Gulf. After the Gulf War broke out in 1991, the US military presence grew considerably while base facilities in the region began to mushroom, centering in particular on Saudi Arabia, the most powerful GCC state flanked by the waters of the Gulf, the Gulf of Aden, and the Red Sea. There was also a presence in other GCC states.[13] During the Gulf War, as many as 334,000 troops were stationed in the Kingdom, which was clearly the US's most important security, economic and political partner in the Gulf. Between August 1990 and the end of 1992, Saudi Arabia placed orders worth more than $25 billion with US arms manufacturers.[14]

In 1993, newly-elected President William Clinton defined US military doctrine in the Gulf in terms of military deployment aimed at containing both Iran and Iraq, the so-called "dual containment." In 1995, the US Navy expanded forces further in the Middle East by reactivating its Fifth Fleet and headquartering this in Manama, Bahrain.[15] In 1997-1998, the United States had approximately 4,000 troops in the region, mostly in Kuwait, Bahrain, and Saudi Arabia under the pretext of "guarding against an Iraqi attack", despite the fact that Iraq was weakened due to the severe sanctions the West and the United Nations had imposed on it.[16]

The 9/11 terrorist attacks shocked the US, which resulted in President George W. Bush and his administration launching the Global War on Terror (GWOT). In 2002-2003, the US still maintained a fleet of B-52 bombers in Jeddah to defend the Saudi Kingdom, but relations between the two countries were becoming increasingly strained. Due to the discords between Washington and Riyadh, the Bush administration shifted part of the military presence from Saudi Arabia to Kuwait, Qatar, Bahrain, and later the United Arab Emirates (UAE). [17] The UAE was in fact the first Arab country to provide troops to NATO to fight in Afghanistan, under a partnership arrangement with NATO in keeping with the provisions of the Istanbul Cooperation Initiative for GCC members.[18]

Reversing the Clinton administration's more limited strategies, Bush sought "full spectrum dominance" for the US over all land, surface and sub-surface sea, air, space, electromagnetic spectrum and information systems, with enough overwhelming power to fight and win global wars against any adversary. [19] This ambitious plan brought a new round of military expansion abroad. Under Bush's preemptive doctrine, Secretary of Defense Donald Rumsfeld unveiled his "1-4-2-1 defense strategy" in August 2002. This new military doctrine expressed the US's determination to safeguard homeland security while at the same time keeping substantial military presence in four "critical regions": Europe, Northeast Asia, East Asia, and the Middle East. The rationale for this was to be able to defeat aggression in two of these regions simultaneously, and "win decisively" in one of those conflicts at a time and place of US choosing.[20] In pursuit of this military doctrine, the US stationed more forces and deployed more military personnel in the GCC countries, ostensibly to fight the GWOT.

The United States war against the Taliban regime in Afghanistan and thereafter the Saddam Hussein regime in Iraq not only damaged America's image, but involved the US expending huge amounts in military and political resources. When President Barack Obama entered the White House in January 2009, the immediate task of the bases in the GCC states shifted away from safeguarding post-war reconstruction in Iraq and combating Taliban militants in Afghanistan and along the Afghan-Pakistani border, towards confronting Iran and preserving regional stability. The status of the military presence in the Gulf evolved from an offensive to a defensive posture. In September 2009, Secretary of Defense Robert Gates declared that the United States had already formed a Gulf missile defensive network composed of PAC-3 missiles and Aegis sea-based missile systems in Saudi Arabia, UAE, Kuwait, and Qatar to deter potential Iranian attacks.[21]

3. The New Posture of US Military Deployment in the GCC Countries

With the transformation of the functions of the deployment in the GCC countries from fighting the GWOT to containing Iran and maintaining regional stability, the bases have since exhibited five new attributes: they have expanded geographically, diminished in size, come closer to their potential enemies, grown more adept in maneuverability, and become gradually interlinked. Below, we will discuss these attributes in more detail.

First, the bases, with the attached military personnel, have spread geographically, and across the GCC they have been distributed more evenly. Saudi Arabia was initially the most important host nation for US military bases in the GCC. In spite of its abundant oil reserves, the Saudi government sees itself as inherently vulnerable to both internal and external threats. To meet its security needs, the Saudi government acted pragmatically in the 1980s and 1990s, and effectively made itself heavily dependent on US military support – seen by the Saudi leadership as a deterrent against radical elements. However, because many of those involved in the 9/11 attacks were Saudi nationals, Saudi Arabia then came to be seen by the US as a hotbed of terrorism. Consequently, the US began seeking bases elsewhere within the region. In the post-9/11 period, the United States gradually withdrew 200 military aircraft and other supporting troops from Saudi Arabia, with only 500 military personnel remaining, mostly for training purposes. The rest of the troops were redeployed to Qatar, Bahrain, Kuwait, Oman and the UAE, and to Central Asian countries.

In practice military cooperation with Saudi Arabia continued in some fields. In due course, it formed part of the US-supported network combatting the Taliban and al-Qaida within the framework of Obama's new anti-terrorist campaign.[22] John O. Brennan, Obama's senior advisor on antiterrorism, articulated this strategy when he stated in 2009 that the Obama administration would be "committed to ending the military action in Iraq and reopening a new battle for countering terrorism on the border of Afghanistan and Pakistan to eliminate the remaining terrorists."[23] In fact the focus was broader than that: the network of military bases was seen as aiding the United States in confronting multifaceted threats in the region, including the long-lasting alleged threat from Iran, as well as the more recent threats of terrorism and social unrest in Iraq and Yemen. By "putting eggs into different baskets," the United States supposedly avoided the risk of intimidation by a single host nation if the two countries' relations deteriorated.

As for Kuwait, the traumatizing impact of the Iraqi 1990 invasion of Kuwait led the Kuwaiti Amir to ask for security protection from the United States. On the eve of the Iraq War in 2003, Kuwait was the most resolute GCC country in its support for the US military campaign to topple Saddam Hussein. The Kuwaiti government not only provided fuel free of charge, but it also allowed US forces to occupy as much as one quarter of the nation's territory for military purposes.[24] In 2008, the United States and Kuwait signed an arms sale agreement worth $328 million; the Bush administration declared that it would also sell Kuwait laser-guided missiles.[25] Since then, the United States has maintained about ten base facilities in Kuwait, the largest ones being Camp Buehring and Camp Arifjan. Under the Obama administration, the number of US troops in the country has stood at approximately 5,000, an unparalleled number relative to other countries in the Gulf region.

The UAE has also seen new US military bases over the last decade. Since its independence in 1971, the UAE has had a territorial dispute with Iran over Abu Musa and the Tunb islands. Partly due to the GCC's weakness and reluctance to offer military aid to the UAE in this matter, the Emirates pinned high expectations on the United States to assist in asserting its claims to the islands. This explains why in the past decade it has allowed Washington to build military bases in the country.[26] In January 2008, President Bush was the first US president to visit the UAE. UAE President Shaykh Khalifa remarked on this occasion that the UAE was committed to partnering with the United States in the war on terrorism and maintaining regional and world stability.[27] In May 2009, Obama ratified the US-UAE Agreement on the Peaceful Use of Nuclear Energy. On 1 February 2010, Obama declared that the United States would send arms to the UAE, including 80 F-16s and Patriot missiles, as well as long-range anti-ballistic missiles. The US facilities at Al-Dhafra air base, near Abu Dhabi, have been developed to host approximately 1,500 US military personnel.[28] Al-Dhafra has a "Special Airborne Operation Centre," which functions as a pilot training centre.[29]

Qatar now houses the forward headquarters of US Central Command, although the overall headquarters still remains in Florida. It was moved from Saudi Arabia to Qatar in 2003. Al Udeid air base (west of Doha) has become one of the US's most critical bases in the Gulf. And, although Qatar was publicly opposed to the war on Iraq, Emir Hamad Bin Khalifa al-Thani reportedly told General Tommy Franks, Commander-in-Chief of the US Central Command, that the United States had an opportunity to "salvage Iraqi people."[30] Hamad Bin Jassim al-Thani, the Foreign Minister of Qatar stated: "We need the US forces to stay here, and the US needs us too."[31]

Bahrain is a tiny Sunni-based monarchy with limited national resources and boasts a majority Shi'a population. It has served as the headquarters and homeport of the Fifth Fleet since the mid-1990s, with a military base covering as much as 60 acres in Manama.[32] During the Gulf War in 1991, Bahrain offered support and acted as a "bridgehead" in the US military campaign against Iraq.[33] In February 2003, on the eve of the Iraq war, bilateral relations reached a new high when Bahrain allowed the United States continued use of its air and navy bases.[34] Today, the number of US troops in Bahrain is approximately 2,000.

After 9/11, the United States also sought to build military bases in Oman, a state which controls the Musandam Peninsula and the waters of the Hormuz Strait. In 2002, the two countries renewed the Collective Defense Treaty under whose terms Oman permits the United States to use the three air bases of Seeb, Masirah, and Thumrait.[35] In return, the US government has offered military assistance to Oman totaling $9.4 million in 2009 and $20.27 million in 2010.[36]

When Barack Obama became US president in 2009, the US global military reach had risen to unprecedented and unparalleled levels: more than 190,000 troops and 115,000 civilian employees were massed in approximately 900 military facilities in 46 countries and territories outside the US. The Pentagon owned or rented 795,000 acres of land, with 26,000 buildings and structures, valued at $146 billion.[37] The majority of the bases are located in three vital regions: East Asia, the Gulf, and Europe. According to statistics, there are 200 institutions in the US that train foreign military personnel, and a significant number of trainees are from the GCC countries. Any nation that buys US military equipment - there are about 150 such countries - gets trainers with the deal.[38]

The second attribute of the developing US strategy on military bases in the GCC states is that they are decreasing in number and size. The Department of Defense's 2014 *Base Structure Report* states that bases and smaller military sites can be listed in five categories, according to whether they host facilities for the army, navy, air force, marines or Washington Headquarters Service (WHS). They cover 50 US states at home, seven overseas territories, and 40 foreign countries. There are 576 large-scale overseas bases, including 248 army bases, 120 navy bases, 186 air bases, and the majority of the foreign sites for these are located in Germany (174 sites), Japan (113 sites), and the Republic of Korea (83 sites).[39]

As one of the six regional military commands, the Florida-based US Central Command is responsible for a relatively limited area. Since the founding of the Africa Command (AFRICOM) in 2008, states in northeast Africa, such as Somalia, Djibouti, and Ethiopia, have been excluded from the Central Command's area of responsibility. Due to the now smaller geographical area covered from its Gulf regional headquarters, the number of military bases in the GCC countries has shrunk, with a parallel reduction in the number of troops. In September 2013, the number of US troops in the six GCC member states stood at 9,269.[40]

The third attribute of current US military deployment in the Gulf is that it is advancing closer to potential enemies, with the relevant bases being upgraded and more effectively maintained. This relates in particular to the military facilities strategically placed near Iran, such as Camp al-Sayliyah near Doha, which now hosts the regional headquarters of US Central Command. Another Qatari base, al-Udeid, is playing a prominent role in the US containment of Iran. The latter airbase boasts a 14,760-foot-long runway, the longest in the Middle East. Its huge concrete bunkers can house 120 aircraft. Its construction, with advanced electronic facilities, cost $1.4 billion.[41] In 2010, 34 key construction projects were under way at al-Udeid,[42] and most of them had been completed in 2012. A Doha seaport facility is under construction to accommodate US aircraft carriers. Similar to those in Qatar, US military garrisons in Kuwait, the UAE, and Bahrain have also been updated with upgraded infrastructure.

The fourth attribute is that, within the relatively stable military deployment in East Asia and Europe, the US military deployment in the GCC states is increasingly mobile. Cooperative security locations (CSLs) are host nation facilities with little or no permanent

US personnel presence, but which may contain pre-positioned equipment and/or logistical arrangements that aid in security cooperation activities and contingency access.[43] To leave only "light footprints" in the Gulf, the US government has increased the number of CSLs to make substantial use of host countries' military bases and facilities in case of emergency. In 2013, US contractor personnel in Oman numbered 22, while they numbered several hundred in Saudi Arabia. But, should a crisis erupt, this engagement enables the United States to make use of the host states' military facilities and base infrastructure to allow for a quick military deployment.

The fifth attribute is that, to respond to multi-dimensional threats, US military bases and facilities in the GCC states are increasingly interlinked. The US government has integrated all the military facilities and garrisons in the Gulf so that they now form a network of containment against Iran and Al-Qaeda affiliates in the Middle East.[44] Bases in the GCC countries are centered in Kuwait, Qatar, and Bahrain, accompanied by sites in Saudi Arabia, Oman, and the UAE. Together, these have forged an "arc of containment" after the outbreak of the Iranian nuclear crisis.[45] And, under the Obama administration, bases in the GCC countries have been brought under a coordinated framework with those in Afghanistan, Kyrgyzstan, Tajikistan, and Pakistan so that West Asia, Central Asia, and Pakistan under the Central Command can support the counter-terror campaign in Afghanistan and Pakistan while at the same time deterring anti-American forces in the Middle East.[46] These military bases have close ties also with the American military base in Djibouti as well as other military facilities in Egypt (a designated area of responsibility under the Central Command), Kenya, and East Africa, the designated area of responsibility under the Africa Command.

4. Internal and External Motives for the Pentagon's Adjustment of its Military Deployment in the GCC Countries

The reasons for the United States' readjustment of its military deployment and bases in the GCC countries are multifaceted. First, there has been continuing change in US national security strategy since 2001. As mentioned previously, after 9/11 the United States designated terrorism and the proliferation of weapons of mass destruction (WMD) as primary threats and regarded the greater Middle East, including Central Asia, West Asia, and part of South Asia, as an "arc of instability."[47] The Obama administration shifted its focus on antiterrorism from Iraq to Central Asia in 2009 and from Central Asia to Iraq again in 2014 to combat the Islamic State in Iraq and Syria (ISIS), which gave rise to the readjustment of its military bases in the region.

In late 2009, the National Security Forum in Chicago noted that the future security challenge to the United States will include both states and non-state entities. The former includes Iran, North Korea, and Venezuela, while the latter includes religious extremists, ethnic radicals, and terrorists. What is most challenging, according to the Forum's analysis, is the situation in which there is a confluence of the two categories. When they converge, anti-American coalitions may support an asymmetrical threat to overseas US facilities.[48] After riots in Kyrgyzstan on 9 April 2010, the US government was concerned that the new pro-Russian government might close US military bases on its territory. This made military bases in the GCC grow in importance. The US readjustment of its military bases in the GCC could be seen as an attempt to better meet the diversity of security threats to the United States in the region. After the Bahrain riots broke out in 2011, US values (democracy, human rights etc) and interests came into direct clash. Ultimately, interests won out. The US was clearly concerned that Iran might be playing a role behind the largely Shi'a uprising, and that this might have adverse effects for US military bases in the kingdom. The US therefore adopted a cautious and pragmatic approach and supported the GCC forces in stabilizing the situation in Bahrain.[49]

Second, the transformation of the United States' military objectives specifically in the Gulf also gave rise to a readjustment of its military deployment and bases. After the new Iraqi leadership was elected, under US supervision, Iran became the United States' main target - being regarded as the supreme challenger to US power in the region.

Iran did not seek to dispel this perception. For example, from 22 to 26 April 2010, for the commemoration of the thirty-first anniversary of the founding of the Islamic Revolutionary Guards, Iran initiated a large military manoeuvre of joint army, naval, and air forces near the Hormuz Strait, testing homemade cruise missiles. Over 300 warships of various kinds participated in the manoeuvre, which was regarded as a measure to offset US influence in the region. On 5 May of the same year, Iran initiated another eight-day military manoeuvre. Due to these dynamics, Kuwait, Qatar, Bahrain, and the UAE, as neighbors of Iran, became even more important non-NATO allies of the United States in the region.[50] To prevent Iran from shutting the Strait of Hormuz, the US has since 2012 moved F-22 and F-15C warplanes into Al Dhafra Air Base in the UAE to bolster the combat jets already in the region and the carrier strike groups that are on constant tours of the area.[51] It is also likely that the US Navy may deploy futuristic military lasers to the Fifth Fleet in the Gulf, with the intention that these could be used to deter Iran from using small boats to attack American warships.[52]

Third, after 9/11, US-Saudi relations worsened. The US media (if not US governmental bodies) accused Saudi Arabia of being a covert sponsor of terrorism. Due to the bilateral discord which followed, Saudi Arabia withdrew its commitment to allow the United States to use certain military facilities in the country, and US air force command and communication centers were forced to move to Qatar. After the outbreak of the 2003 Iraq War, the US air force personnel in Riyadh and the personnel supporting the Patriot missile provision eventually withdrew from Saudi Arabia, with the remaining small number of military personnel only undertaking defensive and training tasks.[53] From the Saudi perspective, the rise of domestic anti-Americanism, which compelled the government to emphasize its diplomatic independence from Washington, overlapped with US criticism of Saudi Arabia and thereby damaged the US-Saudi special relationship. The United States had no choice but find new bases elsewhere.[54]

Finally, US readjustment of its military bases in the GCC also resulted from its economic slowdown. The worldwide financial crisis, whose epicentre was in the United States, forced Washington to make budget cuts. In order to aid the national budget, the Bush and Obama administrations, respectively, reduced the size and number of military bases in the region. By late 2010, the United States maintained only 50 military facilities in Iraq with less than 50,000 troops in the country, which were all closed by the end of 2011. The Main Operating Bases in the GCC were also cut to minimize budgets. The Obama administration put forward a "lighter footprint" concept to reduce the cost of overseas military deployment.[55] The Pentagon's decision to deploy a fleet of Cyclone-class patrol coastal ships to the Gulf is the outcome of Obama's "lighter footprint" strategy.

5. The Impact of US Military Deployment in the GCC Countries after the Arab Uprisings

Due to the volatile Gulf situation, the last three decades have witnessed overwhelming challenges to the GCC collective security mechanism. The frequent failure of the mechanism is due to its lack of enforcement power in conflicts, as was evident in regard to the Iran-Iraq War, Iraq's invasion of Kuwait, the Gulf War in 1991, the Iraq War in 2003, and the rise of ISIS in 2014. After the outbreak of the Gulf War, the Saudi government even disbanded GCC troops in Hafr al Batin in order to make way for US deployment of armed forces in the Gulf.[56] The last two decades have seen a substantial readjustment in the US deployment in the Gulf. However, although this readjustment has given the impression of reduced US engagement in the region, in reality the engagement has remained intact.

The readjustment of the military bases in the GCC has in fact consolidated US predominance in the region. In recent years, three different notions of the Gulf security order have been at play: the first is a Western-dominated framework advocated by the United States; the second is a collective security framework covering all of the eight Gulf States, advocated by Iran; and, the third is a Saudi-led arrangement based on the GCC countries only. It is the first arrangement that still remains operative. In 2005, the GCC rapid response force was formally disbanded (the force was restored after the Arab Uprisings). As such, the GCC internal security mechanism is often more symbolic than real.[57]

On 27 January 2010, President Obama stated in his State of the Union Address that the United States would deal with Iran through both military and diplomatic means.[58] In February 2010, David Petraeus, Commander-in-Chief of the Central Command, said that the United States would deploy eight Patriot PAC-3 missile companies in Qatar, the UAE, Bahrain, and Kuwait, with each country having two. These missile defence systems were operational by July 2010. To foster military integration between the GCC and the United States, the Obama administration sought to integrate the six countries into its economic orbit, initially suggesting the creation in 2013 of the US-Greater Middle East Free Trade Area.[59] Since then, however, it has become clear that this would not materialize due to the Arab uprisings from late 2010. Despite the relaxation of US-Iran relations after Hassan Rouhani took office, the tense Saudi-Iranian discord has remained unchanged, and this too has maintained the space for a US role. Emboldened by a call to arms by the top Shi'a cleric, Iranian-backed militias moved quickly to the centre of Iraq's political landscape in 2014; in response, the USS Mesa Verde, carrying about 550 Marines, entered the Gulf to counterbalance possible Iranian interference in Iraqi internal affairs.[60]

Another aspect of the readjustment is that it has caused more uncertainty in the region. With the intensification of conflicts over Iranian nuclear developments and oil issues and the renewed deployment of US military bases closer to Iran, the GCC countries are captives of US foreign policy. The worsening of tensions between the United States and Iran or between Israel and Iran may make US military bases in the GCC potential Iranian targets. Former Iranian President Mahmoud Ahmadinejad often appealed to the GCC countries not to allow the United States to set up military bases on their soil. On 25 April 2010, Kazem Jalali, spokesman for Iran's National Security and Foreign Policy Commission, said, "The continued presence of foreign military forces in the region has caused insecurity and instability in our region. Under these conditions, Middle East countries, particularly those in the Gulf, should join one another in a collective security treaty to ensure regional safety."[61] In spite of this realistic proposal, which highlights Iranian concerns for the region, the pro-US GCC countries ignored it.

Anti-Americanism in the region, moreover, has intensified due to the readjustment of US policy. Since the end of the Second World War, Muslims have generally resented the deployment of armed forces on Muslim lands by the United States and the Soviet Union.[62] After the Soviet invasion of Afghanistan in 1979, a number of Islamic radicals, supported and funded by the United States, launched a "holy war" to force Soviet forces to withdraw from the country. Since the 1990s, Al-Qaida has initiated a series of attacks, including those on 9/11, in part to put pressure on the United States to close its military bases in Saudi Arabia. More recent terrorist activity includes the 28 August 2009 attack on Saudi Arabia's Interior Minister Mohammed bin Nayef, by suicide bombers.[63] On 28 April 2010, the UAE's Supreme Court ordered the arrest of five citizens and one Afghan for allegedly financing the Taliban and attempting to set up a terrorist organization in the Gulf.[64] Issues over US military bases in the GCC countries are thus being politicized and becoming a source of anti-Americanism.[65] Osama Bin Laden reiterated time and again his view that all Muslims in the world shoulder the "glorious mission" to launch terrorist attacks against the US military and civilian targets because US military bases have spread throughout the holy Islamic lands.[66] To lessen domestic resentment and dissatisfaction, the GCC countries began to encourage the United States to use their military facilities as CSLs rather than full-fledged bases in order to reduce the number of US troops in their countries. In June 2014, President Obama declared that the United States would deploy 300 military personnel to advise the Iraqi security forces, but would not restore bases in the state. These special forces will secure the US embassy and personnel operating inside Iraq, assess the situation on the ground, help evaluate gaps in Iraqi security forces, and increase their capacity to counter the threat posed by ISIS.[67] Meanwhile, the US dispatched an aircraft carrier (the George H.W. Bush) and two guided missile ships into the Gulf to foster US striking capacity against ISIS rather than enlarging its bases in the GCC countries.[68] Moreover, the US Marine Corps is currently planning to deploy 2,300 troops to Kuwait in a new unit designed to quickly respond to crises in the volatile region – again in the context of combating ISIS.[69]

6. The US Military Deployment in the GCC Countries and Other Powers' Responses

The Gulf has played host to the Iran-Iraq War from 1980 to 1988, the first Gulf War in 1991, the second Gulf War in 2003, the Iranian nuclear crisis since 2006 and the rise of extremist groups since 2011. The area is thus a powder keg, and a number of powers have responded to this by escalating their military presence in the Gulf. As has been shown, the US has taken a lead in this. Further measures are likely to follow. However, the United States has not taken any concrete steps yet due to the cut of military spending and Obama administration's shift of the strategic focus to the Asia-Pacific regions. In addition to the military bases mentioned above, in 2012, the US Navy announced the launch of a floating mother-ship base to be deployed in the Gulf. The converted warship USS Ponce is slated to be used by the Navy on anti-piracy missions and for containing Iran. While aircraft carriers must move regularly around the Gulf, the new ship will be able to remain in the same location for weeks. There are approximately 16,000 personnel at sea aboard more than 40 US Navy, Coast Guard and fleet auxiliary ships in the US Fifth Fleet.[70]

Other Western powers have followed this lead. On 26 May 2009, French President Nicolas Sarkozy declared that France would build the first permanent military base in Abu Dhabi, with the capacity to house 500 army, navy, and air personnel. This meant that France would play a more essential role in Gulf affairs.[71]

The United Kingdom is also considering returning to the Gulf region. In 2010, it was negotiating to reopen a military base in Oman, but the negotiation has yet to produce an agreement. The Blair and Brown governments were frequently accused by the GCC countries of having neglected the partnership with the Gulf countries. The government of Prime Minister David Cameron intends to build up a strong "shadow presence" around the Gulf, which, allegedly, would not exhibit an imperial-style footprint, but a smart presence with facilities, defence agreements, rotation of training, transit, and jumping-off points for British forces. Bahrain was de facto home to the UK Maritime Component Command (UKMCC) before 2013. In late 2014, the United Kingdom announced the establishment of a permanent naval base in Bahrain, while the Minhad airbase at Dubai, UAE, has also emerged as a key element in the "smart presence". The Amir of Qatar has reportedly been assured by Cameron of the UK's commitment to the gas-rich emirate, with Doha a favored location for UK military liaison and coordination activities in the Gulf.[72]

Canada is also participating in Gulf security affairs. In June 2011, Canada established a new "hub" military base in Kuwait; Canadian military personnel were also posted to the al-Udeid US military base in Qatar.[73] In 2013, the Canadian government stated that it would extend military deployment in the Gulf until 2015.

It is clear from this that the US military bases in the GCC countries will serve as a hub for Western powers in general to interact and cooperate in the Gulf. Moreover, France, the United States, and Japan have built military bases in Djibouti, close to the Gulf regions. It appears that interaction among the Western powers will be more frequent in the region in the next decade and will inevitably entice other countries, such as China, Russia and India, to set up bases to defend their interests. Furthermore, in response to these developments Iran is planning to build a navy base at Jask, near the Hormuz Strait.[74] At present, instead of establishing a hard military presence, Asian powers such as China, South Korea and India have built up a "soft military presence" in the Gulf to safeguard their geo-economic interests, such as energy, investments and trade, which are the outcome of their development-oriented geo-economic strategies. The forms of China's soft military presence consists of the Chinese naval fleet active in Somali waters, logistic bases in Djibouti and Port Sudan, international peace-keeping forces in the two Sudans and Lebanon, and military attaché offices and military training agencies in the Middle East aimed at protecting Beijing's practical interests. This soft military presence coheres with China's geo-economic strategies. To avoid being demonized as a "China threat", Beijing has highlighted that it is a responsible rising power, and its soft military presence is different from the hard military bases of the US in the region, because it forms a contribution of "public security goods", compatible with the western hard military bases in the Middle East.

7. Conclusion

As suggested throughout this chapter, US military deployments in the GCC regions can be divided into three historical periods, and the posture of the US military bases is evolving continuously. From 1991 to 2001, the US military bases in the GCC states were mostly in Saudi Arabia and Kuwait, aimed at the dual containment of Iran and Iraq. From 2001 to 2011, the US readjusted its military bases in the GCC states, and the US military deployments were moved from Saudi Arabia to the arc of Kuwait-Bahrain-Qatar. The task of the bases was transformed from "dual containment" to the more complex and enduring tasks of safeguarding Gulf security, countering terrorists and containing Iran. From 2011 onward, the US military bases in the GCC countries have acted as stabilizing forces to guarantee the regime security of the pro-Western monarchies and address non-traditional challenges, including those posed by ISIS and Al-Qaida affiliates. In terms of the personnel size, the US military troops in the GCC countries can be divided into different levels: naval forces afloat (level 1); bases in Kuwait (level 2); bases in Qatar and Bahrain (level 3); bases in the UAE and Saudi Arabia (level 4); and a presence in Oman (level 5).

From a historical perspective, US military deployment in the GCC regions features three trends: from hard military bases towards a less visible military presence; from static deployments to stronger mobility (the US military deployment in the GCC countries is being interlinked with other US bases in Central Asia, Turkey and Djibouti in the Horn of Africa); and from global priority to regional priority (the US strategic focus is shifting towards the Asia-Pacific regions). The effects of the US military bases in the GCC are three-fold: first, from the US perspective, they will bring the battlefield closer to the enemies' front-door; second, the US military deployments will deepen Sunni-Shi'a rivalry and enhance competitive power struggles between Saudi Arabia and Iran, worsening the security dilemma in the Gulf region; and third, the US military presence will probably invite further involvement and interaction from outside powers, with increasing rivalry.

Notes

1   This research was jointly supported by the Research Program of the National Social Science Foundation "The US Military Deployment and the Trend of Adjustment in the Middle East and Islamic Regions" (13CGJ042), by "the Program for New Century Excellent Talents in Universities" (NCET), by "Shanghai Pujiang Talent Program" (14PJC092) and by Shanghai International Studies University innovation research team.

2   The strategy was spelled out by National Security Affairs Advisor Anthony Lake in his article, "Confronting Backlash States," *Foreign Affairs*, 73, 2 (March-April 1994), pp. 45-55. For a good critique of that policy, see, F. Gregory Gause III, "The Illogic of Dual Containment," *Foreign Affairs*, 73, 2 (March-April 1994), Web version available at: http://www.foreignaffairs.com/articles/49686/f-gregory-gause-iii/the-illogic-of-dual-containment (accessed 15 November 2014).

3   This is reflected in the classical works of thinkers, such as H. Mackinder, N. Spykman, R. Strausz-Hupé and C. Gray.

4   Stephen Lendman, America's "Bases of Empire," *Global Research*, 27 June 2009.

5   Catherine Lutz, "US Bases and Empire: Global Perspectives on the Asia Pacific," *Global Research*, 21 July 2009.

6   Jacqueline Cabasso, "Strategic Command (StratCom) in Context: The Hidden Architecture of US Militarism," *Global Research*, 26 April 2008.

7   See, Robert E. Harkavy, "Thinking about Basing *Naval War College Review*, 2 June 2005, available at: http://www.thefreelibrary.com/Thinking+about+basing.-a0134999430 (accessed 2 September 2014).

8   US Department of Defense, "Sustaining US Global Leadership: Priorities for 21st Century Defense" (Washington, DC, 2012), p. 4, available at: http://www.defense.gov/news/Defense_Strategic_Guidance. pdf (accessed 20 January 2014).

9   See, http://www.centcom.mil/en/about-centcom-en/area-of-responsibility-countries-en (accessed 20 October 2014).

10 Jules Dufour, "The Worldwide Network of US Military Bases: The Global Deployment of US Military Personnel," *Global Research*, 24 December 2013.

11 Ann Williams, *Britain and France in the Middle East and North Africa* (London: Macmillan, 1968), 38-55.

12 Alvin J. Cottrell and Frank Bray, *Military Forces in the Persian Gulf* (London: SAGE Publications, 1978), 7-8.

13 Anthony H. Cordesman and Khalid R. al-Rodhan, *Gulf Military Forces in an Era of Asymmetric Wars* (Washington, D.C.: Praeger Security International, 2007), 163.

14 David W. Lesch and Mark L. Haas, eds., *The Middle East and the United States: History, Politics, and Ideologies* (Boulder: Westview Press, 2014), 336.

15 Stacie L. Pettyjohn, *US Global Defense Posture, 1783-2011: Prepared for the United States Air Force* (Washington D.C.: RAND, 2012), 87.

16 Ivan Eland, "The US Military: Overextended Overseas," July 24, 1998. http://www.cato.org/publications/commentary/us-military-overextended-overseas (accessed 20 October 2014).

17 Yahia H. Zoubir and Louisa Ait-Hamadouche, "Saudi Arabia's Bilateral Relations with the Gulf War Protagonists," *Journal of Third World Studies*, 24, No. 1 (Spring 2007): 109-135.

18 Rick Rozoff, "Bases, Missiles, Wars: US Consolidates Global Military Network," *Global Research*, 27 January 2010.

19 Stephen Lendman, America's "Bases of Empire", *Global Research*, 27 June 2009.

20 Thomas Donnelly and Frederick W. Kagan, *Ground Truth: The Future of US Land Power* (Washington D.C.: AEI Press, 2008), 12; See also Chalmers Johnson, *Nemesis: The Last Days of the American Republic* (New York: Metropolitan Books, 2007).

21 Rick Rozoff, "Bases, Missiles, Wars: US Consolidates Global Military Network," *Global Research*, 27 January 2010.

22 Sherifa Zuhur, *Saudi Arabia: Islamic Threat, Political Reform, and the Global War on Terror* (Carlisle Barracks, PA: Strategic Studies Institute, US Army War College, 2005), 32.

23 John Brennan, "A New Approach to Safeguarding Americans," *Foreign Policy*, 6 August 2009.

24 Anthony H. Cordesman and Khalid R. al-Rodhan, *Gulf Military Forces in an Era of Asymmetric Wars*, op. cit., 87-88.

25 Robert E. Looney, *Handbook of US-Middle East Relations: Formative Factors and Regional Perspectives* (London and New York: Routledge, 2009), 459.

26 Anthony H. Cordesman and Khalid R. al-Rodhan, *Gulf Military Forces in an Era of Asymmetric Wars*, op. cit., 284.

27 Robert E. Looney, *Handbook of US-Middle East Relations: Formative Factors and Regional Perspectives*, op. cit., 387.

28 David S. Cloud, "US Sees Emirates as Both Ally and, Since 9/11, a Foe," *New York Times*, 23 February 2006.

29 Michael Sirak, "Interview: US Air Force Lieutenant General Walter Buchanan," *Jane's Defense Weekly* (29 September 2004): 32-37.

30 Tommy Franks, *American Soldier* (New York: HarperCollins, 2004), 404.

31 Greg Jaffe, "Desert Maneuvers: Pentagon Boosts US Military Presence in the Gulf," *Wall Street Journal*, 24 June 2002.

32 Anthony H. Cordesman and Khalid R. al-Rodhan, *Gulf Military Forces in an Era of Asymmetric Wars*, op. cit., 65-67.

33 Ed Blanche, "Getting Smart: Gulf States Go for US Wonder Weapons," *The Middle East* 4 (2002): 24.

34 Han Zhibin, *Bahrain* (Beijing: Social Science Academic Press, 2009), 179.

35 Ed Blanche, "Regional Briefing — Gulf States: Winds of Change," *Jane's Defense Weekly* (9 February 2005): 15.

36 Kenneth Katzman, "Oman: Reform, Security, and US Policy," *Congressional Research Service*, 29 June 2009.

37 Catherine Lutz, "Obama's Empire," *The New Statesman*, 30 July 2009.

38 Joan Roelofs, "Bases of Empire: Casting a Global Shadow: US military installations around the World," *Global Research*, February 20, 2010.

39 Office of the Deputy Undersecretary of Defense, *Base Structure Report, Fiscal Year 2014 Baseline* (Washington D.C.: US Department of Defense, 2014), 6.

40 Office of the Deputy Undersecretary of Defense, *Base Structure Report, Fiscal Year 2014 Baseline* (Washington D.C.: US Department of Defense, 2014), 13-18.

41 Kent E. Calder, *Embattled Garrisons: Comparative Base Politics and American Globalism* (Princeton, NJ: Princeton University Press, 2007), 30.

42 Department of Defense, "United States DOD Contracts for April 16, 2010," *Defense Professionals*, 19 April 2010.

43 C. T. Sandars, *America's Overseas Garrisons: The Leasehold Empire*, (New York: Oxford University Press, 2000), 301.

44 "States such as China and Iran will continue to pursue asymmetric means to counter our power projection capabilities, while the proliferation of sophisticated weapons and technology will extend to non-state actors as well," in, "Sustaining US Global Leadership: Priorities for 21st Century Defense," op. cit., p. 4.

45 David F. Winkler, *Amirs, Admirals and Desert Sailors: Bahrain, the US Navy, and the Arabian Gulf* (Annapolis, MD: Naval Institute Press, 2007), 181-198.

46 Liu Jinqian, "Analysis of the US Afghanistan-Pakistan Strategy of Anti-terrorism," *Arab World Studies* 29 (2009): 38. See also, Robert D. Kaplan, "Obama Takes Asia by Sea", *The New York Times*, 11 November 2010.

47 Clive Moore, *Happy Isles in Crisis* (Canberra: Asia Pacific Press, 2004), 9.

48 John Allen Williams, "The US Military: Balancing Old and New Challenges of US National Security Strategy 2010," *National Strategy Forum Review* 19 (2009): 1-3.

49 William B. Quandt, "U.S. Policy and the Arab Revolutions of 2011," in Fawaz A. Gerges ed., *The New Middle East: Protest and Revolution in the Arab World* (Cambridge: Cambridge University Press, 2014), 426-427.

50 Charles Aldinger, "US Honors Kuwait as Major Non-NATO Ally," *Reuters*, 1 April 2004.

51 Thom Shanker, Eric Schmitt and David E. Sanger, "US Adds Forces in Persian Gulf, a Signal to Iran," *New York Times*, 3 July 2012.

52 David Sharp, "US Navy to deploy futuristic military laser to Persian Gulf," *Times of Israel*, 18 February 2014; Dion Nissenbaum, "US Plans New Laser Weapon for Persian Gulf," *Wall Street Journal*, 8 April 2013.

53 Anthony H. Cordesman, *The Military Balance in the Middle East* (Westport, Conn.: Praeger, 2004), 312-324.

54 Charles M. Perry and Toshi Yoshihara, *The US-Japan Alliance: Preparing for Korean Reconciliation & Beyond* (Dulles, VA: Brassey's Inc., 2004), 12.

55 Bilal Y. Saab and Joseph Singh, "Forget the Second Carrier, It's Time to Rethink the Fifth Fleet in the Persian Gulf," *Defense One*, 13 August 2013.

56 W. Andrew Terrill, *Regional Fears of Western Primacy and the Future of US Middle Eastern Basing Policy* (Carlisle, PA: US Army War College, December 2006), 45, 244.

57 Anthony H. Cordesman and Khalid R. al-Rodhan, *Gulf Military Forces in An Era of Asymmetric Wars*, op. cit., 11.

58 "Obama's State of the Union Address," *New York Times*, 28 January 2010; Tariq Saeedi, "Pakistan, Iran Set to Face Hot July," *Daily Mail*, 21 April 2010.

59 Robert E. Looney, *Handbook of US-Middle East Relations: Formative Factors and Regional Perspectives*, op. cit., 430.

60 Jon Harper, "Marines Deployed to Persian Gulf for Potential Iraq Operations," *Stars and Stripes*, 16 June 2014.

61 "Iran Calls for Collective Security Treaty," *Iran Times*, 26 April 2010.

62 Kylie Baxter and Shahram Akbarzadeh, *US Foreign Policy in the Middle East: The Roots of Anti-Americanism* (London and New York: Routledge, 2008), 3.

63 Abdullah al-Shihri, "Prince Mohammed bin Nayef, Saudi Prince, Injured in Suicide Attack, Vows To Continue Fight Against Terrorism," *The Huffington Post*, 28 August 2009.

64 "UAE Jails Five Emiratis on Terrorism Charges," *Maktoob News*, 28 April 2010.

65 Alexander Cooley, *Base Politics: Democratic Change and the US Military Overseas* (Ithaca, NY: Cornell University Press, 2008), 10-11.

66 Bradley L. Bowman, "After Iraq: Future US Military Posture in the Middle East," *The Washington Quarterly*, 31(2), 2008: 84.

67 Barbara Salazar Torreon, "Instances of Use of United States Armed Forces Abroad, 1798-2014," *Congressional Research Service*, (15 September 2014): 33.
68 Spencer Ackerma, "US Sends Aircraft Carrier to Persian Gulf as Obama Considers Air Strikes in Iraq," *The Guardian*, 14 June 14 2014.
69 "US Marines' Crisis Unit to Deploy to Kuwait – 2,300 Troops Arriving - US Crewmember Missing in Gulf," *The Kuwait Times*, 1 October 2014.
70 http://www.aljazeera.com/indepth/interactive/2012/04/2012417131242767298.html.
71 "http://www UAE Over French Military Bases," *Tehran Times*, 27 May 2009.
72 Gareth Stansfield and Saul Kelly, "A Return to East of Suez? UK Military Deployment to the Gulf," *RUSI Briefing Paper*, (April 2013): 2-4.
73 Tony Seed, "Harper Extends Military Deployment in Persian Gulf to 2015", *Crescent*, November 2013.
74 Nazila Fathi, "Iran Opens Naval Base Near Routes for Gulf Oil," *New York Times*, 28 October 2008.

Bibliography

Baxter, Kylie and Shahram Akbarzadeh, *US Foreign Policy in the Middle East: The Roots of Anti-Americanism* (London and New York: Routledge, 2008).

Calder, K, *Embattled Garrisons, Comparative Base Politics and American Globalism* (Princeton, NJ: Princeton University Press, 2009).

Cooley, Alexander, *Base Politics: Democratic Change and the US Military Overseas* (Ithaca: Cornell University Press, 2008).

Cordesman, Anthony and Khalid al-Rodhan, *Gulf Military Forces in An Era of Asymmetric Wars* (Washington, DC: Praeger Security International, 2004).

Cottrell, Alvin and Frank Bray, *Military Forces in the Persian Gulf* (London: SAGE Publications, 1978).

Lesch, David W. and Mark L. Haas, eds., *The Middle East and the United States: History, Politics, and Ideologies* (Boulder: Westview Press, 2014).

Donnelly, Thomas and Frederick W. Kagan, *Ground Truth: The Future of US Land Power* (Washington D.C.: AEI Press, 2008).

Emirates Center for Strategic Studies and Research (ed.), *Arabian Gulf Security: Internal and External Challenges* (Abu Dhabi, UAE: Emirates Center for Strategic Studies and Research, 2008).

Harkavy, Robert, *Strategic Basing and the Great Powers, 1200-2000* (New York: Routledge, 2007).

Looney, Robert, *Handbook of US-Middle East Relations: Formative Factors and Regional Perspectives* (London and New York: Routledge, 2009).

Office of the Deputy Undersecretary of Defense, *Base Structure Report, Fiscal Year 2014 Baseline* (Washington D.C.: US Department of Defense, 2014).

Pettyjohn, Stacie L., *US Global Defense Posture, 1783-2011: Prepared for the United States Air Force* (Washington D.C.: RAND, 2012).

Sun Degang, "U.S. Military Bases in the Gulf and the Dynamics of Redeployment" in Michael C. Hudson and Mimi Kirk eds., *Gulf Politics and Economics in a Changing World* (Singapore: World Knowledge, 2014).

Winkler, David, *Amirs, Admirals and Desert Sailors: Bahrain, the US Navy, and the Arabian Gulf* (Annapolis, MD: Naval Institute Press, 2007).

Zuhur, Sherifa, *Saudi Arabia: Islamic Threat, Political Reform, and the Global War on Terror* (Carlisle Barracks, PA: Strategic Studies Institute, US Army War College, 2005.

Appendix: Tables on US Bases and Personnel

Table 1 US Military Bases at Home and Abroad (as of September 2013)

Area	Army	Navy	Air Force	Marine Corps	Washington Headquarters Service	Total
United States	1,590	802	1,536	147	94	4,169
Territories	40	60	10	0	0	110
Overseas	248	120	186	22	0	576
Department of Defence Total	1,878	982	1,732	169	94	4,855

Source: Office of the Deputy Undersecretary of Defense, *Base Structure Report, Fiscal Year 2014 Baseline* (Washington D.C.: US Department of Defense, 2014), 6.

Table 2 US Military Personnel in the GCC and Turkey (as of September 2013)

Host Nations	Qatar	Bahrain	Saudi Arabia	Kuwait	UAE	Oman	Turkey
Active Duty	592	911	305	944	4449	17	1629
Selected Reserve	0	0	0	30	1252	0	2
Civilians	35	189	195	190	155	5	236
Total	627	1100	500	1164	5856	22	1867

Source: Office of the Deputy Undersecretary of Defense, *Base Structure Report, Fiscal Year 2014 Baseline* (Washington D.C.: US Department of Defense, 2014), 13-18.

Table 3 Major US Military Installations and Units in the GCC Countries (as of 2013)

Installation	Country	Service	Major Units
Ali Al Salem	Kuwait	Air Force	386th AEW(Air Expeditionary Wing)
Al Dhafra	UAE	Air Force	380th AEW
Al Udeid	Qatar	Air Force	379th AEW, 609th CAOC (Combined Air and Space Operations Center), 8th Expeditionary Air Mobility Squadron
Camp Arifjan	Kuwait	Army	N/A
Camp As Saliyah	Qatar	Army	N/A
Camp Buehring	Kuwait	Army	3rd Brigade, 3rd Infantry Division, 35th Combat Aviation Brigade
Fujariah	UAE	Navy	N/A
Jebel Ali Port	UAE	Navy	N/A
NSA Bahrain	Bahrain	Navy	5th Fleet Headquarters

Source: Michael J. Lostumbo, Michael J. McNerney, and Eric Peltz, *Overseas Basing of US Military Forces: An Assessment of Relative Costs*, Prepared for the Office of the Secretary of Defense (Washington D.C.: RAND Corporation, 2013), 24.

Table 4 US Military Dependents in the GCC and Turkey (as of 2014)

Country	Total	Army	Navy	USMC	USAF
Kuwait	13,021	10,768	291	140	1,822
Bahrain	3,227	19	3,023	153	32
Turkey	1,539	122	7	2	1,408
Qatar	592	339	5	0	248
Saudi Arabia	332	208	27	0	97
UAE	313	26	16	187	84

Source: "Total Military Personnel and Dependent End Strength By Service, Regional Area, and Country," Defense Manpower Data Center, 31 July 2014.

6

The Future of a Critical US Relationship in the Gulf: US-Saudi Relations and the Rise of the Saudi "Garrison State"

Mohammed Turki Al-Sudairi

1. Introduction

The future of the US presence in the Gulf will inevitably be dependent on how it relates to the leading powers of the Gulf. Saudi Arabia is of key importance here. This chapter aims to provide readers with a general overview of the state of the US-Saudi relationship, and its sustainability over the long-run. It argues that the traditional strategic basis for the US-Saudi relationship is eroding, but structural and geostrategic impediments, continued utility and mutual benefit as well short-term reinforcing factors are sustaining it for the time being. The next decade or two should be construed as a transitional period during which time the Kingdom's relationship with the US will probably assume a more normalized undertone, a process that will be catalyzed not only by Saudi Arabia's declining strategic relevance to US interests but, more significantly, as a direct outcome of the emergence of what can be termed as a 'garrison state' mentality defining Saudi strategic calculations/approaches.[1]

This 'garrison state' mentality reflects the state's core concern for regime preservation in an environment of instability on the one hand, and a crisis of confidence in Washington's ability and willingness to uphold it if and when the need arises on the other. It is marked necessarily by a growing assertiveness in foreign policy-making (departing from traditional *status quo* approaches and embracing adventurism) and a new-found emphasis on the transformation of Saudi Arabia into a military power capable – supposedly - of safeguarding the regime and protecting the state, as well as decreasing dependence on US military support. Initially, this assertiveness will operate within the parameters of the "abandonment-entrapment" paradigm in which omnibalancing will serve to signal and maximize Saudi options whilst maintaining the current US-Saudi security structure in place. In time however, and as a byproduct of its own internal dynamics (which will work to intensify differences with Washington) it will pave the way for a normalized relationship, albeit one in which the long-term security problems facing the Saudi state will probably remain unresolved despite the major efforts that will be expended to resolve them. It should be noted that this mentality – and the assertiveness arising from it as a result - feeds on a growing sense of insecurity compounded by the mounting social, economic, and political domestic challenges which Saudi Arabia faces, and a regional environment embroiled in instability. All of this may in turn lead to a rupture in the US-Saudi relationship sometime in the coming decades.

The writer maintains that many of the security problems (or more properly insecurities) facing the Kingdom are an outcome of its own political culture which is inherently opposed to the emergence of a more representative polity and chiefly consumed by the need to safeguard the regime and its current monopoly on power. This is not to suggest that the challenges facing Saudi Arabia are contrived or an extension of regime and not national interests (there can be, and there is, a degree of overlap), but that many of these threats are projections of the inherent weakness and frailty of the Saudi political order, which seeks to compensate for this through an assertive foreign policy. A shift in the existing political paradigm is, therefore, a necessary component to resolving the Kingdom's various security issues and bringing about a more realistic assessment of the threats and challenges it faces. However, the 'garrison state' mentality mentioned above makes political reform less likely, serving to deepen suppressive and adventurist tendencies within the state, as can already be observed. This, coupled with the very makeup of the elite, marred by a succession crisis and undergoing fragmentation within the context of a decentralizing political system, will make the prospect of genuine political reform unlikely. This is an especially disastrous prospect as the resultant instabilities are further enhanced by the unsustainability of the rentier political-economic model. The chief problem Saudi Arabia must contend with, therefore, is not the character of its future relationship with the US itself, but how it will go about handling the governance crisis whose resolution is vital for its long-term stability and prosperity. The maintenance of its relationship with Washington will depend on whether the governance crisis is successfully resolved.

2. The Determinants and Parameters of the US-Saudi Relationship

The US-Saudi relationship has been defined since the mid-1940s in terms of an "energy-security" compact by which the United States guarantees the Kingdom's integrity and security through its "off-shore balancing capacity" in exchange for the latter's effective utilization of its energy reserves in service of American global interests (under a variety of capacities, including as a dependable provider of energy supplies, as a swing-producer capable of influencing global prices, and as an actor willing to deploy its petro-dollars and ideological influence abroad in the fight against 'common enemies').[2] The "energy-security" compact carries with it the implication that "the defence of Saudi Arabia is vital to the defence of the United States" and that Saudi/Gulf energy reserves constitute a significant "strategic asset", access to which has to be denied to hostile camps and regional powers (spelt out more clearly in the Carter

Doctrine).[3] While the transactionary logic of this compact is clear enough, its character and parameters have undergone considerable change over the past sixty years, mainly as an outcome to the interplay of four major determinants that have served to reinforce – as well as erode – the underlying basis for this long-standing political-economic-security arrangement between Saudi Arabia and the US: (1) the changing dynamic of energy, (2) the geo-strategic considerations of Riyadh and Washington, (3) common threat perceptions and (4) the lack of feasible alternative arrangements for both parties.

It should be noted that these determinants have been largely subject to the omnibalancing imperatives (Gerd Nonneman's term referring to the state's efforts to "carve out and maintain a measure of relative autonomy, all the while securing external protection and access to resources") of Saudi Arabia, which emanate from a desire to satisfy four key interests: (1) regime survival, (2) accessing resources for modernization objectives, (3) ensuring a relative degree of autonomy for the state, and lastly, (4) the maintenance of the regional *status quo*.[4] For the Saudi elite, then, the US-Saudi relationship is circumscribed both by the four determinants mentioned above and by the confluence of the omnibalancing imperatives. Collectively, these define the considerations, goals, perceptions, and strategic calculations of the Kingdom.

The special relationship with the US has generally implied for the Saudi elite a guarantee for the survival of the regime itself - i.e. "the defence of Saudi Arabia" implies not only a defence of the national sovereignty and territorial integrity of the state, but encompasses that of the regime as well. This is achieved by the US aiding in the modernization of the country's military and providing an externalized "off-shore balancing" military presence which gives access to global resources, markets, and technologies, pursues a policy of non-involvement in the Kingdom's internal affairs, and neutralises potential threats to the regional *status quo*. Perceptions that the US is failing or unwilling to uphold these interests have fueled, during different episodes since the 1970s, tensions in the US-Saudi relationship, engendering in turn the emergence of an omnibalancing foreign policy.

Given the lack of any real alternatives to the US, and long-standing Saudi vulnerabilities *viz-a-viz* its regional rivals (population size and makeup, military capacity, geographic exposure of its oil facilities…etc.), however, this omnibalancing tendency should be understood as not only a continuation of a general 'hedging' strategy that has always been part and parcel of the Kingdom's attempts to safeguard its autonomy, but more importantly as a way to 'signal' Saudi displeasure with US actions and policies. In essence, therefore, the satisfaction of the Kingdom's core interest – the preservation of the regime – has always been identified with remaining under the umbrella of US military protection. Thus, while cyclical crises may emerge, "they are inherent to the very nature of the asymmetric alliance between a stronger power and a weaker power, [with the weaker power] always caught between the opposition fears of 'entrapment and abandonment.'"[5] Omnibalancing operates accordingly within the structural limits of the global balance of power – the Kingdom seeks to maximize its options and autonomy while ensuring that the US-Saudi alliance remains largely intact.

3. The Present State of US-Saudi Relations:
Reinforcing and Eroding Factors

In light of the four determinants discussed above, it could be said that the strategic-security contours of the US-Saudi relationship are still operative. Energy remains a major pillar in this relationship, although the US itself is no longer heavily dependent on Saudi/Gulf energy as such (this is by no means an exceptional state of affairs, and is in fact a return to the situation that prevailed from the 1940s to the early 1960s.) Saudi Arabia remains the world's 'energy gas pump' with an estimated 16% of all global reserves located within its borders, constituting nearly 13% of all current global production.[6] Its spare capacity, estimated at around 2.5 million barrels-per-day, ensures that the Kingdom exercises a considerable – while diminished – influence in determining global price and supply.[7] Safeguarding international access to Saudi/Gulf oil/LNG remains an established objective of US strategy which identifies the continued health of the global economy (and that of its allies), and its access to energy, as integral for its long-term security. This situation, needless to say, is aligned with Saudi interests to the fullest extent.

The role played by energy in the context of US-Saudi ties does not end here by any means. As an established policy, the Kingdom has, over the past decades, 'recycled' significant portions of its petrodollars in the US in the form of treasury bonds and investments exceeding US $6 trillion.[8] These investments make the maintenance of the relationship a rather profitable affair for the American and Saudi elites, and act furthermore as a form of insurance guaranteeing long-term US involvement in the region. Additionally, Saudi military procurements from the US – the unprecedented 2010 US $60.5 billion deal for instance – also fall under this rubric.[9] Given maintenance and training needs, the arms cycle ensures a long-term US commitment on one level or the other.

It should be noted of course in the meantime that the US-Saudi relationship is facing a changing energy topography - characterized by the proliferation of new technologies, the expansion of unconventional sources, the emergence of new potential energy powerhouses (including the possible re-appearance of Libya, Iraq and Iran as major exporters in time), and changing consumption patterns. Domestic consumption in Saudi Arabia currently takes up 24% of annual production and threatens, with a 7% growth rate per annum (according to various reports), to turn the country into a net oil importer some time between 2022 and 2038. There is also the dimension of a Saudi 'pivot to Asia', with non-OECD countries expected to add another 19.3 million barrels to their consumption between 2010 and 2040, according to the EIA. These factors could potentially, notwithstanding various countermeasures and unanticipated shifts, undermine the 'energy' pillar in the relationship over the medium and long-terms.[10]

Beyond the energy dynamic, there has been a degree of convergence in the viewpoints held by both parties regarding regional-security issues – a convergence very much expressed in their counterterrorism cooperation (through intelligence sharing, tightening funding streams, and utilizing Saudi Arabia's spiritual authority in ideological struggles with militant groups, etc.), and more recently in their common efforts to contain Iran.[11] This is supplemented by the strategic context in which the two countries find themselves in, defined as it is, as noted above, by:

(a) the lack of any alternative partners for both sides

(b) long-standing US commitments to the security of Saudi Arabia and the Gulf at large, upon which US credibility is staked, and

(c) an existing US military infrastructure in the Gulf that has made it, according to Frederic Wehrey, "a door-way for US power projection into the rest of the region."[12]

While Saudi Arabia has not had a US troop presence since 2003, it remains subsumed – through its military procurements and extended ties with the GCC - within this military superstructure regardless.

In all, these residual and transitional factors have worked to reinforce US-Saudi relations, and will likely continue to exercise such an influence for a few more decades to come. And yet, despite their positive effect, there has been a gradual but clear erosion – since the end of the Cold War but more specifically from the early 2000s onwards – to the logic underpinning the 'special' US-Saudi relationship which was been increasingly assuming, as Thomas Lipmann and F. Gregory Gause III, have observed elsewhere, a more transactional and problematic character.[13] This development was assumed to follow an established cyclical pattern in US-Saudi relations, emanating from its inherent structural 'asymmetry' that generates tensions. The most recent developments in the US-Saudi relationship however, while echoing past episodes, suggests that a qualitative break or departure from the past is taking place, driven largely by the emergence of what can be termed as the 'garrison state' mentality in Saudi geostrategic assessments (or alternatively, an amplification of the 'structural contradictions' that have always existed between asymmetric allies.)[14]

The garrison state mentality, which stems from deep apprehensions regarding the collapse of the Saudi state (or more specifically the overthrow of the current regime or an end to its monopoly on power) coupled with a fear of US abandonment during a period of heightened political upheaval and instability, accentuates and exaggerates existing threats while seeking to resolve them *via* the utilization of brute force. Within this framework, as Kiren Chaudhry has observed, "fortification has become the governing idiom of Saudi foreign policy" whereby the state seeks to address its sense of insecurity (both internal and external) as well as its sense of encirclement. It does this not only through increased allocations of funding for defence but also by a more robust, and offensive-oriented foreign policy (of which the invasion of Bahrain or the 2009 war against the Houthis are the most representative.)[15] Defence expenditure currently constitutes around 10-20% of the present Saudi budget, and forms the world's fourth largest military budget as of 2014 according to a study by SIPRI. The 'Saudi Defense Doctrine', as conceived by analyst Nawaf Al-Obeid, exemplifies this vision of a more militarized Saudi foreign policy as a response to regional instability.[16]

Additionally, the garrison state mentality paradoxically both produces greater dependency on the US (as an outcome of the recognition that Saudi capabilities are, and will remain, limited for some time to come), and multiplies the points of difference between Washington and Riyadh. The latter outcome arises because the Saudi government identifies its 'regime survival' interests in starker terms than Washington does. As it projects the regime's rejection of any internal political change into the wider regional arena, it obstructs any real cooperation or concordance of views with the US over how best the two states can secure the long-term stability of the region.[17] In that sense, the 'garrison state' mentality becomes a self-fulfilling prophecy, which could, over a considerable period, bring about the scenario of US-Saudi disengagement.

As can be gleaned from the above, there are three main sources driving the formation of a more assertive Saudi foreign policy and the so-called 'garrison state' mentality: (1) the reality of the Saudi domestic political context, (2) the regional context (or more simply, the collapse of the Saudi-dominated Arab order), and (3) lowered confidence in US commitments towards Saudi Arabia arising from US behaviour in dealing with regional events/upheavals. These sources are in a constant interaction with one another, accentuating and relieving each other's pressures as well as reinforcing multiple debilitating tendencies. The issues of the Saudi domestic context are affected to a large extent by the Arab regional environment and its discourses: US actions, both towards the Saudi domestic context and the wider region, in turn determine official Saudi assessments on the durability of their strategic relationship with the US. This then impacts the regime's assessments of its security/insecurity, particularly with regards to its own internal situation. Deterioration in any of these three arenas impacts negatively on the other two and strengthens the 'garrison state' tendency which, while being construed as a solution to the state of insecurity facing the Kingdom, only worsens its overall predicament and exercises a negative influence on the US-Saudi relationship over the long term.

The following section will offer a thorough examination of the first and second sources, with the third being subsumed under the analysis of the second.

3.1. The Saudi Domestic Political Context

The core political values underlining regime behaviour in the domestic context (although by no means limited to it) are the regime's desire for preservation and the maintenance of its power monopoly within the system. Through various periods, the regime has sought to accomplish this by bolstering and reinforcing its 'latent' legitimacy (along different terms directed at different constituencies), by active suppression and political violence, by shows of political reform (the 1992 Basic Laws, and the symbolic reforms of the 2003-2006 period) and by way of co-optation through the rentier order and the 'social contract'. Despite these efforts, however, the Saudi state has faced mounting, albeit ideologically diverse, political challenges emanating from different sectors of Saudi society that have been influenced to a high degree by regional events as well as access to new streams of information thanks to increasing education and exposure to the media and the internet. The most problematic of these challenges have usually been those identified as coming from three quarters: (1) the Islamist opposition, (2) the liberal opposition, and (3) the Shia of the Eastern province.

Each of these threats has been traditionally appraised and dealt with according to the 'balancing' needs of the monarchy at any given time, although the Islamist challenge has in recent decades been deemed the most threatening to the regime, which fears the supposed resonance of its discourse and politics within the wider Saudi public, its inherently 'religious' challenge to the regime, and its links with other groups abroad. Additionally, the regime has also paid special attention to pre-empting the emergence of an 'alliance of interest' between the various dissident groups. In the 1990s for example, the regime sought to address Shia grievances (inviting its leadership from abroad, promising to extend state largesse) at a time when Islamist/*sahwa* opposition to the monarchy's decision to invite foreign troops was mounting. More recently by contrast, the regime's violent response to the ongoing Shia uprising in the Eastern Province – which remains marginalized as a societal and political issue – serves "to demonstrate to [the regime's] wider Sunni constituency the need to support it against a suspect minority."[18]

In all, the monarchy has been successful to a degree since the 2000s in suppressing these various groups, or at the very least ensuring that a wider coalition which might pose a threat against its stranglehold on power does not emerge. Its goals have been largely facilitated by three developments. The first of these is the appearance of the Al-Qaeda threat, which took the form of a major bombing/terror campaign from 2002 to 2007 against government, security, and oil installations. The trauma arising from these bombings served to consolidate support for the monarchy (a rallying around the flag effect) and, more significantly, helped validate the expansion of a more sophisticated 'security state' within the Kingdom that would be later utilized against oppositional voices. The Al-Qaida threat planted the seeds of the 'garrison state'. In other words, the spectre of terrorism, including the recent capture of an ISIS cell, has been a relative god-send for the regime. This does not imply that terrorism does not constitute a threat to the regime – it is – but it is not an existential one by any means.[19] The second key development was the ascension of King Abdullah, whose reign was identified initially by middle class liberal Saudis as one heralding dramatic change in the country's politics. The establishment of National Dialogue Centres, the brief liberalization of the press, the economic 'opening up' including the country's entry into the WTO in 2005, and the enactment of municipal elections, were seen as evidence of this reform direction. Overall this strengthened and sustained popular support for the regime over a considerable 'grace' period and allowed it to push for a security-oriented project relatively unopposed

The third and perhaps most important development was the surge in oil prices since 2003-2004, which expanded the resource streams at the disposal of the state. The budget in 2013, for example, was estimated at around US \$230-270 billion. This allowed the state to control populist sentiments more effectively (through co-optation, re-distribution, patronage, and suppression) and to deal with potential challengers. The 2011 'royal grant' was perhaps the most flagrant expression of this tactic.[20] However, given the spiraling of the state's expenditure, aimed at propping up the rentier system and maintaining public security, it is unclear whether this model is sustainable. The break-even price needed for oil has been constantly revised upwards, and as it stands the Saudi budget is expected to go into the red as early as 2017 (this was originally written prior to the subsequent decline in oil prices experienced in late 2014 – the Saudi budget is probably going to show a deficit in the actual budget of 2015).[21] More worrying than this is that there is an emergent energy crisis brought about by natural depletion (that will be felt, according to Aramco, by 2028) and by uncontrolled domestic consumption abetted by subsidization as noted above. Furthermore, uncertainty exists surrounding the state's efforts to create a sustainable non-oil based economy through massive investments in education (including the dispatch of over 207,000 students abroad), intensified industrialization, promotion of alternative energy, attracting FDI, and the establishment of 'new economic zones' amongst many other ventures. The continued viability of the rentier model is in doubt, although even in the worst outcomes this model could be sustained for a little while longer - the country's surplus reserves of nearly \$270-290 billion can finance its deficits for a few more years before spending will have to be reined in.

It is clear that the past ten years have witnessed a gradual growth in Saudi societal discontent, suggesting that traditional mechanisms are proving inadequate to address the issues confronting Saudi society's aspirations. This discontent has been fueled by a number of factors, primarily by the demographic makeup of Saudi society, where 60% of the population is under the age of 30, which makes it susceptible to upheaval.[22]

The palpable increase in the number of "losers" in the context of the Saudi economic system poses a threat to the survival of the regime. Unemployment remains chronically high, estimated to be somewhere between 10 to 26% for males and potentially at around 85% for females. According to the Labour Minister Adel Al-Fakih in 2012, the Kingdom would have to create a further 3 million jobs by 2015 in order to absorb graduates, returnees to the workforce, and current job seekers.[23] For those with employment, salaries have been generally seen as insufficient in the face of rising inflation. A Twitter campaign launched in 2013, stating 'the salary is not enough for anything!', is worth taking note of as it gained over 17 million Twitter users. More recently there has been another sustained YouTube campaign by unemployed Saudi men complaining about their marginalization and deplorable economic circumstances. This situation has contributed, amongst other socio-economic factors, to the erosion of the Saudi middle class over the last decade, with all that entails for political stability, and an increase in the number of native Saudis living on the poverty line - somewhere between 2 to 4 million.[24] These problems are compounded by the fact that less than 50% of the Saudi population own their own housing, and some studies have suggested that the number of those renting their current residences could be as high as 80%.[25]

No doubt many of these issues can be attributed to the stresses arising from unchecked population growth and the after-effects of Saudi neo-liberal reforms, but they have nonetheless fueled public anger against the state. The latter, in turn, has sought to alleviate the problems through such measures as Saudization, expanding the scope of the social security net (currently costing in excess of US $100 billion), increasing salaries, and launching housing programmes.. [26] The effectiveness of these measures, however, is undermined considerably by the systemic dislocations being experienced by Saudi society, pervasive perception of rampant corruption and extravagance within the royal family and, of course, new ideational discourses espoused by a new generation of Saudis not necessarily swayed by royal largesse.

Furthermore, a strengthening human rights' discourse, coupled with the emergence of a 'new consciousness' regarding the prevailing political paradigm in Saudi Arabia, is fueling a new generation of activists expressing discontent. While drawing on liberal streams within Saudi Arabia (some of which, ironically, have been promoted by the state as an ameliorating strategy of its own) and constituting a form of disillusionment with the early reform promises of King Abdullah's reign, the 'new consciousness' stems largely from growing dissatisfaction with (and awareness of), the social and political disenfranchisement prevailing within the country. It reflects new aspirations and new articulations regarding how the relationship between the ruler and the ruled should be, as well as the popularisation of the norms of citizenship, political participation, and *huquq* (rights) and a gradual rejection of paternalistic tribal politics.

Much of the activism arising from this new consciousness remains localized and concerned with particular issues – exemplified by ongoing sit-ins by women and children protesting the incarceration of the Saudi 'War on Terror' prisoners, class-action suits by Saudi rights' lawyers, and women's suffrage 'driving campaigns'. But increasingly the activism reflects a more national orientation as indicated by the emergence of such organisations as the Saudi Civil and Political Rights Association and the Human Rights First Society, repeated 'mass petition' campaigns calling for a constitutional monarchy (with signatories from across the country), and recent cross-sectarian cross-regional attempts at solidarity – bringing mainline elements together with Shia in the Eastern province, the Buraydah prison families etc.. This is aided immensely by the utilisation of new communication mediums such as Twitter, YouTube, and Facebook, which have facilitated the quick dissemination of news/rumours regarding the government to a wider segment of the Saudi population than ever before. It is worth noting that Saudi Arabia has the highest per capita usage rate for Twitter and YouTube globally.[27] All this suggests that the political attitudes within the wider Saudi public are changing, with increasing dissatisfaction with (aspects of) the current political order as it exists.

While the situation overall appeared to be somewhat stable and contained prior to 2011, the eruption of the Arab Spring uprisings in late 2010 proved to be deeply unsettling for the monarchy. It offered an 'Arab' precedent (or inspiration), fueled by similar social and political grievances as those discussed above, for the overthrow of the regime. The uprising in Bahrain constituted by far the most substantial threat, given Manama's political resemblance to Riyadh, and its supposed susceptibility to Iranian influence. The Muslim Brotherhood's ascension to power in Egypt amplified the worries further as it offered, for a duration at least, a concrete political platform for (what were perceived to be) the aspirations of some Saudi Islamists. Sensing in these a real threat to the security regime and the political *status quo*, the Kingdom quickly assumed the mantle of the counter-revolution abroad (to be discussed below), while clamping down heavily on potential dissent within. Its response, while regurgitating traditional mechanisms of cooption and suppression, also involved a more vigorous and unjustified security component coupled with markedly less tolerance for some forms of dissent which had previously been acceptable.[28] Abdulmajeed al-Buluwi has described this as a "securitizing [of] the public domain and classifying many peaceful actions as threats to security."[29] On the side of cooption and suppression, the regime significantly increased social welfare and other benefits, utilised religious discourse discouraging protests, and relied on scare-tactics in the media associating the uprisings with chaos and the advance of Iranian interests.[30]

Interestingly, while the Arab Spring has clearly energized some elements within the Saudi activist community (such as in the rights' movement in Awamiyyah, calls for mass protests in 2011, the establishment of pro-reform parties, and the women's driving campaign, etc.) Saudi society itself has remained rather acquiescent.[31] Nonetheless, state suppression/intimidation has intensified significantly from 2011 onwards, typified by mass arrests against Saudi activists (including Abdullah al-Hamid, Muhammad al-Qahtani, and Waleed Abulkhair), the promulgation of draconian anti-terrorism laws in 2014 severely curtailing the scope of (already limited) freedoms within the Kingdom, the banning of petitions, increased surveillance, and the use of violence against protestors (in the Eastern Province mostly), amongst many other measures and actions.[32] This comprehensive response not only reveals that the monarchy in Saudi Arabia is, as Madawi Al-Rasheed correctly notes, "out of touch with the serious changes that swept the Arab world over the last three years,"[33] but that it is unwilling to alter the basic and unsustainable political formula within the country. This obstinacy with regards to maintaining the political *status quo*, hand in hand with the regime's decision to securitise and suppress the political debate within the Kingdom, will only serve to breed further discontent within the Saudi public, entrenching regime paranoia (or the 'garrison state' mentality) even further.

A shift in the political paradigm further down the line remains doubtful, and this has much to do with the nature of the Saudi system itself, which is not only dominated by a conservative and aged leadership ill-disposed towards a substantive change in their paternal rule (with, it should be stressed, a wide generational gap between its senior ruling members – mostly in their 70s and 80s – and the youthful population they rule), but is increasingly assuming an oligarchic character with multiple centres of power. While the Kingdom may have exhibited the characteristics of an absolute monarchy at one point during the 1960s and 1970s, the rentierest-clientalist nature of the system (i.e. tendencies to re-distribute wealth and create localized fiefdoms) as well as the segmentalised/personalised tendencies of the elite has generally pushed the political order towards greater decentralisation, where the King rules ceremonially.[34] This tendency towards decentralisation, has been strengthened significantly by the upcoming succession process. Various first generation princes, including King Abdullah himself, have placed their sons and relatives in positions of high authority, overseeing a variety of 'feudal holdings', so as to facilitate their subsequent ascension when the time comes (this chapter was first written prior to the passing of King Abdullah in January 2015, but the dynamic holds equally under King Salman who has actively concentrated power in the hands of his son Mohammed).[35] This competition already appears to be aggravating elements of conflict within the royal family and its various branches,[36] and will probably expend the family's political energy/capital, as well as undermine the leadership's unity over the next decade.

In all, we are faced with a situation in which a divided, sclerotic, and insecure leadership, unwilling to forego its stranglehold on the system, will have to contend with growing centrifugal pressures on it. Its response to this societal challenge will embrace the well-tried formulas of re-distribution, patronage and securitisation, with the latter incrementally adding greater pressure on the system as a whole due to the general ineffectiveness of the system. Given the long-term trajectory of declining resources at the disposal of the state, the regime may opt for a 'Chinese option' by which it seeks to deepen its neo-liberal reform path and transform the country socially and economically in ways that could potentially revitalize its legitimacy and fortunes. This in fact has already been taking place since the late 1990s. The regime operates furthermore under the added urgency that there is a closing 'window of opportunity' during which time the system could be salvaged – before state resources begin to decline (potentially by the early 2020s). Regardless, these measures will probably prove ineffective. The political gap between the ruling elite and the population (or more precisely segments of it) is likely to widen in the coming decades, feeding into the garrison state mentality and reinforcing the tendency towards suppression and the exercise of state violence as a way to check political demands emanating from Saudi society. While willing to bargain, the regime's structural inability and unwillingness to give up on its full monopoly of power will probably only solidify the securitization impulse as an easy resort. Hence, the 'garrison state.'

3.2. The Regional Context

The regional security environment surrounding the Kingdom has undergone considerable deterioration over the past decade in so far as Saudi security/regime interests are concerned. The three major drivers behind this deterioration are the following: (i) the ascendancy of Iran, (ii) the eruption of the Arab Spring (and the subsequent fallout arising from it), and

(iii) US failure to maintain the *status quo*. The convergence of these three developments, particularly in the past few years, has prompted the emergence of – in conjunction with some of the internal developments recounted above – a more assertive foreign policy seeking to contain, if not roll back, the worst excesses or byproducts of these developments, as well as 'filling the vacuum' left by perceived US inaction and blundering.

Iran has been traditionally perceived in Saudi circles – whether under the Pahlavi monarchy or the subsequent Islamic republic – as a historical regional rival and potential threat to the Kingdom. This threat is defined not only in terms of Iran's regional clout and size (population, economic modifiers, military) but by its proximity to the Eastern province which holds nearly all of the Kingdom's oil fields and infrastructure, as well as most if not all of its Shia communities that are perceived by Riyadh to be "vulnerable to external influence."[37] Containment has defined Saudi Arabia's longstanding approach, a policy it could safely pursue given US backing and support. Prior to 2003 this was pursued, in particular, by playing off Iraq (another historical adversary) against Iran, as seen in Riyadh's active support for Saddam in the 1980s followed by its sustained engagement with Rafsanjani and Khatami in the 1990s. However, the 2003 US invasion of Iraq – which the Kingdom had counselled against – overturned the tenuous balance of power in the Gulf, and allowed for a significant expansion of Iranian influence in the region. This was facilitated, it should be added, by a series of US governing blunders and sectarian policies enacted during the occupation. The re-activation of the Iranian nuclear enrichment program, which was viewed in Riyadh as an explicitly 'weaponized program', served to exacerbate Saudi fears of Iran's growing clout. Saudi fears were also fuelled by Iran's apparent success in forging a unified 'Shia crescent' throughout the Middle East, as witnessed in the consolidation of Hezbollah's power following the 2006 Lebanon War (with Hezbollah viewed as a proxy for Tehran), Al-Maliki's control of Iraq, and the tensions with Damascus (which had deepened its relations with Iran due to shared threat perceptions of the US) following the assassination of the Lebanese prime minister Rafik Al-Hariri, and the Houthi rebellion in Yemen (with whom Saudi forces clashed directly in 2009) which has assumed effective control over the country as of February 2015.

Confronting this hegemonic encirclement was deemed vital for the preservation of Saudi interests and this enabled, for a time, close cooperation between Saudi Arabia and the US, with a focus on shutting down the Iranian nuclear programme.[38] However, it should be stressed that this convergence was in many ways a rather momentary phenomenon aided largely by the ideological and strategic calculations of the neo-conservative Bush administration and long-standing US apprehensions regarding Iran post-1979. Increasingly over the past few years, there has been evidence to suggest that US policymakers are interested in the possibility of a US-Iranian rapprochement or 'grand bargain' that could potentially lead to the normalization of diplomatic ties between Washington and Tehran.[39] This line has been pursued in the face of strong opposition by both Israeli and Saudi lobbyists and pundits, coupled with signals from the Israeli and Saudi governments aimed at deterring

Washington, such as Tel Aviv's threats to attack Iran and Riyadh's flirtations with nuclear developments. The US view was borne to a large extent by a more sober (and rational) reading of Iranian approaches in the region. There was an appreciation of the "missed opportunity" in 2001 when the Iranians willingly cooperated with the US against the Taliban, and the possibilities which had been opened up by the 2007 Iraq-Iran-US talks, as well as a growing understanding of Iran's significance as a major regional player that is key to solving many of the region's problems (most recently, as a means to help contain ISIS). The US was also becoming more conscious that Iran constitutes in its own right a "strategic prize" that is currently courting the budding interest of various Asian powers seeking to integrate West Asia into their own economic strategies.

This shift towards Iran was very noticeable in the early overtures extended by the Obama administration, strengthened considerably with the election of Rouhani, and Obama's push for renewed nuclear talks - culminating in the conclusion of the 2013 Geneva Interim Agreement. Despite Obama's assertions during his March 2014 visit to Riyadh that he would not pursue a 'bad deal' with Tehran, for Saudi Arabia these flirtations were, hand in hand with the secret nature of the negotiations overseen by Oman, indicative of a strategic recalibration on the part of Washington that would end in sacrificing Saudi security interests while legitimizing Iran's gains over the last decade. Such an outcome was not favourable for Riyadh by any stretch of the imagination.[40]

The timing, moreover, could not have been more problematic. Iranian influence was already deeply entrenched in Iraq and Lebanon, and was now making significant advances in Syria with what appeared to be a re-consolidation of Assad's rule. The latter development was clearly due, in the prevailing Saudi view, to Obama's failure to live up to his 'Red Line' regarding the use of chemical weapons, thus aborting a Saudi push to overthrow the regime. This state of affairs was heavily suggestive, it was contended, of a potential US departure from the region.

Yet the prospect of a US-Iranian rapprochement had attracted considerable global - and more importantly GCC – support, so the now isolated Kingdom was forced to assume a more conciliatory tone. It extended an invitation for the Iranian Foreign Minister Mohammad Javad Zarif to come to Riyadh.[41] While this may suggest a coming 'shift' (or return to normalcy) in Saudi policy, it is more likely that Riyadh's current strategy is to make a show of sustaining diplomatic talks with Iran while waiting for 2016 when US elections might bring a more acceptable administration to the White House. Additionally, the Saudi government's assertive posturing *viz-a-viz* Iran - as exemplified in its own strengthening ties with Pakistan, its continued backing of militias and non-state groups in Lebanon and Syria against Iranian-backed forces/clients, the expanding military budget, and the displays of power such as in the 'Sword of Abdullah' military exercise - will probably continue.[42] This is only to be expected given the long-standing perception of Iran as an ascendant enemy whose power has grown unchecked for several years and which poses a direct threat to Saudi dominance in the Gulf and the wider region. Accommodation at this current stage is unthinkable given the existing balance of power regionally. Accordingly, a muscular Saudi approach to Iran will endure for some time to come, even though Iran is currently somewhat cowed due to recent events and cognizant of the limits of 'going it alone'. When linked to the Iranian domestic context, the 'Iranian threat' serves as a propagandistic tool to cement regime support.

The Iranian issue to a large extent also intersects with the events of the Arab Spring, which were viewed in Riyadh as extremely disruptive and threatening to the survival of the regime, both in terms of upending the 'moderate Arab camp' which Saudi Arabia saw as an integral part of its regional 'security' architecture, and as an ideational challenge to its own political order - particularly so following the eruption of protests in neighboring Bahrain. The successes experienced by various branches of the Qatari/Turkish-backed Muslim Brotherhood in a number of Arab countries, moreover, were disconcerting: they brought to the fore a 'political Islamist' challenge backed by regional competitors antithetical to the Saudi order. Furthermore, the regional chaos and instability was perceived to offer Iran – the primary competitor - an opportunity to maximize its gains. This was witnessed, for instance, in Mohamed Morsi's diplomatic recognition of the Islamic Republic, and the 'Shia' character of the protests in Bahrain. Aggravating Saudi assessments of the regional situation was the strong perception of US 'withdrawal' and abandonment of the Kingdom: the US failure to back Hosni Mubarak at the height of the Egyptian revolution in 2011, its slow recognition of Abdul Fattah Al-Sisi's July 2013 coup, and its opposition to the deployment of Saudi troops in Bahrain in 2011. In addition, its overtly cautious policy towards involvement in the Syrian civil war revealed, according to Marc Lync "a more general disconnect between Washington and Riyadh on regional order."[43]

The Saudi state, while initially shaken by these various events, quickly assumed the mantle of the counter-revolution, subverting the popular uprisings abroad and striking against its regional competitors - principally Iran, but also encompassing Qatar. Its principal approach has been to restore or shore up its regional influence through a projection of its securitization strategy, whether by active military participation through its own forces or that of its regional allies (in Bahrain, Kuwait, and Syria), its de-legitimization of certain political forces such as the Muslim Brotherhood, and through intense subsidisation of its 'new-found' or old clients across the region, including Bahrain, Lebanon, Yemen, Jordan, Morocco, and now Egypt. According to Bruce Riedel, an American counter-terrorism expert quoted in the *Economist*, Saudi Arabia spent nearly $25 billion in 2012 to support allied regimes.[44] This has probably increased significantly with Egypt now becoming a major recipient of Gulf largesse and support.[45] In addition to these efforts, Saudi strategy has also subsumed a more radical attempt to create a cohesive regional security bloc - either through a 'League of Monarchies' or a more consolidated 'Gulf Union' - that would take on a more active role in bolstering regional stability. It is, however, unclear whether conditions will ever - due to the lack of institutional frameworks and perhaps the deep (but never acknowledged) suspicions held by the smaller Gulf states regarding Saudi Arabia's oversized role – allow for it to come to fruition. It is very clear that many of these measures constitute a temporary fix and are part of a general desire to restore the pre-Arab Spring *status quo*.[46] Given regional trends, the transformations that are taking place across various Arab societies, and the regional spillover from a number of conflicts (most notably Syria-Iraq), it is likely that the Kingdom will quickly face the limitations (in terms of resources, political capital etc.) of its strategy as well as in its ability to control regional developments. Despite this, however, Riyadh has as yet no alternative strategy to pursue, and will most likely continue committing itself to this approach, with all that entails in working against the 'regional flow', its impact on US-Saudi relations (with the two parties diverging regarding their goals and visions for the region), and on Saudi Arabia's regional position.

4. Conclusion

The Saudi regime faces a changing domestic and regional context that it is unable to deal with. This stems from the 'makeup' of the Saudi political order, which is unwilling to address the core political issues at hand. Instead, the regime has opted to securitize its solutions both at home and abroad in a bid to ensure regime survival. This strategy has only served to compound its dilemmas even further and to entrench the 'garrison state' mentality. Perceptions of withering or weakened US support, moreover, have strengthened the recourse to a more assertive (and compensatory) foreign policy, negatively shaping Saudi calculations. The 'special' US-Saudi relationship, still defined by a number of strategic determinants, will continue to retain its traditional relevance, although erosion of influence, hand in hand with the new emergent 'mentality' will serve to widen the gap and force, over the next decade or two, a 'normalization' of the relationship.

Long-term stability will make it necessary for the regime to adjust to the realities on the ground and respond to the aspirations and demands of the Saudi public, especially since the current strategy is not sustainable in the face of mounting political pressures and declining resources. A more 'representative' Kingdom will enable the recalibration of Saudi Arabia's security assessments along more rational lines, strengthen Saudi's position *viz-a-viz* its regional challengers (backed as it would be by solid popular support), liberate Saudi resources, and most significantly revitalize the US-Saudi relationship along more favorable lines. Otherwise, as Madawi Al-Rasheed points out, Saudi Arabia will have "to revisit its new foreign policy doctrine and accept the limitations of its ability to lessen its military dependence on the United States"[47] while also contending with a (self-imposed) worsening security environment both internally and externally. It cannot hope to win such a fight so long as the leadership remains unwilling to change the political formula. Most importantly, it has a limited time frame to pursue such a decision with any hope of a soft landing. Unfortunately, it is unlikely that the reign of King Salman – which has so far seen the empowerment of security institutions – will augur such a change anytime soon.

Notes

1   The term 'garrison state' is borrowed from Kiran Chaudhry. Please refer to: Chaudhry, Kiran. "Kingdom of the Terrified" *Aljazeera* (English). 5 March, 2012.

2   "US is ultimate 'offshore balancer in the Gulf'" International Institute for Strategic Studies, last modified 10 December, 2012.

3   Ottaway, David. "The U.S. and Saudi Arabia Since the 1930s" Foreign Policy Research Institute Wachman Centre 14, no. 21, 2009.

4   Nonneman, Gerd. "Patterns in Saudi-British relations: continuity and change" Institute of Diplomatic Studies, Riyadh., 3-4 May, 2008.

5   Gause III, F. Gregory. "Tensions in the Saudi-American Relationship." The Brookings Institution., 27 April, 2014.

6   Ramady, Mohammed. A. *The Saudi Arabian Economy: Policies, Achievements and Challenges*. 2nd ed. New York: Springer, 2008.; "Saudi Arabia: Selected Issues." 2013 International Monetary Fund. June 2013. Web. 18 May 2014. <http://www.imf.org/external/pubs/ft/scr/2013/cr13230.pdf>.

7   Ibid.

8   Al-Labbad, Mustapha. "Obama's Presidency Brings Uncertainty to Saudi-US Relations." *Al-Monitor*, 12 March, 2013.

9   Cordesman, Anthony H.. *Saudi National Security and the Saudi-US Strategic Partnership*. Centre for Strategic and International Studies., 2008. Al-Saadi, Yazan. "Saudi-US Relations: Between Tension and Profit." Al Akhbar (English), 6 February, 2014.

10   "Saudi Arabia: Country Analysis Briefs," US Energy Information Administration.; Sfakianakis, John. "Saudi Arabia's Essential Oil." Foreign Affairs. 8 January. 2014.; Hamdan, Sara. "Demand Booms Among Saudis." *The New York Times*, 18 June 2014.; Al-Tamimi, Naser. "Saudi Arabia's Oil Policy: The Challenges Ahead" *Al Arabiyya*, 18 December, 2012.

11   Worth, Robert. "U.S. and Saudis in Growing Rift as Power Shifts." The New York Times, 25 Nov. 2013.; Gause III, F. Gregory. "Saudi-American Relations ." Middle East Institute, 1 October, 2009.

12   Al-Saadi, Yazan. "Saudi-US Relations: Between Tension and Profit." *Al Akhbar* (English), 6 February, 2014.

13   Gause, F. Gregory. *Saudi Arabia in the new Middle East*. New York: Council on Foreign Relations, 2011; Lippman, Thomas W.. *Saudi Arabia on the Edge: The Uncertain Future of an American Ally*. Washington, DC: Potomac Books, 2012.

14   Gause III, F. Gregory. "Tensions in the Saudi-American Relationship." The Brookings Institution., 27 April, 2014.

15   Chaudhry, Kiren. "Kingdom of the Terrified" *Aljazeera* (English). 5th March, 2012.; "Military spending continues to fall in the West but rises everywhere else, says SIPRI." Stockholm International Peace Research Institute. 14, April. 2014.

16   Obaid, Nawaf. "Saudi Arabia shifts to more assertive defense doctrine." *Al-Monitor*, 3 June 2014.

17   Al-Buluwi, Abdulmajeed. "US, Saudi still far apart on regional issues." *Al-Monitor*, 28 February, 2014.

18   Al-Rasheed, Madawi. "Saudi reform could include elected legislature." *Al-Monitor*, 6 June, 2014.

19   Al-Buluwi, Abdulmajeed. "Saudis fear Syria blowback after discovering ISIS cell." *Al-Monitor*, 8 May, 2014.

20   Hertog, Steffen. "A Rentier Social Contract: The Saudi Political Economy since 1979." Middle East Institute, 28 February, 2012.; "Saudi king boosts economic benefits to citizens." *The Washington Times*, 23 February, 2011.

21   "Gulf 2013: The Constant and the Changing," Gulf Centre for Development Policies, 2013.

22   Nafjan, Eman. "Saudi Arabia is losing its fear." *The Guardian*, 8 March, 2011.

23   McDowall, Angus. "More than 1 million Saudis on unemployment benefit." *Reuters*, 28 March, 2012.

24   Alnuaim, Mishary. "The Composition of the Saudi Middle Class." GRC Gulf Papers, October 2013.; Carrington, Daisy. "Twitter campaign highlights poverty in Saudi Arabia." *CNN*, 6 September, 2013. Al-Rasheed, Madawi. "Marginalized Saudi youth launch virtual protests." *Al-Monitor*, 9 April, 2014.;

Sullivan, Kevin. "Saudi Arabia's riches conceal a growing problem of poverty." *Guardian Weekly*, 1 January, 2013.

25   Dohman, Ahmad. "Poverty in the Kingdom of Gold." *Al-Monitor*, 2 November, 2012. "Gulf 2013: The Constant and the Changing," Gulf Centre for Development Policies, 2013.

26   Ibid.

27   Black, Ian. "Saudi digital generation takes on Twitter, YouTube ... and authorities." *The Guardian*, 18 December, 2013.

28   Al-Alawi, Irfan "Saudi Arabia's anti-protest fatwa is transparent". *The Guardian*, 1 April 2011.

29   Al-Buluwi, Abdulmajeed. "Saudi anti-terrorism law casts wide net." *Al-Monitor*, 4 June 2014.

30   Al-Rasheed, Madawi. "The Saudi Leadership Crisis." *Al-Monitor*, 1 November, 2013.

31   Laessing, Ulf "Pro-reform Saudi activists launch political party". *Reuters*, 10 February, 2011.

32   Nafjan, Eman. "Saudi Arabia is losing its fear." *The Guardian*, 8 March, 2011.

33   Al-Rasheed, Madawi. "The Saudi Leadership Crisis." *Al-Monitor*, 1 November, 2013.

34   Al-Rasheed, Madawi. "The coming Saudi decentralization." *Al-Monitor*, 28 March, 2014.

35   "Saudi ruling royal family moves to pre-empt succession crisis." *Middle East Monitor*, 31 March, 2014.; Aziz, Jean. "Changes in Saudi Defense Ministry a matter of family politics." *Al-Monitor*, 27 May 2014.

36   Al-Rasheed, Madawi. "Saudi Arabia's Unpredictable Succession Plan." *Al-Monitor*, 23 April, 2013.; Al-Rasheed, Madawi. "The coming Saudi decentralization." *Al-Monitor*, 28 March, 2014.

37   Burke, Jason. "Riyadh will build nuclear weapons if Iran gets them, Saudi prince warns." *The Guardian*, 30 June, 2011.

38   Ibid.

39   Leverett, Flynt Lawrence, and Hillary Mann Leverett. *Going to Tehran: why the United States must come to terms with the Islamic Republic of Iran*. Picador, 2013.

40   Al-Buluwi, Abdulmajeed. "US, Saudi drifting apart despite Obama visit." *Al-Monitor*, 14 April, 2014.

41   Al-Rasheed, Madawi. "Saudi reform could include elected legislature." *Al-Monitor*, 6 June 2014.

42   Al-Rasheed, Madawi. "Saudi strategy includes alliance with Pakistan." *Al-Monitor*, 8 January, 2014.; Al-Labbad, Mustapha. "Obama's Presidency Brings Uncertainty to Saudi-US Relations." *Al-Monitor*, 12 March. 2013.

43   Gause III, F. Gregory. "Tensions in the Saudi-American Relationship." The Brookings Institution., 27 Apr. 2014.; Lynch, Marc. "America's Saudi Problem." *Foreign Policy*, 24 January, 2013.

44   "Awkward relations." *The Economist*, 29 Mar. 2014.

45   Al-Rasheed, Madawi. "Saudi reform could include elected legislature." *Al-Monitor*, 6 June, 2014.

46   Ibid.

47   Ibid.

Bibliography

Aarts, Paul. *Saudi Arabia in the Balance: Political Economy, Society, Foreign Affairs*. New York: New York University Press, 2005.

Cooper, Andrew Scott. *The Oil Kings: How the US, Iran, and Saudi Arabia Changed the Balance of Power in the Middle East*. New York: Simon & Schuster, 2011.

Cordesman, Anthony H. Saudi National Security and the Saudi-US Strategic Partnership. Centre for Strategic and International Studies, December 2008.

Gause, F. Gregory. *Saudi Arabia in the New Middle East*. New York: Council on Foreign Relations, 2011.

Lippman, Thomas W. *Saudi Arabia on the Edge: The Uncertain Future of an American Ally*. Washington, D.C.: Potomac Books, 2012.

Nonneman, Gerd. Patterns in Saudi-British relations: Continuity and Change. Riyadh: Institute of Diplomatic Studies,, 3-4 May 2008.

Rasheed, Madawi. *A History of Saudi Arabia.* New York: Cambridge University Press, 2002.

Ulrichsen, Kristian. *Gulf Security: Changing Internal and External Dynamics.* Working Paper, Kuwait Programme on Development, Governance and Globalisation in the Gulf States. London: London School of Economics, 2009.

Ulrichsen, Kristian. *Insecure Gulf: The End of Certainty and the Transition to the Post-oil Era.* New York: Columbia University Press, 2011.

Vitalis, Robert. *America's Kingdom: Mythmaking on the Saudi Oil Frontier.* Stanford, Calif.: Stanford University Press, 2007.

7

America's Monetary Stake in the Gulf and the Looming Challenge of the Petro*yuan*

Flynt Leverett and Hillary Mann Leverett

1. Introduction

Thinking clearly about the future of US commitments and alignments in the Persian Gulf requires appreciation of America's monetary stake in this critical part of the world. That stake is embodied most saliently in a strategically vital link between the dollar and international oil trading.

Since World War II, America's geopolitical supremacy has rested not only on military preponderance, but also on two critical geoeconomic foundations. One has been the ability to exercise dispositive strategic influence over the security, production, and marketing of Persian Gulf hydrocarbons. From its origins in World War II, US interest in Gulf oil has never been primarily about America's own energy needs. The United States came out of World War II self-sufficient, and then some, in oil production. It would not become a net oil importer until the early 1970s. Even after becoming a net importer, it has never met that high a percentage of its own oil demand with Middle Eastern imports. Washington's interest in the Gulf has been primarily about controlling who gets access to its oil, thereby bolstering US influence in other important parts of the world. Coming out of World War II, America wanted to guarantee Gulf oil flows to Western Europe and Japan, judging (well before the Cold War) that secure and cheap energy supplies would be essential to their postwar recovery – which was deemed essential to America's own long-term economic prospects. Moreover, US-provided energy security would lock Europe and Japan into economic and security partnerships with the United States. For nearly seventy years – even after the OPEC revolution of the 1970s ended the West's ability to control energy prices – shoring up America's strategic standing in other regions has remained the real root of its interest in Gulf hydrocarbons.[1]

The other geo-economic mainstay of American supremacy has been the dollar's standing as the world's leading transactional and reserve currency. In narrowly economic terms, dollar primacy allows the United States to extract seigniorage from other countries and to minimize exchange rate risk in international transactions by using its own currency to settle them.[2] Far more significantly, dollar primacy allows the United States to cover its chronic current account and fiscal deficits simply by issuing more of its own currency. This "exorbitant privilege," as then French Finance Minister Valery Giscard d'Estaing described it almost half a century ago, remains an indispensable prerogative for an American superpower that has, for more than fifty years, funded its worldwide projection of hard power in precisely this way – making dollar primacy effectively synonymous with dollar hegemony.

Over the last forty years, these two geo-economic foundations for America's global preeminence have been inextricably bound up with one another – because, for the last four decades, one of the main pillars undergirding dollar primacy has been the dollar's role as the overwhelmingly dominant currency in which oil and gas volumes are priced on international markets and in which cross-border oil and gas sales are invoiced and settled. In energy markets around the world, the dollar functions as the ultimate vehicle – a currency used to denominate and execute foreign trade transactions and capital transfers that do not directly involve its issuing country – helping keep global demand for dollars high.[3] In turn, the dollar's transactional dominance in energy markets conditions the accumulation of large dollar surpluses by major energy producers. These surpluses reinforce the dollar's standing as the world's premier reserve currency. Moreover, they can be – and to a large extent are – "recycled" back into the US economy to cover America's never-ending current account and fiscal deficits.

Many analysts assume that dollar dominance in international energy markets is a natural result of the dollar's wider status as the world's foremost transactional and reserve currency. But the dollar's leading role as invoice and settlement currency in transnational oil and gas sales is neither economically "natural" nor, historically, a function of more generalized dollar dominance. Rather, it was deliberately engineered by Washington as a foundational element in the reconstitution of dollar primacy after the collapse of the Bretton Woods monetary order in the early 1970s. As the United States worked to reconstitute dollar primacy, its strategic ties to Gulf Arab hydrocarbon producers proved central to forging the contemporary oil-dollar nexus; these ties have remained critical to maintaining this nexus. As we will see, since the 1970s – that is, during the Cold War's last two decades as well as after its end – Gulf Arab threat perceptions have been heavily focused on Iran and its regional and global standing. Structurally, Saudi Arabia and some of its Gulf Arab neighbors fear the rise of a modern, economically advanced, and militarily capable Iran, almost regardless of the political order presiding over it. Washington's ability to leverage these concerns through its security partnerships with Gulf Arab states has been vital to the recasting and perpetuation of post-Bretton Woods dollar hegemony.

The rise of China as a global economic power, and as the leading market for energy producers in the Persian Gulf and the former Soviet Union, is posing the biggest challenge yet to America's indefinite prolongation of dollar dominance and wider hegemony.

On one level, currency politics between China and the United States can play out in what is popularly described as "currency war," the competitive management of exchange rates.[4] On another level, it plays out through what might be called "currency contestation" – the competitive promotion of national currencies as international transactional and reserve currencies.[5] As part of its long-term strategy for moving the international order from a condition of American-dominated unipolarity to a more genuinely multipolar distribution of power, China wants the *renminbi* to become a major transactional and reserve currency in its own right. To this end, Beijing is working to encourage major hydrocarbon producers in the Persian Gulf to begin accepting *renminbi* as a transactional currency, including for settlement of hydrocarbon purchases, and to begin incorporating *renminbi* in their central bank reserve portfolios. How Sino-American competition for influence in the Persian Gulf plays out in the realm of currency politics will strongly shape international relations in the Middle East and globally in the 21st century.

This chapter, organized in five sections, explores the "petro*yuan*" challenge and its ramifications for the relative positions of the United States and China *vis-à-vis* Persian Gulf energy producers. The first section reviews the financial and monetary components of modern American grand strategy and how Washington's decision to abandon the Bretton Woods system in the early 1970s compelled it to reconstitute the bases of dollar hegemony. The second section examines US policymakers' intensifying focus on consolidating the dollar's status as the chief currency in which international oil transactions are priced and settled and on the recycling of petrodollars into the American economy as keys to recasting dollar hegemony. The third section considers how Washington's ability to leverage its strategic ties to Gulf Arab energy producers was essential to forging the oil-dollar nexus, and how these ties remain indispensable to upholding dollar dominance in international energy markets. The fourth section assesses the motivations for China's ongoing efforts to persuade major hydrocarbon producers, including in the Persian Gulf, to accept the *renminbi* as a transactional currency for Chinese hydrocarbon purchases. The fifth section offers concluding observations.

2. Economic Foundations of US Grand Strategy

To understand the origins and evolution of the oil-dollar nexus, it is necessary to look at the oil-dollar relationship through the prism of post-World War II American grand strategy. From the war's early stages, US policymakers knew that their country would come out of it in an overwhelmingly powerful position, with uniquely favorable opportunities to shape the postwar world. Over a year and a half before US entry into the war, Washington had started planning how to remake economic and political orders in Europe and East Asia to lock in these regions as economic and strategic partners of the United States – and, in the process, to consolidate America's position as the world's leading power. In pursuit of this goal, US officials were out not just to reduce permanently the standing of Germany and Japan, but also to weaken Britain sufficiently to eliminate it as a potential postwar competitor.[6] (The project of "containing" the Soviet Union would only later be added to Washington's core foreign policy objectives.)

As part of their vision for an open-ended *Pax Americana*, US policymakers were determined to create a dollar-centered postwar economic order.[7] This agenda shaped America's approach to the 1944 United Nations Monetary and Financial Conference at Bretton Woods, New Hampshire, where dollar primacy was first enshrined. At Bretton Woods, representatives of the United States and its wartime allies debated two options for providing liquidity after the war. One, advanced by Britain and favored by virtually every other participating country save the United States, was to create a new international currency, issued and governed multilaterally by the fledgling International Monetary Fund (IMF). The other option, pushed strongly by Washington, was for the dollar to serve as the main form of international liquidity. Although almost all participants at Bretton Woods preferred the multilateral option, the overwhelming relative power of the United States ensured that its preferences would prevail.[8] In the end, America's non-communist allies acceded to a gold exchange standard – pegging their currencies to the dollar at fixed exchange rates with the dollar pegged, also at a fixed rate, to gold – laying the ground for a dollar-centered monetary order.

Once these arrangements came into effect after World War II, it became clear that there was a fatal contradiction in Washington's dollar-based vision: US policymakers found it impossible to reconcile their grand strategy's material demands with the monetary and fiscal strictures of the gold exchange standard.[9] As US administrations promoted rising consumption and a growing welfare state at home and as they were pursuing an expansive and highly militarized foreign policy, America's money supply quickly outstripped its official gold reserves. Along with Washington's disdain for facing fiscal tradeoffs between guns and butter, the only way the United States could diffuse enough dollars to provide adequate liquidity for the global economy was by running open-ended current account deficits. As economically significant countries in Western Europe and Japan recovered from the war, rebuilt, and regained their competitiveness, these deficits grew. Given the logic of Bretton Woods, combining a generalized commitment to fixed exchange rates with an American commitment to dollar-gold convertibility, maintaining dollar primacy under these circumstances required that a critical mass of foreign dollar holders be persuaded and/or coerced to refrain from changing their dollars into gold. From the late 1950s, this was an increasingly urgent imperative for US policymakers.[10]

Over the course of the 1960s, the United States made concerted efforts to keep foreign holders of dollars from exchanging them for gold. The White House put considerable pressure on allied governments to limit the extent to which West European and Japanese dollar holders would actually cash in their greenbacks.[11] Washington also worked with the British government to create the Eurodollar market, so that foreign dollar holders could use their holdings to purchase dollar-denominated investment instruments – technically issued outside US jurisdiction – instead of exchanging them for gold from official US reserves.[12] Ultimately, though, US policymakers could never resolve the fundamental contradictions between America's seemingly limitless appetite for guns and butter simultaneously and the discipline inherent in commodity-based money. In August 1971, with monetary insolvency looming, the Nixon administration suspended the convertibility of dollars into gold, terminating the Bretton Woods gold exchange standard. By late 1973, fixed exchange rates were gone too.

The American decision to end dollar-gold convertibility, along with the final implosion of fixed exchange rates, challenged Washington to reconstitute the bases for continued dollar primacy. To preserve its role as the chief provider of international liquidity, thereby maintaining its strategic autonomy unbounded by ordinary financial constraints, the United States would have to continue running current account deficits. But those deficits were ballooning, for America's abandonment of the Bretton Woods system intersected with two other important developments. First, the United States became a net oil importer in the early 1970s. Second, Middle Easterners' perceived profound flaws in American policy toward their region that triggered the world's first major oil crisis in 1973-1974, resulting in a 500 percent increase in the price of oil. The dramatic rise in oil prices severely exacerbated the strain on the US balance of payments. With the link between the dollar and gold now severed and exchange rates no longer fixed, the prospect of the United States running ever larger deficits with no end in sight raised concerns about the dollar's long-term value. In this environment, several of America's Western European allies revived the idea, first broached by Britain at Bretton Woods thirty years earlier, of providing international liquidity in the form of an international currency issued by the IMF. In particular, these countries pushed to expand the use of Special Drawing Rights (SDRs), which the IMF had created just a few years earlier.[13]

By circumscribing Washington's ability to keep creating as many dollars as American politicians deemed necessary to support rising consumption and welfare expenditures at home and hard power projection abroad, such a multilateral system would have gutted the financial foundations of America's post-World War II grand strategy. To fend this off, US officials had to devise new ways to incentivize foreigners to continue holding ever-larger surpluses of what were now fiat dollars. The approach they settled on – initially forged across the Nixon, Ford, and Carter administrations, consolidated by the Reagan administration, and continued by every subsequent US administration – had two main components. One was to incentivize countries to accumulate and maintain dollar surpluses by maximizing demand for dollars as a transactional currency. The other was to reverse Bretton Woods' endorsement of restrictions on transnational portfolio investment and push for financial liberalization on an increasingly global basis. With financial globalization, the United States could leverage the superiority of its financial markets – then, as now, the world's largest and most liquid – to cover its chronic fiscal and current account deficits by accessing international capital stocks at relatively low cost.[14] US policymakers calculated that, taken together, these two initiatives would also have a corresponding effect of renewing the dollar's standing as the world's foremost reserve asset. As we will see, these policymakers judged that consolidating a more clearly dominant role for the dollar in international energy markets was critical to both dimensions of their approach to rebooting dollar hegemony after the demise of Bretton Woods.

3. Forging the Oil-Dollar Nexus

Though crucial to the emergence of the oil-dollar nexus, the strategic motivations of American policymakers and the role of US diplomacy in promoting dollar dominance in international energy markets are almost wholly neglected in conventional economic analyses. In assessing the dollar's role in these markets, economists and economic historians have emphasized two propositions. The first holds that dollar primacy in transnational energy markets is economically "natural" because of the efficiency gains from employing a dominant invoice and settlement currency in transnational oil and gas sales. The second proposition holds that dollar primacy is historically conditioned, to a point of near-inevitability, by America's prominent role in the development of the international energy industry and by its longstanding status as the world's leading economy.[15]

In reality, the oil-dollar nexus is neither economically natural nor historically inevitable. The dollar did not emerge as the clearly dominant currency in international oil markets until the late 1970s, well over a century after the beginning of the modern hydrocarbon era. Notwithstanding the vital role of American companies in the oil industry's internationalization, some of the earliest oil concessions granted by non-Western sovereigns to Western oil interests – including concessions obtained by US as well as British firms – specified payment of royalties, taxes, and other obligations in sterling or sterling-related currencies rather than in dollars.[16] To be sure, the 1928 Achnacarry Agreement – the initial "roadmap" for oligopolistic collaboration among internationally active American and European energy companies – specified a dollar-based pricing formula for international oil transactions, with US Gulf Coast prices as a benchmark.[17] Still, data on oil import payments show that, in the 1930s – after the dollar had already replaced sterling as the world's premier transactional currency – slightly more than half such payments were made in sterling and other non-US currencies. Furthermore, the data show that this pattern continued well after World War II, through the 1950s, 1960s, and even into the 1970s – after the dollar had replaced the pound as the world's leading reserve currency as well as the world's leading invoice and settlement currency for international trade – under the "posted price" system administered by Western energy companies holding concessions in major non-Western hydrocarbon basins.[18]

So what explains the dollar's ascendance, from the late 1970s, as the overwhelmingly dominant currency in international energy markets? Two factors are particularly noteworthy. The first is essentially economic in character. The second – and more important – is intensely political.

Economically, US-led dissolution of fixed exchange rates in the early 1970s raised the transaction costs and associated risks of using multiple currencies for invoicing and settling cross-border oil sales. Employing sterling alongside dollars for these purposes was economically rational in a world operating under fixed exchange rates. This was clearly the case before World War I and, somewhat more problematically, during the interwar period, when the international monetary system was predicated on a more or less classical gold standard. It was also the case after World War II, under the Bretton Woods gold exchange standard. Under a fixed exchange rate regime, dollar-sterling rates – that is, the price of sterling in dollars and the price of dollars in sterling – were set, with the force of law. While exchange rates were sometimes adjusted, revaluations were relatively rare. This meant that, as long as the price of sterling was pegged to the value of the dollar and the dollar was "as good as gold," the exchange rate risk entailed in using pounds and dollars in more or less equal proportion for international oil trading was manageably low. With the end of Bretton Woods in the early 1970s, the currency regime for international oil trading was bound to come up for grabs, as the shift from fixed to floating exchange rates created incentives to move toward a single-currency regime for cross-border oil sales.[19]

But with the dollar no longer backed by any underlying asset, there was no *a priori* reason to assume that, as a new regime emerged, it would be dollar-based. Certainly, the initial reaction of America's major oil-producing allies in the Persian Gulf – including Saudi Arabia and the Shah's Iran – to the end of Bretton Woods was not encouraging on this point. In 1971-1972, America's major allies in the Persian Gulf all favored shifting the Organization of Petroleum Exporting Countries' (OPECs') administered price system for oil exports from denominating prices in dollars to denominating them in a basket of currencies. By 1975, OPEC had reached a consensus to begin pricing oil in IMF-administered Special Drawing Rights.

A temporary resumption of dollar appreciation delayed implementation of this consensus. By 1977, the dollar's renewed depreciation revived OPEC's active consideration of SDR- and currency basket-based options for oil pricing. Moreover, after the dramatic rise in oil prices engorged Persian Gulf producers' current accounts, Saudi Arabia and other Gulf Arab allies of the United States all supported British and West European proposals to recycle petrodollar surpluses through the IMF – in part to encourage the Fund's emergence as the main provider of international liquidity in a post-Bretton Woods world.[20]

Thus, the economic environment in the 1970s was, on its own, not at all clearly conducive to establishing a dollar-based regime for international oil trading. This points to the more important – and more explicitly political – factor conditioning the dollar's rise to preeminence in international energy markets during the period. From the early 1970s, the United States worked assiduously and purposefully to promote it. Jonathan Kirshner notes that monetary choices "are *always* and *everywhere* political." As a result, consequential monetary outcomes are inevitably driven at least as much by political forces as by market dynamics.[21] America's role in establishing the oil-dollar nexus, its motivations for doing so, and the means it applied to the task underscore the truth of Kirshner's observation. For strategic reasons – to reconstitute dollar hegemony for the larger purpose of preserving its economic and foreign policy autonomy – the United States strove to induce major energy producers to accept fiat dollars as the sole currency in which they would denominate oil and gas prices on international markets and to recycle substantial portions of their "petrodollar" surpluses back into the US economy. These outcomes were foreordained neither by prior practice nor by economic rationality. They were, rather, the product of strategic bargains struck between US administrations and the leaderships of oil-rich Gulf Arab states, especially Saudi Arabia.

4. Focusing on the Gulf

The complexity of the partnerships that the United States has established with Saudi Arabia and other Gulf Arab energy producers is obscured by the simplistic "oil for security" formula through which they are often described. Washington does indeed guarantee the security of Saudi Arabia and other Gulf Arab states – "security," in these cases, meaning not just territorial integrity but also their ruling families' hold on power. Yet Gulf Arab producers are not significantly committed to supplying the US market. Rather, they have deployed their hydrocarbon assets to serve US interests – i.e., by reliably supplying international energy markets and, at times, adjusting production levels to moderate prices. They also provide political support for US initiatives in the Middle East and, in different ways and to varying degrees, make themselves part of America's regional military infrastructure.

From the mid-1970s – that is, since Washington's abandonment of Bretton Woods – the United States has, with considerable success, sought to make support for post-Bretton Woods dollar hegemony another constitutive element of these partnerships. This started in 1974-1975, when the Nixon and Ford administrations reneged on pledges to America's West European and Japanese allies and quietly encouraged Saudi Arabia and other Gulf Arab energy producers to recycle substantial parts of their petrodollar surpluses into the US economy through private (largely American) financial intermediaries, rather than through the IMF.[22] These commitments provided critical support for Washington's determination to prevent the IMF from supplanting the United States as the main provider of international liquidity. Once US officials had leveraged Gulf Arab decision-making on petrodollar recycling, America's West European allies had no hand to play in pushing an alternative to the dollar as the main form of international liquidity.[23] Gulf Arab cooperation also gave a meaningful early boost to Washington's ambitions to finance US current account deficits by recycling foreign dollar surpluses back into the US economy through private capital markets.

America's financial diplomacy with Gulf Arab energy producers went further, as Washington began eliciting their support for its strained finances. These efforts bore their first fruit in 1974, in the form of another secret deal with Saudi Arabia, whereby the Kingdom's central bank committed to buy substantial volumes of US Treasury securities outside the normal auction process; soon afterward, the United Arab Emirates apparently agreed to a similar arrangement.[24] Most immediately, Gulf Arab purchases of US treasury bills reduced the impact of government borrowing on domestic capital markets in the United States.[25] In the longer term, Gulf Arab bypassing of normal auction processes in buying US treasury bills helped actualize the financing of American fiscal deficits through purchases of US government securities by foreign holders of dollar surpluses By reducing the amounts that the United States needed to finance through public auctions, Gulf Arab states buttressed an initial international image of US treasury bills as the world's safest investment instrument.

The incentives offered by the Nixon and Ford administrations for Saudi and Emirati accession to US requests regarding petrodollar recycling and for direct financial support were threefold. First, while all details of the secret deals are not known, Washington almost certainly offered preferential terms for Gulf Arab purchases of US government securities. Second, Washington agreed to support an increase in Saudi Arabia's allocation of weighted voting power at the IMF while preserving America's *de facto* "veto." Third – and most importantly – US officials did not hesitate to link Gulf Arab states' willingness to help the United States financially with American willingness to guarantee their security against threats perceived by Gulf Arab elites.[26]

In the 1970s, Saudi Arabia was concerned primarily not about Cold War threats from the Soviet Union and its regional partners, but rather about the rising power of Iran. During this period, Gulf Arab states watched as Iran grew richer from higher oil prices, converted much of its wealth into a large, sophisticated, and mostly US-supplied military apparatus, and began asserting power around the Persian Gulf.[27] Though the last shah, Mohammad Reza Pahlavi, had become America's leading regional military partner, he was more hawkish on oil prices than Saudi Arabia and other Gulf Arab states and less interested in recycling Iran's petrodollar surplus into the US economy, preferring to fund domestic spending and investment programs, mega-development projects, and military expansion.[28] These conditions both enabled and incentivized Washington to leverage Gulf Arab states' concerns about Iranian power to influence their financial and monetary decision-making.

Taken together, the willingness of Saudi Arabia and the UAE to recycle large parts of their petrodollar surpluses into the US economy and to finance American deficits by buying US government securities proved critical to consolidating the dollar's post-Bretton Woods status as the world's premier reserve currency. In 1978, the Carter administration struck yet another secret deal with Saudi Arabia, whereby the Saudis agreed to exert their influence to ensure that OPEC abandoned plans to price oil in a basket of currencies or in SDRs and instead, continued pricing oil in dollars under its administered price system.[29] To elicit a positive Saudi response, the Carter administration moved to implement the Ford administration's commitment to increase the Kingdom's IMF quota. Continued US-Saudi security cooperation was, once again, another important incentive for Saudi cooperation on currency choice in oil pricing.[30]

Spurred by Gulf Arab producers, OPEC's commitment to the dollar was key to its broader embrace as the oil market's reigning transactional currency. Once OPEC dropped plans to begin pricing oil in a basket of currencies or in SDRs, this virtually guaranteed that OPEC member states would keep denominating oil prices in dollars.[31] After OPEC's posted price system collapsed in the first half of the 1980s, use of the dollar for invoicing international oil transactions was universalized with the emergence of international oil exchanges in London and New York.[32] Nearly universal pricing of oil – and, later on, natural gas – in dollars has, in turn, conditioned transactional path dependencies and network effects raising the likelihood that international hydrocarbon sales would not just be denominated in dollars but settled in them as well. This has made the dollar a true vehicle currency in international energy markets, generating ongoing and substantial support for worldwide dollar demand.

The simultaneously financial, monetary, and military arrangements between US administrations and Gulf Arab energy producers have held up despite periodic and intensifying dissatisfaction with America's Middle East policy by Saudi Arabia and other Gulf Arab states and more fundamental US estrangement from other major Gulf producers (e.g., Saddam Hussein's Iraq and the Islamic Republic of Iran). Ongoing concern about the perceived threat of Iran has been key to maintaining these bargains. Since Iran's 1979 revolution, the Saudis and some of their Gulf Arab neighbors have been even more worried about Iran under the Islamic Republic than under the last shah. While Iran's conventional military capabilities have atrophied since the revolution, the Islamic Republic's model of participatory Islamist governance combined with indigenous technological advancement and foreign policy independence represents a different – and, in many ways, more potent – threat to Gulf Arab polities.[33]

Under these circumstances, US security commitments to its Persian Gulf allies, especially *vis-à-vis* the perceived threat of Islamist Iran, have elicited sustained Gulf Arab support for the oil-dollar nexus.[34] While Saudi Arabia and other Gulf Arab producers now accept euros in payment from some of their European customers, they continue pricing their energy exports exclusively in dollars.[35] In response to US pressure, they have also limited the extent to which they have diversified their reserve portfolios with euros.[36] Over the years, Saudi Arabia and other Gulf Arab energy producers have supplemented their support for the oil-dollar nexus with sizable purchases of advanced US weapons systems and other military equipment.[37] Most Gulf Cooperation Council states further complement their contributions to covering America's current account and fiscal deficits by pegging their national currencies to the dollar. In this context, senior Saudi officials say that the Kingdom's continuing commitment to the dollar is fundamentally a "strategic decision," not an economic one.[38]

5. The *Petroyuan* and the Gulf

The commitment of major Gulf Arab producers to the oil-dollar nexus remains critical to perpetuating dollar hegemony. While Iraq moved away from pricing its oil exports in dollars prior to the 2003 US invasion and occupation, and Iran no longer accepted dollars in payment for its oil exports, the larger share of the world's hydrocarbon transactions continued to be settled in dollars, bolstering the dollar's ongoing status as the world's top transactional currency. Despite a drop in the dollar's share of overall global reserve assets, it remains the world's leading reserve currency. Nevertheless – and notwithstanding the array of transactional path dependencies, network effects, and strategic considerations sustaining the oil-dollar nexus – the fact that international energy markets, for much of their history, made room for more than one currency suggests that current dollar-based practices are not set in stone, and that movement toward a different system is possible.[39] Indeed, with the rise of the "petro*yuan*," movement toward a different system appears to be already underway.

China has clearly emerged as a major player in international energy markets. From the late 1970s, economic reform spawned a rapidly growing industrial base and rising living standards for burgeoning numbers of Chinese, sparking exponential increases in energy demand. Though China was (and is) a major oil producer, its production could not keep up and, in 1993 it became a net oil importer. Within a decade, the People's Republic became the world's third-largest consumer of foreign oil, after the United States and Japan. It pulled past Japan into the number-two spot in 2008 and, according to OPEC and the US Energy Information Administration, would surpass America as the world's biggest oil importer in 2014.[40] Today, sixty percent of China's oil imports are sourced from the Persian Gulf, making relations with Gulf producers an especially high priority for Chinese foreign policy.[41] This also makes relations with China – the most important incremental market for energy producers for the next quarter century and beyond – a high priority for Gulf states. China's quest to access overseas hydrocarbons, moreover, puts it in an escalating competition with America for influence in key energy-producing regions – particularly the Persian Gulf.

As it faces these challenges, the People's Republic has embarked on a long-term campaign to internationalize its currency (*renminbi*, denominated in *yuan*).[42] A steadily rising share of China's external trade is being denominated and settled in *renminbi*; the issuance of *renminbi*-denominated financial instruments for foreign investors is also growing. China is making progress in an extended process of capital account liberalization, which many Western observers deem essential to the *renminbi's* full internationalization. Likewise, it is allowing greater exchange rage flexibility, with the eventual goal of floating the *renminbi*. *Renminbi* are already being held in central bank reserve portfolios in some of China's trading partners. Beyond this, the People's Bank of China now has currency swap arrangements with more than thirty other central banks – which means that *renminbi* are, for all intents and purposes, functioning more widely as a reserve currency.[43] Longer term, Beijing is laying the ground for a multipolar international monetary order.

As for dollar hegemony, China's goal is not for *renminbi* to replace dollars, but for *renminbi* to function alongside the dollar as an important international transactional and reserve currency. Beyond economic gains, Beijing seeks a range of strategic benefits from internationalizing its currency, particularly *vis-à-vis* the United States.[44] Chinese policymakers have watched Washington's increasing propensity to cut off countries from the American financial system as a foreign policy tool and are concerned about the prospect of Washington seeking to leverage the People's Republic in this way. They have also watched as the United States has undertaken economic, military, and political initiatives aimed, from Beijing's vantage, at constraining China's emergence as a legitimately influential player.[45] Chinese officials calculate that *renminbi* internationalization helps mitigate China's potential vulnerability to such pressure. More broadly, Chinese policymakers understand the importance of dollar hegemony to America's capacity for unilateral global power projection. By chipping away at the dollar's relative standing as the world's premier transactional and reserve currency, Beijing can constrain what it sees as excessive US unilateralism in international affairs.

China has long incorporated financial instruments into its strategy for securing access to foreign hydrocarbon resources.[46] Now, as part of its campaign to internationalize the *renminbi*, Beijing is working to persuade major hydrocarbon producers, including Persian Gulf producers, to begin accepting *renminbi* as a transactional currency – not just to pay for Chinese imports, but also to settle Chinese hydrocarbon purchases – and to begin incorporating *renminbi* in their central bank reserve portfolios.[47] Besides contributing to *renminbi* internationalization, the petro*yuan* is a valuable addition to Beijing's financial tool kit for implementing the "going out" policy. It is also a new resource for China to deploy in its intensifying competition with America for influence in key energy-producing regions – including in the Gulf.

Promotion of the petro*yuan* lets China expand the financial, monetary, and strategic options available to major energy producers.[48] The incentives for Gulf Arab receptivity are threefold. First, given widespread expectations that the long-term trend in the value of China's currency runs strongly toward appreciation, accumulating *renminbi* seems a virtual "no brainer" in terms of portfolio diversification. Second, as noted, China is clearly the major incremental market for Persian Gulf hydrocarbon producers for the vastly foreseeable future. While knowledgeable Gulf Arab elites recognize that America's "shale revolution" will not imperil the Gulf's unique place in international energy markets, the rise in US shale oil and gas production is further focusing the attention of major energy producers, in the Middle East and elsewhere, on China and other East Asian markets.[49]

Finally, as the United States is seen more and more as a hegemon in relative decline, China is viewed in the market for Persian Gulf, as elsewhere in the world, as the preeminent rising power. Conversations with Saudi and other Gulf Arab elites indicate that, even for Persian Gulf states that have long relied on Washington as the ultimate guarantor of their security, the shifting balance of power between the United States and China makes closer relations with Beijing an ever more imperative strategic hedge. China's growing ties to the Islamic Republic are problematic for some Gulf Arab states.[50] Nevertheless, they increasingly realize that China will not be induced to pull back from these ties by Saudi proposals for expanded and oil supplies for the People's Republic, making the imperative for Gulf Arabs to broaden and deepen their own ties to Beijing even more compelling.

6. Looking Ahead

While Saudi Arabia may not yet be ready to embrace the petro*yuan*, other Persian Gulf energy producers are warming to it. China has already shifted some of its payments for Iranian oil into *renminbi* to help Chinese banks and importers avoid Iran-related US secondary sanctions.[51] Chinese and Iranian interlocutors say that discussions are underway about expanding Sino-Iranian energy and financial ties, including through *renminbi*-based transactions. Among Gulf Arab states, China is making currency swaps part of its partnerships with energy producers. From China's perspective, such arrangements are meant in part to pave the way for using petro*yuan* to pay for Gulf Arab hydrocarbons. The extraordinary expansion of Sino-Russian energy ties – with Russia's growing embrace of the petro*yuan* a salient aspect – will further boost receptivity to the petro*yuan* among Persian Gulf hydrocarbon producers.[52]

Of course, these are just opening skirmishes in the battle between the petrodollar and the petro*yuan*. Anxious speculation aside, America is not going to leave the Persian Gulf. Even with its shale revolution, the United States continues to operate in an international energy market, especially for oil. It cannot fundamentally separate its own energy security, much less its international standing and influence, from developments in the Middle East. But just as surely, China will continue working to expand its influence in the region. And by promoting the petro*yuan*, Chinese policymakers calculate that they can slowly erode America's longstanding hegemonic dominance in the Gulf without firing a shot.

Notes

1   For discussion, see Robert Keohane, *After Hegemony: Cooperation and Discord in the World Political Economy* (Princeton: Princeton University Press, 1984/2005), 139-141, 150-181, 190-195, and 202-206; Stephen Randall, *United States Foreign Oil Policy Since World War II: For Profits and Security* (Montreal and Kingston: McGill-Queen's University Press, 2005), 110-318; Rashid Khalidi, *Sowing Crisis: The Cold War and American Dominance in the Middle East* (Boston: Beacon, 2009), 40-62; Doug Stokes and Sam Raphael, *Global Energy Security and American Hegemony* (Baltimore: Johns Hopkins University Press, 2010), 1-53; and Flynt Leverett and Hillary Mann Leverett, "The Balance of Power, Public Goods, and the Lost Art of Grand Strategy: American Policy Toward the Persian Gulf and Rising Asia in the 21st Century," *Penn State Journal of Law and International Affairs* 1, no. 2 (Nov. 2012), 210-211.
2   Seigniorage is the revenue generated by governments from the difference between the cost of printing paper money – or, historically, minting coins – and the money's market value. The internationalization of a country's currency increases opportunities from earning seigniorage.
3   The definition is adapted from George Tavlas, "Vehicle Currencies," in *The New Palgrave Dictionary of Money and Finance*, ed. Peter Newman *et al.* (London: Macmillan, 1992), 754-757.
4   James Rickards, *Currency Wars: The Making of the Next Global Crisis* (New York: Penguin, 2011).

5   Flynt Leverett and Hillary Mann Leverett, Strategic Ambition and the Politics of Currency Choice in International Energy Markets: The Birth of the Petroyuan and the Slow Erosion of the Oil-Dollar Nexus, Working Paper, Penn State School of International Affairs and School of Law, June 2015, 4.

6   Christopher Layne, *The Peace of Illusions: American Grand Strategy from 1940 to the Present* (Ithaca: Cornell University Press, 2006), 39-50.

7   Richard Gardner, *Sterling-Dollar Diplomacy in Current Perspective: The Origins and the Prospects of our International Economic Order* (New York: Columbia University Press, 1980), 71-100, 110-114; Robert Skidelsky, *John Maynard Keynes: Fighting for Freedom, 1937-1946* (New York: Penguin, 2001), 89-133, 233-256, 300-336; Benn Steil, *The Battle of Bretton Woods: John Maynard Keynes, Harry Dexter White, and the Making of a New World Order* (Princeton: Princeton University Press, 2013), 99-124.

8   On this debate, see, *inter alia*, Barry Eichengreen, *Exorbitant Privilege: The Rise and Fall of the Dollar and the Future of the International Monetary System* (Oxford: Oxford University Press, 2011), 45-47 and, with greater granularity, Skidelsky, *John Maynard Keynes*, 337-358 and Steil, *The Battle of Bretton Woods*, 1-5, 61-98, 125-149.

9   Leverett and Mann Leverett, *Strategic Ambition and the Politics of Currency Choice in International Energy Markets*, 12-13.

10 Fred Block, *The Origins of International Economic Disorder: A Study of United States International Monetary Policy from World War II to the Present* (Berkeley and Los Angeles: University of California Press, 1977), 164-199 and Michael Webb, *The Political Economy of Policy Coordination: International Adjustment Since 1945* (Ithaca: Cornell University Press, 1995), 119-121.

11 Francis Gavin, *Gold, Dollars, and Power: The Politics of International Monetary Relations, 1958-1971* (Chapel Hill: University of North Carolina Press, 2004).

12 Eric Helleiner, *States and the Reemergence of Global Finance: From Bretton Woods to the 1990s* (Ithaca: Cornell University Press, 1994), 1-21, 81-100.

13 Leverett and Mann Leverett, *Strategic Ambition and the Politics of Currency Choice in International Energy Markets*, 13 and the sources cited therein.

14 *Ibid.*, 15 and the sources cited therein.

15 For a more detailed exposition of these propositions and a critique of their application to analyzing currency choice in international energy markets, see *ibid.*, 6-9 and the sources cited therein.

16 For example, the 1933 Saudi oil concession, granted to two American companies (Standard Oil of California and Texaco, both forerunners of today's Chevron), stipulated an upfront signing payment of 50,000 pounds and a subsequent royalty of four gold shillings per English ton of oil. (For many years, Saudi King 'Abd al-Aziz ibn Saud insisted that the royalty be paid in four-shilling gold pieces.) Likewise, the 1939 onshore oil concession in Abu Dhabi stipulated a royalty of three rupees per English ton of oil. See Ernest Smith and John Dzienkowski, "A Fifty-Year Perspective on World Petroleum Arrangements," *Texas International Law Journal*, 24, no. 1 (Winter 1989), 18.

17 See "Draft Achnacarry Agreement, 18 August 1928" in J.H. Bamberg, *The History of the British Petroleum Company*, vol. 2, *The Anglo-Iranian Years, 1928-1954* (Cambridge: Cambridge University Press, 1994), 528-534; the text is also available at https://www.mtholyoke.edu/acad/intrel/energy/achnacarry.htm.

18 Barry Eichengreen, Livia Chiţu, and Arnaud Mehl, *Network Effects, Homogeneous Goods and International Currency Choice: New Evidence on Oil Markets from an Earlier Era*, Working Paper Series 1651 (Frankfurt: European Central Bank, March 2014), 2, 6-12. On the posted price system, see, *inter alia*, Ian Skeet, *OPEC: Twenty-Five Years of Prices and Politics* (Cambridge: Cambridge University Press, 1988), 1-6; Robert Mabro, "The International Oil Price Regime: Origins, Rationale, and Assessment," *Journal of Energy Literature* 11, no. 1 (June 2005), accessed at http://graduateinstitute.ch/files/live/sites/iheid/files/sites/mia/users/Rachelle_Cloutier/public/International%20Energy/Mabro%20International%20oil%20price%20regime.pdf, 3-5; and Bassem Fattouh, *An Anatomy of the Crude Oil Pricing System*, WPM 40 (Oxford: Oxford Institute for Energy Studies, Jan. 2011), 14-15.

19 Leverett and Mann Leverett, *Strategic Ambition and the Politics of Currency Choice in International Energy Markets*, 14.

20 On these points, see Skeet, *OPEC*, 71-72, 131; David Spiro, *The Hidden Hand of American Hegemony: Petrodollar Recycling and International Markets* (Ithaca: Cornell University Press, 1999), 122 and the sources cited therein; Daniel Sargent, "The United States and Globalization in the 1970s," in *The Shock of the Global: The 1970s in Perspective*, ed. Niall Ferguson *et al.* (Cambridge: Harvard University Press, 2010), 59 and the sources cited therein; and Leverett and Mann Leverett, *Strategic Ambition and the Politics of Currency Choice in International Energy Markets*, 14-15.

21 Jonathan Kirshner, "The Inescapable Politics of Money," and "Explaining Choices About Money: Disentangling Power, Ideas, and Conflict," in *Monetary Order: Ambiguous Economics, Ubiquitous Politics*, ed. Jonathan Kirshner (Ithaca: Cornell University Press, 2003), 1, 260-262.

22 Spiro, *The Hidden Hand of American Hegemony*, 23-48, 105-107, 146-147 and Andrew Scott Cooper, *The Oil Kings: How the U.S., Iran, and Saudi Arabia Changed the Balance of Power in the Middle East* (New York: Simon and Schuster, 2011), 169-170, 174-175.

23 Leverett and Mann Leverett, *Strategic Ambition and the Politics of Currency Choice in International Energy Markets*, 17.

24 Spiro, *The Hidden Hand of American Hegemony*, 107-109, 110-113.

25 *Ibid.*, 110.

26 *Ibid.*, 103-105, 109-110, 113-116.

27 Faisal bin Salman Al-Saud, *Iran, Saudi Arabia and the Gulf: Power Politics in Transition* (London: I.B. Tauris, 2003), 57-124; Joseph Kéchichian, *Faysal: Saudi Arabia's King for All Seasons* (Gainesville: University Press of Florida, 2008), 188; and Cooper, *The Oil Kings*, 219-220, 275.

28 Cooper, *The Oil Kings*, 181-186, 229, 263.

29 On OPEC's administered price system, see Mabro, "The International Oil Price Regime," 5-6 and Fattouh, *An Anatomy of the Crude Oil Pricing System*, 15-16.

30 Spiro, *The Hidden Hand of American Hegemony*, 103, 121-122, 123-124, 147-148.

31 During the 1970s, OPEC included Algeria, Gabon (from 1975), Indonesia, Iran, Iraq, Kuwait, Libya, Nigeria (from 1971), Qatar, Saudi Arabia, the United Arab Emirates, and Venezuela.

32 On the emergence of the exchanges in London and New York in the 1980s, see Mabro, "The International Oil Price Regime," 7-17.

33 For discussion of these points, see Flynt Leverett and Hillary Mann Leverett, *Going to Tehran: Why America Must Accept the Islamic Republic of Iran* (New York: Metropolitan/Picador, 2013), 31-37, 64-78, 90-101, 165-177, 185-194.

34 On this point, a recent study notes that "GCC countries do not hide their dependence on US military protection in confronting the threat of Iran" in explaining their continuing commitment to the dollar; see Miguel Otero-Iglesias and Federico Steinberg, "Reframing the Euro Vs. Dollar Debate Through the Perceptions of Financial Elites in Key Dollar-Holding Countries," *Review of International Political Economy*, 20, no. 1 (Jan./Feb. 2013), 197.

35 *Ibid.*, 192.

36 *Ibid.*, 197.

37 U.S. Secretary of Defense Chuck Hagel said at the International Institute for Strategic Studies' 2013 Manama Dialogue that, during 2007-2013, Gulf Arab states purchased over $75 billion in U.S. weaponry and military equipment; see "Remarks by Secretary Hagel at the Manama Dialogue from Manama, Bahrain" (news transcript), U.S. Department of Defense, Dec. 7, 2013, http://www.defense. gov/transcripts/transcript.aspx?transcriptid=5336.

38 Flynt Leverett, "Black Is the New Green," *The National Interest*, No. 94 (Jan./Feb. 2008).

39 Eichengreen *et al.*, *Network Effects, Homogeneous Goods, and International Currency Choice*, 5

40 On an annualized basis; see Asjylyn Loder, "China to Surpass U.S. Was World's Top Crude Importer, OPEC Says," *Bloomberg*, Apr. 2, 2013, http://www.bloomberg.com/news/2013-04-02/china-to-surpass-u-s-as-world-s-top-crude-importer-opec-says.html; "China Poised to Become the World's Largest Net Oil Importer Later This Year," *Today in Energy* (U.S. Energy Information Administration), Aug. 9, 2013, http://www.eia.gov/todayinenergy/detail.cfm?id=12471; Liang Fei, "China Set to Become Largest Net Oil Importer," *People's Daily*, Aug. 12, 2013, http://english.peopledaily.com.cn/90778/8360667.html;

and "Red October: China to Overtake US as World's Largest Oil Importer – EIA," *Russia Today*, Aug. 12, 2013, http://rt.com/business/china-us-oil-october-379/.

41 See Flynt Leverett and Jeffrey Bader, "Managing China-U.S. Energy Competition in the Middle East," *Washington Quarterly*, 29, no. 1 (Winter 2005-2006); Flynt Leverett, "Resource Mercantilism and the Militarization of Resource Management: Rising Asia and the Future of American Primacy in the Persian Gulf," in *Energy Security and Global Politics: The Militarization of Resource Management*, ed. Daniel Moran and James Russell (Oxford: Routledge, 2008); and Manochehr Dorraj and Carrie Currier, "China's Quest for Energy Security in the Middle East: Strategic Implications," in *China's Energy Relations with the Developing World*, ed. Manochehr Dorraj and Carrie Currier (London: Continuum, 2011).

42 Leverett and Mann Leverett, *Strategic Ambition and the Politics of Currency Choice in International Energy Markets*, 20-22 and the sources cited therein.

43 This is so even though, because China has not fully liberalized its capital account, *renminbi* are not captured in IMF surveys on the composition of nationally-held reserve assets around the world. For a (nearly complete) list of the PBOC's swap arrangements, see Yang Jiang, "The Limits of China's Monetary Diplomacy," in *The Great Wall of Money: Power and Politics in China's International Monetary Relations*, ed. Eric Helleiner and Jonathan Kirshner (Ithaca: Cornell University Press, 2014), 169.

44 Leverett and Mann Leverett, *Strategic Ambition and the Politics of Currency Choice in International Energy Markets*, 24, 25.

45 Leverett and Mann Leverett, "The Balance of Power, Public Goods, and the Lost Art of Grand Strategy," 233-236.

46 The state-owned China Development Bank (CDB) has made long-term "loans for oil" in Venezuela, Kazakhstan, and Russia; concessional financing from CDB and other "policy banks" has also been an important asset for China's three state-owned energy companies in their efforts to acquire equity stakes in upstream oil and gas reserves overseas. See Henry Sanderson and Michael Forsythe, *China's Superbank: Debt, Oil and Influence – How China Development Bank Is Rewriting the Rules of Finance* (Hoboken: Wiley/Bloomberg, 2013), 123-146.

47 *Strategic Ambition and the Politics of Currency Choice in International Energy Markets, 23* and the sources cited therein.

48 *Ibid.*, 22 and the sources cited therein.

49 For analysis explaining why America's so-called shale revolution is not the geopolitical "game-changer" that some claim, see Flynt Leverett and Hillary Mann Leverett, "America's Shale Revolution and the Dangerous Myth of Energy Independence," *The World Financial Review* (May/June 2014).

50 For discussion, see Flynt Leverett and Hillary Mann Leverett, "American Hegemony (and Hubris), the Iranian Nuclear Issue, and the Future of Sino-Iranian Relations," in *The Emerging Middle East-East Asia Nexus*, ed. Anoush Ehteshami, Raymond Hinnebusch, and Yukiko Miyagi (Oxford: Routledge, 2015); available as Penn State Law Legal Studies Research Paper 39-2014, http://papers.ssrn.com/sol3/papers.cfm?abstract_id=2501476.

51 Henny Sender, "Iran Accepts Renminbi for Crude Oil," *Financial Times*, May 7, 2012; Raissa Kasolowsky, "Iran Accepts Chinese Yuan in Exchange for Oil," Reuters, May 8, 2012, http://www.reuters.com/article/2012/05/08/iran-china-oil-idUSL5E8G85WW20120508.

52 Leverett and Mann Leverett, *Strategic Ambition and the Politics of Currency Choice in International Energy Markets*, 24-25.

Bibliography

Andrew Scott Cooper, *The Oil Kings: How the U.S., Iran, and Saudi Arabia Changed the Balance of Power in the Middle East* (New York: Simon and Schuster, 2011)

Barry Eichengreen, Livia Chiṭu, and Arnaud Mehl, *Network Effects, Homogeneous Goods and International Currency Choice: New Evidence on Oil Markets from an Earlier Era,* Working Paper Series 1651 (Frankfurt: European Central Bank, March 2014)

Eric Helleiner and Jonathan Kirshner, eds., The Great Wall of Money: Power and Politics in China's International Monetary Relations (Ithaca: Cornell University Press, 2014)

Gardner, Richard. *Sterling-Dollar Diplomacy in Current Perspective: The Origins and the Prospects of our International Economic Order.* New York: Columbia University Press, 1980.

Gavin, Francis. *Gold, Dollars, and Power: The Politics of International Monetary Relations, 1958-197.* Chapel Hill: University of North Carolina Press, 2004.

Keohane, Robert. *After Hegemony: Cooperation and Discord in the World Political Economy.* Princeton: Princeton University Press, 1984.

Khalidi, Rashidi. *Sowing Crisis: The Cold War and American Dominance in the Middle East.* Boston: Beacon, 2009.

Leverett, Flynt, and Hillary Mann Leverett. Strategic Ambition and the Politics of Currency Choice in International Energy Markets: The Birth of the Petroyuan and the Slow Erosion of the Oil-Dollar Nexus. Working Paper, Penn State School of International Affairs and School of Law, June 2015.

Randall, Stephen, *United States Foreign Oil Policy Since World War II: For Profits and Security.* Montreal: McGill-Queen's University Press.

Raphael, Sam. *Global Energy Security and American Hegemony.* Baltimore: Johns Hopkins University Press, 2010.

Sargent, Daniel. "The United States and Globalization in the 1970s," in *The Shock of the Global: The 1970s in Perspective*, ed. Niall Ferguson *et al.* Cambridge: Harvard University Press, 2010.

Skidelsky, Robert. *John Maynard Keynes: Fighting for Freedom, 1937-1946.* New York: Penguin, 2001.

Spiro, David. *The Hidden Hand of American Hegemony: Petrodollar Recycling and International Markets.* Ithaca: Cornell University Press, 1999.

8

Emerging Dynamics of US-Gulf Engagement: India's Policy Options

Girijesh Pant

1. Introduction

The subtle but defined shift in US –GCC engagement triggered by the ramifications of the Arab uprisings experienced an unexpected twist on 29 June 2014 when, out of the fumes of the regional conflict, emerged the Islamic State with ISIS leader Abu Bakr Al-Baghdadi as Caliph. The declaration transformed the security–stability matrix by placing political Islam and terrorism as the defining parameters, thus posing a challenge to the political authority of those whose rule is based on their Islamic legitimacy. The Gulf regimes saw this as primarily an ideological threat to their existence, rather than a simple matter of terrorism. The fallout from the politics of ISIS terror, however, has not been confined to the region. It has been finding resonance in the Islamic space across countries. Recognising it as a global security threat, the US along with its coalition, which includes the Gulf countries, has launched a war 'to degrade and destroy' ISIS. This appears to have led to a re-engagement of the US in the regional security architecture and reaffirmed US-GCC relations, as outlined in the Jeddah Communiqué issued after the meeting held between President Obama and the King of Saudi Arabia.[1]

However whether this new development in US Gulf policy amounts to a revision of the policy in its substance remains a matter of interpretation. Although the US and the Gulf countries have been able to synchronise their strategy to fight against ISIS, the same can not be argued for their medium- to long-term vision about the region. In fact the Gulf countries themselves do not share among themselves a common strategic vision for the future security and stability of the region. It can be argued that although in the short-run US engagement with the Gulf countries will be influenced by its war against the ISIS, in the medium- to long-term the US would like the region to initiate a regional solution with internal structural reforms – something which the Gulf regimes might find difficult to agree on. The divergence in perception between the two has been publicly admitted by US policy-makers, while at the same time they express appreciation of the time-tested relationship. William J. Burns, the Deputy Secretary-of-State speaking at the Center for Strategic and International Studies, minced no words when he stated that:

> The reality is that in our conversations with our Gulf partners, we don't always see eye-to-eye on what has caused the revolutions and transitions spurred by the second Arab Awakening. We don't always see eye-to-eye on the direction these transitions should take. And we don't always see eye-to-eye on how best to respond to them.[2]

Clearly the US will not be abandoning the region but it would not like to be the sole bearer of the security burden of the region. This means a consensus needs to be arrived at on a new security regime with new players. The central argument of this chapter is that despite the reengagement of the US in the regional security complex, a sustainable future regional security arrangement would require a wider engagement of diverse stakeholders, which would include the domestic population being part of the solution. This means a new space for Asia, including India, as stake holders in the emerging regional order.

India is not new to the region but its engagement with the region has been confined to energy and remittances. It needs to revisit its policy, carving a distinct role in the context of emerging imperatives of sustainable security in the region. A major Asian player with high stakes in the region, it can not be oblivious to the momentous changes taking place in the region. The spill-over of the rise of ISIS impinges on its security frame because its 'Islamic' dimension carries a sectarian import. With Pakistan and Bangladesh as troubled neighbours, and Muslims being its largest minority (of whom a significant proportion are of the Shia sect), India's Islamic space becomes vulnerable and susceptible to sectarian conflict. Clearly this is no more a question of securing energy supplies from the region but one which involves wider adversarial influences, with a potential to add to the security threat to the country. The country needs to evaluate the ramifications of these changes and calibrate its Gulf policy accordingly. The business-as-usual approach is not going to deliver. India needs to visualise a role for itself in promoting processes that could lead to a sustainable regional security architecture. This would require the assessment and imagination of a construct that meets the country's interest in the region. Accordingly it has to position itself and leverage its strength to define the scope and trajectory of its engagement. This raises some new questions, as to whether India would like to be a player in a US Asian pivot policy, or whether it, along with other Asian countries in a similar position, could act as counter-balancers to provide the Gulf countries a symmetrical engagement with the West. This chapter will attempt to address these questions.

2. Regional Security Dynamics since the Arab Uprising

The Arab uprisings have changed the regional security–stability context by unleashing the potential of domestic pressures for change. They have contested the power of authoritarian regimes by the counter-power of non-state players drawn from both the global and local environments. The strength of the non-state players was visibly demonstrated by netizens in the Arab street and later by the extremist militants. A synoptic view of the evolving regional dynamics is desirable so as to put the issues in perspective. In terms of the most recent time-line, it began with the fall of Saddam Hussain's regime in Iraq. The lesson taken away from the US experiment of regime-change in Iraq could be that US power has its limitations. The only uncontested superpower failed to deliver a viable alternative. Consequently it fed the perception that US power no longer possesses the leverage to draw the political cartography for orderly change, as it could do in the past. It also underlined the point that externally imposed democratic frameworks fail to internalise the latent aspirations of domestic social forces. A political solution which fails to engage its citizens in defining the social contract, especially in a region where authoritarian regimes have never built any institutions to articulate popular aspirations in a formal format, can not be sustainable. The perception of the US's low power quotient was further reinforced by its failure in Afghanistan. Thus, following the Arab uprising the dominant view has been that the US, although a powerful player, is not invincible. The perceived limitation of the superpower has emboldened the sense of power felt at the bottom of the pyramid. The structural crisis of neoliberal economies has further exposed the powerlessness of the powerful and the power of the powerless. Consequently a redefinition of the organising principle of the security regime in the region was required.

The US and its West Asian allies did not share the same prognosis for change in the region. Instead, US behaviour over regime-change in Egypt, and its policy toward Syria, made the regional players (especially the Gulf rulers) think afresh about their relationship with the US. This was very eloquently stated by Saudi Arabia's ambassador to the UK:

> The foreign policy choices being made in some Western capitals risk the stability of the region and, potentially, the security of the whole Arab world. This means the Kingdom of Saudi Arabia has no choice but to become more assertive in international affairs: more determined than ever to stand up for the genuine stability our region so desperately needs.[3]

Although not all GCC countries shared the Saudi Arabian position, the apprehension that the US was scaling down its engagement made all of them rejuvenate their collective efforts to ensure the security of the region. The GCC thus did give consideration to the Saudi Arabian call for a Gulf Union, even though such a development was deferred due to a divergence of threat perception among GCC members.[4] The differences among the GCC countries in their assessment of, and response to, the uprisings also impacted on regional relations, as indicated by the withdrawal of the Saudi and UAE ambassadors from Qatar and the proactive role played by Oman in acting as liaison between the US and Iran - leading to Iran's return to the negotiation table.

Another leading factor that has changed, and led to negative consequences for, regional security and peace has been the sharpening and transforming of the Shia-Sunni construct. This has become a political project, enhanced by the emergence of the Shia-led regime in Iraq. It has altered the regional Islamic power balance between Shia and Sunni rulers in the region, with the Iranian engagement in regional affairs escalating the shift. The Syrian imbroglio provided the most effective setting for Iran to influence and manipulate affairs. Ironically, the divide has been used by the Gulf regimes to suppress local popular protests, whether in Saudi Arabia, Bahrain or Iraq. Along with this divide the region is also experiencing a mutation within Sunni Islam, with the rise of multiple competing centres of power contesting the supremacy of the traditional order. Previously the Muslim Brotherhood as a model of Islamic governance by ballot did not pose a serious challenge to the Wahhabi model of Islamic governance. Further, jihadi groups fighting for an authentic Islamic system are questioning the legitimacy of the regimes ruling in the name of Islam. This is most evident in Syria where different Islamic groups are jockeying for power. Consequently the leadership of Islam is no more perceived as resting in the monopoly position of the custodian of the two holy mosques. The plurality in political Islam has become a major factor in regional security affairs following the uprisings.

The Arab uprisings may not have led to regime change in the Gulf countries, but their most fundamental ramification has been the demolition of the insularity created by the Gulf rulers, wherby the rich and poor Arab countries were set apart by the presence or absence of oil wealth. The social and political influences from the uprisings have contributed to a scaling-up of the aspirations of the youth in the Gulf. Similarly their participation in jihadi struggle has demonstrated their potential to destabilise the internal social and political fabric of the region. The regimes are taking cognisance of the new social mood and have been responding, but the challenge that the Gulf regimes face is to evolve mechanisms to connect with society and undertake institutional changes which address the structural obsolescence of their governing systems. Prince Turki Al-Faisal, the former director general of the Saudi National Intelligence Agency and chairman of the King Faisal Center for Research and Islamic Studies, in a recent speech, reportedly observed that. "The first condition to maintain the security of Gulf states and their communities is to further fortify these states from the inside by formulating policies that ensure smooth relations between the leaders and the people"[5]

It needs to be underlined that the security of the rentier state in the Gulf is further undermined by new challenges emanating from the structural rigidities inherent in the continuing dependence on oil revenue.[6] The regimes are being pressed for reforms to face the demographic changes which are occurring. To quote Mohamed al-Harthi:

When the GCC was established three decades ago, the member states had a total population of 13 million people. Now GCC countries have 47 million people, half of whom are non-citizens, including other Arabs. It is clear then that this imbalance has to be considered a major threat, particularly when formulating security tactics and strategies. Many would be dissatisfied with the political and social consequences if this issue remains unresolved.[7]

The huge share of expatriates in the demography, the growing unemployment among the youth, and the low level of female employment, is perceptibly impacting on social security and the pressure for institutional reform. The public discourse is questioning the opportunities lost due to expatriate domination of the jobs market.[8] A new debate has also been triggered on citizenship, as indicated by the uproar following Sultan Saud al-Qassemi's observation that: "Perhaps it is time to consider a path to citizenship...that will open the door to entrepreneurs, scientists, academics and other hardworking individuals who have come to support and care for the country as though it was their own."[9] The latter development would have economic, social and above all political ramifications which could enhance security but perhaps jeopardise it as well.[10] The Gulf regimes are approaching the issue cautiously. The acceleration of labour market reforms and large schemes for human resource development, including restructuring of the education systems, embodies the regimes' response. The new social and political space given to women in particular symbolises the lesson learnt by the ruling regimes from Tahrir square.[11] It can not be ruled out that the reforms in this sphere could trigger differences between the rulers and the clerics, especially in Saudi Arabia. The reality is that

> women are generally more visible, even on the streets of Riyadh, which lies in the heartland dominated by the influence of Wahhabists, who follow an ultra-conservative version of Islam. Since restrictions on women at work have been eased, they operate cash tills everywhere, from lingerie shops to IKEA, a Swedish-founded furniture shop. They take taxis alone and head to the increasing number of facilities dedicated to women, from spas to separate floors of shopping malls.[12]

This opening of the social and political space is viewed with concern by the clerics,[13] which could further contribute to eroding the resilience of the regimes.

3. US Reassessment and Reprioritisation of the Region

In the history of US-Gulf relations, 9/11 is said to be the turning-point. It made the US realise that "authoritarian stability - that is, relying on authoritarian leaders in the region to help create a political order that made it relatively easier for the United States to pursue its interests in the region - was perhaps no longer appropriate."[14] Among policy-makers and public opinion the view began to gain hold that the security of the region no longer needed to be considered a responsibility to be borne by the US alone. This was further reinforced by the failure of the attempt to export democracy. US President Obama pursued the narrative in his famous Cairo speech in 2009. Ironically the message that it conveyed was one of US disengagement and distancing from the region. The US approach to the Arab uprisings and its efforts to support engagement with Iran on the nuclear issue clearly indicated that America would like the region to evolve by its own rhythm. Public discourse in the US also stressed that the US had its own interests to pursue. In his New York Times article entitled 'What About US?' Thomas Friedman wrote that the US convergence of interest lay in moving beyond the status quo. He observed,

> We as America are not just hired lawyers negotiating deals for Israel and the Sunni Gulf Arabs which they alone get the final say on. We in America have our own interests in not only seeing Iran's nuclear weapons capability curtailed but in ending the 34 years old Iran-US cold war which has harmed our interest---- Hence we must not be reluctant about articulating and asserting our interest in the face of Israeli and Arab efforts to block a deal that we think would be good for us and them.[15]

The US re-imagination of the regional construct was seen by its regional allies as implying their strategic marginalisation.

One of the major consequence of the Arab uprising has been an erosion of trust between the US and its allies in the region, particularly Saudi Arabia. The US attitude towards the exit of President Mubarak, the effective endorsement of the Muslim Brotherhood as "good Muslims over bad ones", the reluctunace to support the anti-Asad forces in Syria, and engagement with Iran, clearly demostrate the US perception that ruling regimes have limited capacity to contain destabilising forces. The thrust of the policy has been to facilitate a reconfiguration of the regional power dynamics, seeking to address issues at the structural level by expanding the space for societal engagement in local affairs - although this need not necessarily be described as democracy promotion. The subtext of US Gulf policy in the context of the period after the Arab uprisings is that its regional view is no longer defined by a GCC-Iran binary axis. Despite promoting the GCC as a regional grouping to counter Iran, Iranian engagement with the region is needed not only in the narrow context of the Gulf but in the wider frame of the Middle East. In other words, the nuanced shift has been to look at the GCC not as independent of the developments in the wider region but in conjunction with it.

The underlying US assumption is that the Saudi Arabia's power to influence the politics of Islamic world has been undermined by the rise of other power centres in the Islamic world. There are competing players who may not be able to replace the Kingdom but are certainly contributing to the destruction of the monolithic construct which Saudi Arabian rulers have been promoting with Wahhabi Islam. The radical Islamists are questioning the authencity of the Al Saud and thereby their leverage. The emergence of the Islamic State vindicates this assessment. Thus a Saudi-Iran convergence is seen as the way forward in terms of containing or restraining the increasing radicalisation of political Islam. Whether the US establishment will be able to converse with both players on the wave length needed to bring about convergence remains to be seen. It will critically hinge upon the Iran nuclear deal and US capacity to convince the Saudi esablishment to accept it. The overture by the Saudi foreign minister, inviting his Iranian counterpart to Riyadh, suggests that the two sides are beginning to recognise the declining dividends of mutual hostility.

It may be relevant now to refer to the global contextual shift in US foreign policy orientation, as this has bearing on US policy in West Asia and the Gulf.[16] With the rise of Asia, and specifically China, Asia is projected to constitute the pivot of US foreign policy. This reprioritisation has its obvious implications for West Asia. In the new orientatation, the US views the Gulf region from the perspective of its Asian tilt, rather than as part of the western security ambiance. The Gulf region itself has been articulating its Asian engagement in terms of its Look East Policy. This is a major departure with strategic implications. The US is apparently seeking a low risk, low cost but necessarily visible presence in West Asia – one which would be reassuring enough to its allies in the region. In visualising this new security constuct in the region, the adminstration would, it seems, possibly be willing to concede space in the Gulf to the EU and some Asian powers if their presence strengthens the regional power balance.

The thrust of the US policy seems not to have been well-received in the region, particularly by Saudi Arabia. The high power visits to the region, including one by President Obama himself, clearly shows that the shift in the US approach has not been appreciated in the region. In fact, the reaction from Saudi Arabia has been terse and explicit. The Saudi withdrawal from taking up its Security Council seat was the most explicit indication of the country's belief that the US needs to do more to demonstrate its commitment to the region. Some ground has been made up since then. In March 2014 President Obama visited Saudi Arabia. The defence supplies provided to Saudi Arabia, and the expansion of the US naval fleet in Bahrain, may have helped assusuge the sensitivities of the Gulf countries. The assurance by Hagel that there is no trade-off between the Iranian nuclear deal and Gulf security illustrates the hard work that the US has to do to convince the Gulf governments.[17] Moreover, the Declaration of the Islamic State has escalated the threat to such a degree that the US and Saudi Arabia have been compelled to bridge the gap between them.

4. Perceptions from the Gulf Region

In contrast to the US assessment of the regional security issues emanating from the Arab uprisings, the Gulf countries viewed in these developments the necessity for forging closer strategic ties with the USA. Since 2011 their threat perception and security assessment has evolved from convergence to divergence and then to renewed convergence. Initially the response to the Arab street protests was one of panic, with the intention of forestalling its spread by any means. This led to the richer Gulf states giving support to the more vulnerable states, such as Bahrain and Oman - financing their public expenditure to enable them to co-opt the constituency of discontent. It also led to the assertion of regional resolve to fight collectively, with a declared intent to form a Gulf Union. The second phase was more of engagement with change or agents of change. The most critical phase emerged from the Syrian crisis where not only did the regime survive beyond all expectations, but the rebels lost their unity of purpose. This led on to a rise in extremist militancy.

Divergences of perception among the regional players became apparent over their positions on the rise and fall of the Muslim Brotherhood – especially in Egypt. It was framed in terms of an ideological contest. The decline of the secular nationalist political formation in the region had provided the Muslim Brotherhood with an opportune political space. The electoral victory of the Muslim Brotherhood in Egypt was perceived as an existential threat by Saudi Arabia – and the Brotherhood was declared a terrorist outfit. While the UAE endorsed the Saudi Arabian position, Qatar opposed it. Qatar extended massive financial support to President Morsi, while Saudi Arabia and UAE financed President Sisi. The differences even evoked the possibility of an alliance being formed between Qatar and Turkey against an alliance linking Saudi Arabia, the UAE, Egypt and Jordan.[18] The withdrawal of ambassadors from Qatar by three GCC members (Saudi Arabia, UAE and Bahrain), on the grounds that Qatar was contributing to the threats to regional security, clearly demonstrated the feeble nature of GCC bonding.[19] Though the GCC members are making every effort now to scale down their differences in the context of the threat posed by ISIS, their difference on political Islam remains a matter contention.

Regional divergence can also be seen in their assessments of Iran's possible rehabilitation following progress in the nuclear negotiations. It may be recalled that Iranian President Ahmadinejad participated in a GCC summit meeting in 2007[20], and similar efforts had been made to forge solidarity of sorts during the Rafsanjani and Khatami periods. Therefore their hostility to Iran's rehabilitation is contextual. The prospects of a nuclear Iran, with a depletion of Arab power following the uprisings, raised the possibility of the power balance tilting in favour of the Shia crescent. Though generally apprehensive of Iran's large profile, the Gulf countries have had different threat perceptions of the Islamic Republic. Oman has strong historical ties with Iran, the UAE has thriving trade relations with Iran, and Qatar has a common interest with Iran in harnessing gas from their shared fields. It is the biggest GCC state (Saudi Arabia) and the smallest (Bahrain) which are most concerned about a hegemonic presence of Iran in the region. Due to divergence of perception, the Gulf countries look at US–Iranian engagement on nuclear issues through differing prisms.

Significantly it is Oman which played the back-channel role in breaking the ice. Iranian President Rouhani visited Muscat[21], and Iran and Oman are working on a pipeline to transport gas. With the progress of the nuclear talks other Gulf states are also reassessing possible Iranian roles in the region.

Significantly, following the Arab uprising at least three Gulf countries (Saudi Arabia, UAE and Qatar) have displayed a new sense of assertiveness in their foreign policies beyond the region. They have made ambitious attempts to project their interests through their financial power and ideological strength. In fact the region has witnessed a cold war within the Islamic world not only on the Shia-Sunni axis but within the Sunni orbit as well. With the rise of ISIS, the war has become a military engagement where some of the Gulf countries are participating in the battle directly. The widespread displays of a Saudi prince and a UAE female pilot in fighter planes were no doubt directed more towards the domestic constituencies than a real show of strength, but the public display of weaponry by the Saudi state made clear that the Saudi monarch has the wherewithal to be the Custodian of the Holy Mosques. The Saudi Chief of Staff, General Hussain Al Qubail, reportedly observed that "By conducting this exercise, we are preparing our forces to defend our holy places." This is more a message to regional countries that Saudi Arabia has significant capabilities, especially when compared with Iran's military infrastructure. One Arab official commented that Qatar should be taking note of these exercises and parades. Among the main guests were King Hamad of Bahrain, Shaikh Mohammed bin Zayed (Crown Prince of Abu Dhabi) and the Chief-of-Staff of the Pakistan Army. By also displaying Chinese equipment the Saudi regime apparently wanted to convey to the US establishment the diversity of its strategic engagement as well.

Notwithstanding the differences among the Gulf rulers, there is a strong sentiment in the region that the US is retreating if not withdrawing from the region. This enhances the feeling of security vulnerability. Though this assessment may not be equally shared by all GCC countries, they do feel the need to internationalise their security concern and to retain the intensity of western (to be more precise US) engagement. Among the Gulf countries it is Saudi Arabia which has enjoyed the closest relationship with the US, hence any shift in US policy is bound to be seen most seriously by the Saudi regime. The latter has been most vociferous in critiquing US policy over Iran, Egypt and Syria, as also over the wider frame of Gulf policy. The escalation of extremist threats in the region, especially after the declaration of the Islamic State, served the Saudi interest of bringing US attention back to the region. The Saudi Arabian ambassador to the UK has vehemently denied allegations that Saudi Arabia at some stage financed ISIS.[22] Importantly, the battle that the coalition is fighting is now recognised by the US as a long term project. Further with IS becoming central to regional and global security concerns, the Iranian nuclear deal is now losing its shine. The renewed agenda of US policy thus emphasises the centrality of Gulf security in US foreign policy.

5. Framing the Region: The Asian Pivot and the Multipolar Globe

Terrorism, political Islam, energy and reforms are the key factors which have a critical bearing on the emerging dynamics of the US-Gulf engagement.[23] In the US assessment, the region as an incubator of terrorism poses a serious threat to global security. Yet the US also recognises its loss of leverage. The sectarian divide in political Islam complicates the picture, and the agenda of political Islam is now written by the non-state players. The US sense of security from growing 'energy independence' does not make the hydrocarbon sector free from volatility and uncertainty, and that impacts on the recovery of the global economy. Lastly US neoliberal prescriptions have not helped its regional allies stay in power.

The interface of these factors with the global gravitational shift from the Atlantic to the Pacific makes it necessary to frame Gulf concerns in a much wider context. The shift, however, is affected by the fractured nature of the new power configuration. The US, despite the erosion of its economic strength, remains the only global military power. While others, including China, might have acquired the economic strength they do not possess the corresponding military might. Thus, when confronting terrorism, the US is the only player which can lead the coalition. It is precisely for this reason that the Gulf and the West Asian countries lean towards the US even though their economic engagement is beginning to face elsewhere. The fractured nature of the power configuration, with other powers able to play a role, however, creates the possibility that the security issues facing the region are viewed from diverse vantage points. While Washington might view the region more through the terror lens, others might see the region more in terms of energy security or political Islam. In other words there is likely to be more than one narrative on the security dynamics of the Gulf. Energy-sensitive Europe with visible Muslim immigrants, Muslim-majority countries, culturally diverse Asian, and Muslim minority and energy dependent India are likely to have their own differing perceptions and assessments. Therefore, despite sharing common concerns with the US, they may find it difficult to agree on a common strategy with the US.

With the increasing intertwining of terrorism and political Islam, and its empathetic resonance if not endorsement in different arenas (as illustrated by the fact that individuals from more than sixty nationalities have joined ISIS), the security issues are moving away from being framed exclusively in military terms. Security in the region can not be arrived at by eliminating the militants physically. The killing of militants by air strikes carries the potential of making them martyrs, thereby expanding the constituency for recruitment. The militancy may be degraded by air strikes but it can not be destroyed in this manner when the search is for a 'higher purpose' in human life.[24] The region thus needs a coalition which could contribute by muting the edge of the ideology of jihad along with its physical decimation. It is unlikely that the US can lead this ideological coalition, due to its huge unpopularity and low credibility in the region. Further, the erosion of US soft power (in the form of "liberal democracy"), triggered by the implosion of neoliberal economic programmes, is occurring despite the might of US hard power. The emerging tension between military and ideological power has raised the need for a coalition that contests ISIS ideologically. It is here that the Asian dimension becomes important: the region needs to take advantage of Asian approaches to Islam. Asian Islam is plural in profile and embedded in local culture and traditions. Thus it carries with it the strength and resilience of tolerance, which seemingly is missing in Gulf Islam. The latter tends to be more arrogant, subsuming local diversities into a monolithic construct. The co-existential nature of Asian Islam provides it with the means to counter the militancy flowing from West Asia. Put differently, Asia can be a player in a larger coalition to contest the radical ideology of political Islam.

In the current changing context, a totalising view of terrorism and political Islam fails to grasp the ground realities. It can not be ignored that the ground realities are constructed by the people - their imagination and their concerns. Their sense of security impinges on the security or insecurity of the state. In the follow-up to the Arab uprisings, the regional insecurity (manifested in ghastly violence by extremist organisations) is the product of insecure people and an insecure state. The solution thus lies not only in making the state secure but people as well. US foreign policy conceives the region in a manner which undermines if not ignores the diversity which exists within the region and around the region. A coalition which defines threat in a totalising way is likely to fail in its objective. It will not create the ground for sustainable stability and security in the region. The growing and visible footprint of China in Asia, stretching toWest Asia, is drawing new boundaries on the strategic space, and this has a bearing on US foreign policy. Although China still does not enjoy the leverage in the Gulf to threaten US interests there, its convergence with Russia on Syria has influenced the progression of that crisis. This convergence makes it imperative that the US looks at the region beyond hard security. The Gulf, within the framework of the US-Asian pivot, can be examined as an arena for balancing the expanding profile of China beyond South East Asia.

Asian countries are vulnerable to radicalisation in the region. The footprint of this is in the constituencies of political Islam in Afghanistan, Pakistan, Bangladesh, Indonesia and Malaysia. The stakes of Asian countries in the Gulf are high, but they can not be part of a US military project. At the same time they can not be mute observers. It is possible that, hunted by the US military, the militants will at some stage move on to these countries. Their return to Saudi Arabia has already started to create ripples. The Asian countries thus have to make a strategic choice on how to contain the entry of 'jihadi Islam' to their territories. For Asian countries this is a major political decision because of its domestic consequences.

It is argued here that, given the changing complex of security construct in the region, the need is to supplement US hard power with an Asian engagement, where Asian countries promote reform processes in the Gulf region. Asia enjoys a compatibility of values with the region, with no baggage of hegemony. A benign Gulf effort to encourage ties with powers like India, Japan and Korea could facilitate the transition towards multipolarity also. In the geopolitics of the region, although the three Asian countries do not enjoy the power to provide a security umbrella, their role could be envisaged as that of a de-escalator in the security field: a promoter of empowering processes to address non-traditional insecurities. The rentier states of the Gulf are struggling for a process of transition compatible with local cultural values - one which engages their youth, and the female population, without denting the conservative ethos. The experiences of the Asians would be easier for Gulf people to relate to, hence more acceptable and less subject to change-related trauma. It needs to be reiterated that the constituency of radicalisation has been encouraged by counter-posing local life to the western life-style – reflecting the identity crisis in the region. Asian engagement is likely to make the transition less bumpy, if not smooth.

It is not a matter of semantics to remember that, in terms of cultural and civilizational depth, the Gulf is part of the construct called Asia. While the historicity of the relationship remains a romantic memory and can not be of sufficient weight to provide strategic depth to the contemporary relationship, yet it provides a civilisational space that could be harnessed. The object would be to reconstruct a regional vision which undermines the arbitrarily-drawn cartography of colonial times which perpetuates territorial tensions. This can be argued in the context of globalisation, where economic supply chains are visualised across the political boundaries. The trans-nationalisation of the region provides a case for a new strategic doctrine, involving a more widely-based regionalisation. This could be seen as a working proposition to subvert the hegemonic construct in the region. The Gulf countries have articulated the emerging reality in terms of their Look East policies. These policies, while focused essentially on accelerating economic engagement, have of late carried a strategic dimension too, with China as an important weapon supplier, and India as partner in defence skills and a maritime player on the piracy frontier. The Gulf regimes still look towards the West for security assurances because Asia can not meet their demands, but the Gulf can not resolve its complex security threat by military support alone. Asian powers can play a role by refashioning the demand for security. They can promote regional security dialogue and negotiation.

Asian players have been fence-sitters because they themselves do not have a shared view of the political dimension of the security crisis. They continue to project it as terrorism, where they have nothing to pool together except declarations. An Asian engagement with the crisis becomes the logical corollary in the context of the Asian Century, but it will fail if it is framed in terms of rising Asia competing with the West. Such a parochial imagination of the emerging global order will not be sustainable. The globe is a composite notion. Thus Asian engagement has to be framed as part of global engagement with the crisis, with global ramifications. The Asian "pivot" thus need not be defined in terms of containing China but rather as a proposition to engage Asia's soft power in responding to the ideological challenge posed by the crisis. The point made here is that the Gulf, and the rest of West Asia, need to be framed in a manner which goes beyond that of a binary East-West axis.

6. The Indian Assessment and Policy Options

The Indian response to the Arab uprisings has been noncommittal, reflecting the tone and tenor of its foreign policy objective of non-interference in the domestic affairs of other countries. An editorial published in the Public Diplomacy Division of the Government of India clearly takes this line. The guiding principles of Indian policy, it says, are:

> First, there cannot be one-size-fits-all reactions and our policies must be country, region and issue specific. Reactions, cosmetically attractive in the context of events in distant countries but which convey ambivalent messages to countries which are important substantively, would be counterproductive.
>
> Secondly, the situation in West Asia is exceedingly fluid and uncertain. There are multiple players, both regional and non-regional, who are proactively involved. An indisputable fact is that whatever India says or does is not likely to influence outcomes on the ground. Therefore, in formulating policies India must be fully conscious of this reality and refrain from statements and actions which in the longer term could be prejudicial to national interest.
>
> Thirdly, the principle of non-intervention in internal affairs has always been sacrosanct for India. India would react strongly to outside comments on internal political matters. Reticence or so-called policy passivity in an unpredictably changing environment does not reflect an absence of decision making or an abdication of 'leadership'. India's policy makers should not be deterred by ideologically motivated domestic criticism about supposedly abandoning a so-called 'independent' foreign policy or criticism by foreign countries on this account.[25]

The nuanced shift in US policy towards West Asia and the Gulf is a matter of interest for India.[26] India also recognises the necessity for US re-engagement with the region in the context of the growing violence threatening the peace and security of the region. It can be argued that the US presence, to provide security in the region, contributed in a benign way to expanding India's engagement with the region. India has been successful in promoting and protecting its interest in the Gulf region effectively. The fact that the region has emerged as India's largest trade partner, provided more than 30% of all remittances received in India, constituted a source of employment to nearly 6-7 million Indians, and provided 70 percent of energy, shows the huge Indian stake in the region. The historical and civilisational memories, and the religious links (with nearly 20 percent of the Indian population being Muslim) underline the reach of the engagement. The sustainability of the relationship can also be gauged by the fact that the region no longer looks at its links with India as less important than its Islamic ties with Pakistan. In fact in all of the Gulf countries the number of Indian expatriates exceeds the Pakistani number. This is symptomatic of the fact that the engagement is very vibrant and dynamic. India would no doubt like this dynamic status quo to continue, but the region is changing. The regional political matrix is transforming opening possibilities of inclusion and exclusion. The regimes are not so stable, even if they are not fragile. The forces of exclusion are manifesting themselves in extreme forms of violence. The state institutions are becoming dysfunctional. The prognosis for security and stability is not very favourable. In this phase of uncertainties, India can not be sure of the outcome in pursuing a wait and watch approach.

India has to assess the situation and reposition itself by crafting a policy which is appropriate for when the political map of the region undergoes change. It needs to protect and promote its interest by taking a holistic view. A vision of the regional dynamics in the medium- to long-term is required. Short-term policies, given the dynamics of the current situation, could be detrimental. It has to move away from its reactive mode.

The Indian assessment of its foreign policy approach in the region so far is that this has helped it to protect Indian interests. In the words of the Indian Foreign Minister,

> We have not let the recent uncertainties come in the way of our growing engagement with all countries of the Arabian Peninsula and the broader Middle East. This mutually beneficial engagement is based on a clear-headed assessment of our national interest and our bilateral complementarities. Our successful efforts to upgrade our relations with both Saudi Arabia and Iraq are an illustration of this approach. The cooperation we are getting on counter-terrorism for example is a tribute to the mutual trust and understanding we have been able to build together. Further in the Middle East, another example is the bilateral engagement we have been able to construct with Egypt.[27]

In the assessment of the Indian state, despite the turmoil in the neighbourhood the Gulf regimes have responded effectively in maintaining the status quo. India has appreciated the reform initiatives the regimes have taken in the diversification of the economies and it sees a great opportunity for India to take a role as a partner in these processes. The Indian government recognised the depth of energy relations when the region covered the deficit in India's oil supply caused by sanctions on Iran. The high-level visits from the Gulf since the signing of the Saudi-Indian Delhi Declaration of January 2006, within the context of the region's Look East policies, shows the intent to promote a comprehensive relationship. India, for its part, has a high stake in the region. Thus a nuanced distancing from the uprisings is a reflection of India's Gulf policy. The nightmare of rescuing 11,000 Indian workers from Kuwait in 1990 still haunts policy-makers in New Delhi. It is not in India's interest to see the Arab uprisings have a destabilising effect on the Gulf.

The Indian government does have strong concern over the possible fall-out from Saudi-Iranian differences, the Shia-Sunni conflict, and the enlarging constituency of terror.

It looks at the Iran nuclear negotiations as an important step towards the de-escalation of tension in the region. The Geneva negotiations are seen as an endorsement of India's stand that Iran needs to be talked to. The Indian foreign minister has affirmed that India understands the Iranian need for nuclear energy and believes negotiation is the only way to resolve the issue.[28] Although supporting a legitimate Iranian role in the Gulf, India would not favour Iran having a hegemonic position. Thus on the nuclear issue India has pursued a policy that recognises the Iranian right to have nuclear energy but not nuclear weapons. On Syria, the Indian position has been to oppose regime change by external intervention. India is concerned that its West Asian flank is rapidly moving under the control of fundamentalist forces. The possible terror flow from Syria, Libya, Yemen and Iraq is of great concern for Indian internal security, especially when Pakistan and Afghanistan too are in turmoil.

The security and stability in the extended neighbourhood is very vital for India. The space emanating from flux in the region has posed new challenges for Indian policy-makers. India faces an asymmetry between its stake in the region and its capacity or power to control regional tensions so as to protect its interests. It cannot act as a power-player if the tension along any axis, whether Saudi Arabia-Iran or the Shia-Sunni crescent, escalates. Yet Indian interests would certainly be affected. There are three options for India to choose between. The first would be for India to be a fence–sitter; the second is for it to be a player in the processes of change in the region; and the third is to act as a supporter of the status quo. The third option can be ruled out because the region is, in any case, going to move away from the status quo. The change will be irreversible, but the key issue concerns the nature, scale and pace of the change. Given the high stakes in the region, a traumatic change in the region would be not in India's interest. The fault lines defined by radical Islam, the Shia-Sunni divide or tension between Saudi Arabia and Iran could jeopardise its interests. Similarly it is not in the Indian interest that the region becomes involved in competitive hegemonic politics whether from within the region or from outside. If Saudi-Iran competition harms Indian nterests so would be any prognosis that visualises Sino –US competition.[29] China seems to be calibrating its global ambitions in the region. In the Chinese vision the Gulf region could form part of its projected Silk Road Economic Belt.[30] The region has seemingly responded to these moves positively. Is the Chinese expansion in the region necessarily detrimental to Indian interests? The answer is a complex mixture of yes and no.

It can be argued that given the conflictual mode of Sino-Indian relations, any advance by China in any region which can be considered as lying within India's extended neighbourhood may be seen by India with apprehension. This is best illustrated by Gwadhar port. China has built this port so as to have a land route to the Gulf or perhaps as part of an Indian Ocean "string of pearls" to encircle India. India does see China in the Gulf region as a player with potential to undermine its strategic position. However, it would not like to endorse any competitive engagement with China in the region. It should be mentioned that up till recently India and China shared a common approach on the Gulf, based on non-interference. This paid them good dividends. Their mutual tension was not reflected in any rivalry in the Gulf. There is a school of thought which argues that, in the context of the US Asia pivot, the US would welcome greater engagement by India in sensitive issues related to the security architecture of the region. This flows from the assumption that others should bear some of the burden being born by America. US-India relations have, it could be contended, moved to a stage where India could be trusted with sharing responsibility in the region. The US does see in India an ally to counter Chinese influence, and the Gulf could be an appropriate region. The counter perspective is that, given the low credibility of the US in the Gulf, any defined relationship would restrict India's leverage in the region. Moreover, the China-Pakistan combination, and perhaps Saudi Arabia and Pakistan collectively, could view such a development in Indian policy-making with concern if not anxiety. The security nexus between Pakistan and the Gulf countries may not impact on India-GCC relations, but it does have potential to work as a spoiler.

An alternative view in India has been to take an enlightened view by forging an Asian option in the Gulf countries. Rather than joining a Western alliance or security structure, the leading Asian players could work for a regional security architecture which is inclusive. The feasibility, desirability and legitimacy of such an initiative will lie in identifying a common threat around which the architecture could be conceived. This can not take the form of regime threat or regime security (which underpins the US-Saudi deal). It could be focused on major issues facing the region. The Arab uprising has shown the primacy of domestic sources of insecurity, flowing largely from a failure to institutionalise the organising principle of society. Regime change is no solution by itself. Possibly it is an evolutionary than not a revolutionary path which is needed to address the domestic dimensions of regional security. Clearly external intervention is likely to distort the processes of domestic change. An imaginative way to contribute in empowering the public sphere could be a good option. The region is witnessing the emergence of new constituencies, such as women and youth. The Gulf regimes are currently providing some new space for these parts of society, primarily economically but to some extent socially as well. India, with its oriental cultural heritage, can play an important role in the processes of women's empowerment. Similarly India could leverage its IT power in the youth constituency of the region.

The escalation of tension and violence by radicalising groups could lead the US to solicit those like India to be the part of the campaign,[31] and certainly if the destabilisation reaches a scale where Indian assets are threatened, India will not be in a position to remain a distant spectator. India has expressed concern at the possibilities of its diasporas joining the radicals and bringing it back to the country. This would enhance the vulnerability of the country. [32] Indian diplomacy, thus, needs to work on a counter strategy that mobilises all forces threatened by the radicalisation of the region. If the US sees a security threat, then so also do Russia, Iran and China. As has been argued, the threat posed by ISIS is not one coming from a terrorist organisation but from a political formation which uses terror as an instrument. Its political import is detrimental to the interests of the countries mentioned above, yet ironically the conflict so far has been seen in terms of an American war.

The coalition to confront ISIS thus needs to be more inclusive and comprehensive. Indian diplomacy needs to work in that direction by leveraging its strategic relationship with the US. The present dispensation in India seems to be towards upgrading the strategic depth of India's relations with America, as is evident from the fact that President Obama will be the first US President to be present as Chief Guest at the Indian Republic Day parade. Though symbolic this demonstrates the current inclination of the Indian government.[33]

Notes

1   J. Westphal, "Saudi-US Relations", lecture delivered at The 23rd Annual Arab Policymakers Conference, held on 28-29 October 2014. See http://ncusar.org.

2   William James Burns, "A Renewed Agenda for U.S.-Gulf Partnership". See. http://susris.com/2014/02/19/.

3   Mohammed bin Nawaf bin Abdulaziz al Saud is Saudi Arabia's ambassador to Britain. "Saudi Arabia Will Go It Alone". See, http://www.nytimes.com/2013/12/18, accessed on 10th May 2014.

4   The Omani rejection of GCC union has added insult to injury for Saudi Arabia, see http://www.al-monitor.com/pulse/originals/2013/12, accessed on 10-5-2014.

5   M. F. Al Harthi, "Between the lines: Getting the GCC back on track". in http://www.arabnews.com dated7-5-2014

6   The combined GDP of the GCC reached $1.64 trillion in 2013. This means that the annual revenue of the six nations could plunge by roughly $130 billion. The total revenue of the GCC states — 90 per cent of which come from oil — more than doubled from $317 billion in 2008 to $756 billion in 2012. It declined slightly to $729 billion in 2013, according to IMF estimates. In the IMF scenario, Saudi Arabia, Oman and Bahrain risk running a budget deficit in 2015 if their spending plans do not change to cope with declining crude prices. See "IMF calls for GCC reforms; warns of effect of oil price", drophttp://www.khaleejtimes.com.

7   Mohammed Fahad Al-Harthi, "Between the lines: Getting the GCC Back on Track". http://www.arabnews.com.

8   Ugo Fasano and Rishi Goyal, "Emerging Strains in GCC Labor Markets", IMF Working Paper, Washington.

9   Y. Mahmoud Habboush, "Call to Naturalise Some Expats Stirs Anxiety in the UAE", see http://uk.reuters.com/article/2013/10/10/, accessed on 18/5/2014.

10 Jane Kinninmont, "Citizenship in the Gulf States and The Arab Uprisings", see http://www.chathamhouse.org/.

11 And women are generally more visible, even on the streets of Riyadh, which lies in the heartland dominated by the influence of Wahhabis, who follow an ultra-conservative version of Islam. Since restrictions on women at work have been eased, they operate cash tills everywhere, from lingerie shops to IKEA, a Swedish-founded furniture shop. They take taxis alone and head to the increasing number of facilities dedicated to women, from spas to separate floors of shopping malls. See http://www.economist.com, accessed on 18-5-2014.

12 "Women in Saudi Arabia Unshackling Themselves". See http://www.economist.com/news/middle-east-and-africa/21602249-saudi-women-are-gaining-ground-slowly-unshackling-themselves.

13 J. Burki, "Saudi Arabia's Clerics Challenge King Abdullah's Reform Agenda". http://www.theguardian.com/world/2011/jul/01. For details of reforms see Joseph Kechichian, *Legal and Political Reforms in Saudi Arabia*. Routledge (London: Routledge, 2012), and Anoushiravan Ehteshami and Steven Wright (eds), *Reform in the Middle East Oil Monarchies* (London: Ithaca Press, 2008).

14 See "9/11 Perspectives: Transformation in U.S. Middle East Policy.", http://www.cfr.org/.

15 Thomas Friedman, "What About US?", see http://www.nytimes.com/2013/11/13.

16 See Richard N. Haass, "The Irony of American Strategy: Putting the Middle East in Proper Perspective" *Foreign Affairs*, May-June 2013.

17 "Hagel, in Saudi Arabia, tells Arab states not to Fear Nuclear Talks with Iran", .see http://www.washingtonpost.com. accessed on 18/5/2014.

18 Theodore Karasik, "Shifting Sands and Shifting Security Alliances in the Gulf" See http://english. alarabiya.net, accessedon6/4/2014.

19 David Andrew Weinberg, "Frustration with Qatar adds to GCC Security Dispute". See http://english. alarabiya.net. accessed 6/3/2014.

20 The highlight of the two-day gathering was the presence of Mahmoud Ahmadinejad, the first Iranian president to attend a GCC summit. He offered his GCC neighbours a regional security pact and a 12-point cooperation plan, including free trade and joint investments in oil and gas. See http://www. globalresearch.ca, accessed on 18/5/2014

21 See http://www.thenational.ae, accessed on 18/5/2014.

22 Patrick Cockburn, "Iraq Crisis: How Saudi Arabia Helped Isis Take Over the North of the Country". See http://www.independent.co.uk. See also, Patrick Cockburn, *The Occupation: War and Resistance in Iraq* (London: Verso Books, 2007).

23 See also Stephen Zunes, *Tinderbox: U.S. Middle East Policy and the Roots of Terrorism.* (London: Zed Books, 2003).

24 See "Youths seek higher purpose in Syria", http://www.detroitnews.com/story/news/nation/ 2014/08/27 accessed on 6/11/2014.

25 See "The Arab Spring and West Asia: Challenges for India", http://voiceof.india.com/lectures/the-arab-spring-and-west-asia-challenges-for-india/11313/5.

26 The developing nexus between Pakistan, Qatar, Saudi Arabia and the Taliban in the context of the US withdrawal from Afghanistan could create problems for India. Ibid.

27 Manama Dialogue 2013 Fifth Plenary Session, Salman Khurshid, Minister of External Affairs India. See http://www.iiss.org/en/events, accessed on 19/5/2014.

28 See "India will Always Back Iran's Nuclear Issue: FM", http://www.presstv.com/detail/2014/03/01/ 352746/india-vows-support-for-iran-nissue/, accessed on 20/5/2014.

29 Toshi Yoshi Yoshihara and Richard Sokolsky, "The United States and China in the Persian Gulf: Challenges and Opportunities", Fletcher Forum of World Affairs; Winter/Spring2002, vol. 26, Issue 1, p63.

30 China's President Xi Jinping and Foreign Minister Wang Yi told a visiting high-level delegation from the Gulf Cooperation Council (GCC) that China wanted to work with the GCC to promote the building of the new Silk Road Economic Belt across Asia and Europe. The Silk Road initiatives also included reviving the Maritime Silk Road to connect the Pacific, the Indian Ocean and the Atlantic. See http://www.arabnews.com/news/518966, accessed on 18/5/2014.

31 See "McCain Exhorts India to Join Fight against Islamic State", in *The Hindu* 9/9/2014.

32 In a meeting of senior security officials the head of India's security outfit made a categorical assertion on the possibilities of radicalisation in India, that "the return of battle-hardened youth from these two countries has exposed India to new threats. The Indian diaspora has become increasingly vulnerable to elements having allegiance to terror groups. The Indian Home Minister, however, saw it more as a Pakistani-promoted design. See *The Hindu*, 29/11/2014, and *DNA*, 30/11/ 2014.

33 The Indian media reported it as a diplomatic coup: "'This Republic Day, We Hope to Have a Friend Over... Invited President Obama to be the 1st US President to Grace the Occasion as Chief Guest' Modi Tweeted in a Sudden Development." See http://timesofindia.indiatimes.com, dated 22/11/2014, accessed on 28/11/2014.

Bibliography

Burns, William James. "A Renewed Agenda for US-Gulf Partnership". http://susris.com/2014/02/19/.

Cockbum, Patrick. *The Occupation: War and Resistance in Iraq* . London: Verso Books, 2007.

Ehteshami, Anoushiravan and Wright, Steven (eds) *Reform in the Middle East Oil Monarchies.* London Ithaca Press, 2008.

Fasano, Ugo and Rishi Goyal, "Emerging Strains in GCC Labour Markets", IMF Working Paper, Washington, 2004.

Hass, Richard N. "The Irony of American Strategy: Putting the Middle East in Proper Perspective", *Foreign Affairs*, May-June 2013.

Kinnimont, Jane. "Citizenship in the Gulf States and The Arab Uprisings", http://www.chathamhouse.org.

Toshi Yoshi Yoshihara and Richard Sokolsky, "The United States and China in the Persian Gulf: Challenges and Opportunities", Fletcher Forum of World Affairs; Winter/Spring 2002, vol. 26 Issue 1.

Zunes, Stephen *Tinderbox U.S. Middle East Policy and the Roots of Terrorism.* London: Zed Books, 2003.

9

The European Union in the Gulf: New Opportunities for Cooperation

Cinzia Bianco

1. Introduction

The relationship between the United States (US) and the Gulf Cooperation Council (GCC) countries has been described as a Catholic marriage: one in which, no matter the strains you go through, for the greater good, there is no divorce.[1] Since the 1990s, when the US started functioning as the offshore balancer in the peninsula's power struggles, the relationship has survived several strategic threats, including the 2003 Iraq War and its destabilizing consequences. However, events that took place under Barack Obama's presidency suggested the idea that the United States was willing to re-evaluate its role in the Middle East and North Africa region and even its strategic partnership with the countries of the GCC. As a matter of fact, the gap between the respective strategic interests of the United States and the GCC countries has consistently grown since the 2011 Arab Spring.

Then the Gulf monarchies saw their ally, whom they also consider responsible for their regimes' security, taking a backseat during one of the widest strategic shifts the region has ever experienced. The US detachment even included the abandonment of Egypt's Hosni Mubarak, a historic American ally. In the Gulf itself, America was reluctant to take the government's side during popular demonstrations in Bahrain while arguing in favor of reforms.

Secondly, the Obama administration's policy in Syria attracted substantial discontent. Saudi Arabia read as dangerous the US decision not to follow through on threatened airstrikes against the Syrian regime led by President Bashar al-Assad, a protégé of the Saudis' regional rival, Iran. Some in the region saw Obama's approach of "leading from behind" as a way to hide irresolution and inconsistency, and interpreted American hesitations as a sign of weakness, a view that was reinforced by cuts in the Pentagon budget.[2] A common narrative was that, after a decade of long wars and a harsh financial crisis, the US had no choice but to scale down its global engagement.

Suddenly the whole US military umbrella seemed leaky. The worries were only amplified, especially in Saudi Arabia, by the diplomatic overture that the Obama administration pursued vis-à-vis Iran. The *ad interim* agreement signed in 2013 by the P5 +1 on Iran's nuclear program, and the way in which it was achieved through secret talks in Oman, caused fear that the United States would value a stronger relationship with Iran over GCC interests.[3] Historically dependent on America for their security, the GCC states panicked at this apparent shift in US foreign policy.

It is undeniable that recent US actions have given the impression of a certain fatigue with regards to handling this boiling region. This impression, and all the other factors described, gave substance to a feeling of US disengagement from the Gulf region. This idea was reinforced by the release of the 2012 US Defense Department's Strategic Guidance that stated Washington would "rebalance" its defence policy toward the Pacific.[4] Later background briefings indicated that this rebalancing, which has thus far remained rhetorical, would include only partial cutbacks in US air and naval forces, many of which would be redeployed from Europe.[5]

However, from that statement on, many started wondering whether the strong interests acting as binding agent in the US-GCC marriage still persist. Against this puzzling and opaque backdrop, this chapter considers the status of these interests and how the US posture in the region has changed accordingly toward a declining political presence. Far from implying a US withdrawal from the Gulf, we assess that the envisioned strategic outlook will create the necessity for an allied power to play a role complementary to that of the US. We then ask whether the EU has sufficient material interests and the potential ability to support the transatlantic ally in the endeavors to unravel the region's knots, by virtue of its own strengths and of its longstanding relations with Gulf states. We find that the EU, in spite of its inherent weaknesses, has a significant and unexploited mediation capacity on which to capitalize on, a capacity that would be instrumental in facilitating any meaningful initiative aimed at addressing the fierce sectarian violence that risks tearing the region apart. Among them, the most effective one could be establishing a Gulf-wide dialogue on cooperative security that puts together, under US auspices, discussions among GCC states, Iraq and Iran to confront pressing common concerns that can create a new shared concept of regional security.

2. Balancing Enduring and Emerging Priorities

A close analysis suggests that the United States continues to have enduring interests in this globally geostrategic hub. These interests, chiefly consisting of ensuring the free flow of energy, resources and commerce and dismantling transnational security threats, prevent Washington from disengaging from its security commitments in the region, even when balanced against different, newly emerged and even conflicting priorities. However such conflicting priorities, such as the necessity to refocus on the home front, may set the conditions for the *de facto* creation of a hazardous political vacuum that would allow a significant space for another global player to raise its political profile on the scene.

One of the main factors that, through the years, categorized the Gulf region as globally strategic is the impressive size of its energy reserves. The countries of the Gulf, i.e. the six countries of the GCC, Iraq and Iran, are home to approximately the 60 percent of the world's proven crude oil and natural gas reserves.[6] Every day, 17 million barrels of oil transit through Straits of Hormuz.[7] Admittedly, the security of America's oil supply has always been an element in its national strategic thinking. However, concerns about the domestic market are only part of the story. Indeed, in 1995, the US Security Strategy for the Middle East drafted by the Pentagon openly declared that "an unhindered flow of oil from the Persian Gulf to the world market at a stable price was paramount to US national security interests."[8] The reason for that is that the oil market is not only global, but also inherently linked to other economic sectors.

The United States, the world's second largest consumer of petroleum and first of natural gas, pays market prices for energy. This means it would pay all the increases in energy costs that would come out of a war or crisis in the Gulf, and any reduction or expected reduction in the global supplies will further increase such costs. Moreover, while North America is projected to become energy-independent, it is also going to be increasingly more dependent on the global economy for exports and imports.[9] This represents an immense volume of indirect imports of energy that most statistics don't take into account. In addition, the stability of the global economy, in particular that of the US allies and its major trading partners in Europe, is still dependent on a secure flow of oil from the Gulf, which explains why the Gulf region will still be home to vital American interests.[10]

As an aside, the vast abundance of energy resources has brought to the region commensurate an abundance of financial resources. The strategic implications in the movement of those capitals are increasingly evident today, with $1.7 trillion worth of assets under management, representing 30 percent of the total worth of all sovereign wealth funds in the world.[11] In short, the GCC has emerged as the world's largest net supplier of financial resources. The bulk of the investments have gone west, and in particular, by virtue of the strategic partnership, into US-headquartered companies. But the real strategic relevance of the funds became evident during the global financial crisis, when GCC funds committed considerably, through emergency financing, to give relief to troubled banks in the United States and Europe. In October 2008, in the midst of the US's economic, financial, credit, and liquidity crisis, the Gulf partners operated thinly disguised economic bailouts to tide the world's largest but also most indebted economy. It was at that time that the Abu Dhabi Investment Authority bought a $7.5 billion stake in Citigroup, America's largest bank, becoming the bank's largest shareholder. When the crisis moved to Europe, the Gulf partners stepped in again. Abu Dhabi invested $6 billion in the British Barclays Bank, Qatar announced its country's funds stood ready to invest €300 million in the troubled

Spanish savings banks and €1 billion in a joint fund with Greece to invest in Greek small and medium-sized companies.

The Gulf's dollar diplomacy also guaranteed an unprecedented influence on the strategic reshuffling of the Middle East-North Africa (MENA) region following the 2011 Arab uprisings. Just to cite one example, in 2012, Kuwait, Saudi Arabia, and the UAE deposited $12 billion in support of the military-led Egyptian government, providing a significant comparative advantage to this faction in the power struggle for North Africa's most critical country.[12] The substantial surpluses generated in the past few years are likely to confirm the strategic role of Gulf, thus inevitably confirming the importance of maintaining fruitful relations with the Gulf leaders. Finally, the proximity and connections of the Gulf countries with emerging markets in Asia, the Middle East and Africa is turning the Gulf region into a leading international trading hub, through which transit the most security-sensitive commodities.

Security concerns have always been prominent in the assessment of the Gulf's strategic relevance. Though weakened, al-Qa'ida, and its affiliates and adherents around the world are still considered a preeminent security threat to the United States.[13] Arms proliferation after the revolution in Libya, the conflict in Syria, and its spillovers in Iraq and Lebanon, have significantly contributed to the resurgence and empowerment of jihadism, which still retains the power to attract sponsors and recruits from the Gulf countries. In Yemen, al-Qa'ida in the Arabian Peninsula (AQAP) is a serious threat thriving from the country's instability. In the Mashreq area, the al-Qa'ida-inspired Islamic State of Iraq and Syria[14] (ISIS), emerged from both the Syrian civil war and Iraq's insurgency.[15] The Islamic State proclaimed in June 2014 the establishment of an Islamic Caliphate stretching, according to the group's official statement, from Iraq's Diyala province to Syria's Aleppo, and including Iraq's second largest city Mosul and the northern Syrian province of Raqqa.[16] The alarming advancement of the group, which triggered the formation in September 2014 of a US-led international coalition to fight it, has been one of the most significant threats posed to the Middle East regional order in many years, and one that threatens all Gulf powers equally.

To confront the most cogent of these threats, the United States will need the support of regional powers, and in particular those of the GCC countries, which are directly affected by these conflicts and have proved to be key allies in counter-terrorism activities.[17] Indeed the operational capacity of the US military and intelligence apparatus is effectually complemented by the human and cultural intelligence capabilities, as well as the capacity to project power locally, of Saudi Arabia and the other Gulf states. Other than contributing to counter-terrorism operations and being key partners in the fight against terrorism financing, Gulf leaders have a great potential at an ideological level. Indeed, these rulers contest the ISIS agenda and vigorously refute any legitimacy of linking religious identity to terrorism. Such US-GCC security cooperation is essential both in Yemen and in the fight against ISIS, as having the GCC countries in the US-led coalition fighting the jihadist group facilitates the mission both in operational and politico-ideological terms.

Finally, should America continue on the path of engagement with Tehran, this would not translate into disengagement from the Gulf. As confidence-building is a much slower process than diplomacy, lowering the guard vis-à-vis a country that has been America's archenemy for decades would not be an option among several decision-making circles in Washington, and, even more so, in Tel Aviv. It is a fact that Israel shares with Saudi Arabia fears that overtures may allow Iran to consolidate its regional position or even to buy time to go nuclear.[18] No real *détente* can take place in spite of Israel's concerns that its security is not a US priority anymore. Furthermore, it is not a secret that these concerns resonate clearly through lobbyist groups in Congress, whose approval is necessary to lift sanctions that were passed as U.S federal laws.[19] Keeping in mind these elements, it is difficult to envision any meaningful adjustments to American military forces or military planning in the Gulf region as a result of further agreements with Iran.

Notwithstanding the acknowledgement of persistent critical interests binding Washington to the Gulf region, all of the factors hereby examined have to be balanced against conflicting factors, such as budget constraints and the necessity to examine the challenges and opportunities presented by a quickly evolving Asia-Pacific region. Taking these elements into account, it is reasonable to expect the American posture in the Gulf region to adapt according to old and new interests. Signs of this changing posture, at a security as well as a political level, can already be detected.

At the purely hard security level, the US military has been building since the early 2000s what the Pentagon refers to as "strategic agility."[20] Far from involving any kind of reshuffling of military priorities, this agility in the Gulf materialized as a focus on building allies' capabilities and a renewed emphasis on a multilateral approach with the aim of increasingly dealing with the American Gulf allies through the GCC. On the ground, the reality in terms of allocation of military resources has shown an effort to maintain the traditional security architecture in the region. American military bases in Bahrain, Kuwait, and Qatar, equipped with the most advanced weaponry and surveillance assets, continue to offer concrete security guarantees to the host nations while confronting emerging threats. Additionally, the US Navy maintains a naval presence of more than forty ships in the broader region, investing $580 million to support the expansion of Fifth Fleet capabilities. Meanwhile, thousands of US military personnel, including an extra army brigade stationed in Kuwait since the withdrawal from Iraq, will still serve as a bulwark against aggression.

On top of maintaining a stable asset, the Pentagon seems determined to invest more than ever in building the capacity of the partners, i.e. by upgrading the level and numbers of joint exercises and trainings in all services, perhaps with the long-term objective of empowering them enough to complement America's military presence in the region. Alongside that, and notwithstanding the uncertainty of the outcome, the United States is pushing for better integration within the GCC by enhancing interoperability, channeling the sales of US defense articles directly through the GCC, and encouraging strategic coordination through US-GCC forums.

At a long-term political level, the United States is likely to maintain the "leading from behind" approach experimented in Libya in 2011, thus reducing its direct military presence in the multi-layered regional conflicts. President Obama has often stressed the need to strengthen international relations based on "shared interests" and to place a new emphasis on multilateralism. At a closer look, the hesitations shown by Obama may be read also as a way to encourage allies, especially European allies, to take on a bigger share of the responsibilities connected with international affairs. The president was ready to acknowledge the limits of American influence in the region, underlining the preference to employ all the tools available in external relations rather than resorting exclusively to the use of force.

Obama's foreign policy in the MENA region could be described as inspired by fundamental values and liberal pragmatism. Grounded in the awareness of the country's limits and concrete interests, this approach will likely outlive the Obama administration and consolidate as a long-term strategic paradigm. This approach, however, may create a political vacuum and, subsequently a lack of a coherent leadership from Washington. This could intensify the regional challenges from the on-going state failures in Syria and Iraq to the struggles against ISIS and handling of Iran's reintegration in the region.

3. A New Space for the European Union?

As noted above, the United States is unlikely to withdraw fundamentally from the MENA region given its own strategic needs and priorities. Still, many observers in the region fear an American drawdown that would leave its allies vulnerable. However, it is worth noting that the presence of a heavy-weighted American military umbrella couldn't protect the region from the emergence of the unconventional forces threatening its security. These are, at their roots, political problems that demand comprehensive political solutions.

In this context, the European Union (EU) has the potential, responsibility, and interests to step forward and cooperate with the United States. The EU's interests in the Gulf are substantial and clear-cut. In all ambits explored in the previous section – energy, trade and finance, security – Europe would be considerably more affected than the United States by any possible conflict in the Gulf. Not only is Europe much more dependent on the Gulf for its energy supplies, Gulf ports are also Europe's gateways to trade with Asia. The size of EU-GCC inter-regional investments is far more significant than those involving the United States. Finally, geographic proximity significantly raises the stakes in the fragile security in the Gulf region. Europe is directly affected by mass migrations from the region as well as by transnational terrorism and crime. Such motivations, and their direct and indirect implications, should be sufficiently compelling to encourage the EU to seize the opportunity generated by the current strategic outlook and take on a more proactive and effective role in the region.

Building on its expertise on conflict resolution and undertaking the necessary efforts to overcome some long-standing, well-known weaknesses, the EU would be the most appropriate actor to put forward a comprehensive strategy and to mediate a regional framework of dialogue on cooperative security in which to confront pressing common security concerns that risk enflaming the entire region. The violent conflicts that have emerged in the past few years have created a conflictual atmosphere in the Gulf region. Militarized sectarianism has risen to alarming levels, both in its international and domestic dimensions. Upheavals based upon Sunni and Shi'a rivalries threaten the stability of the Persian Gulf. Given their own security and economic interests and stakes in regional stability, European leaders are in a logical position, in conjunction with the United States, to assume an active role in establishing a multilateral response to the turbulence.

Arguably, given the considerable distrust between the Sunni and Shi'a rulers in the region, only the EU and the US together have enough political capital and influence on the regional actors to pursue such a response. Undertaking such an enterprise, of course, would require a huge effort of diplomatic mediation. The United States, whose recent policies have provoked a widespread discontent and mistrust in the region, considering strains in the relations with Saudi Arabia, its ill-conceived invasion and occupation of Iraq, and its long history of hostility toward Islamist Iran, is clearly no longer best suited to manage this task of mediation alone.

On the other hand, the European Union, especially via the European Commission and the External Action Service, is perceived as a trustworthy diplomatic interlocutor. Despite ups and downs, the EU has a long history of dialogue with the countries of the GCC. It has played a constructive role in post-war Iraq and has almost uninterruptedly maintained communication open with Iran. Notwithstanding sizable economic interests have played a major role, the EU has maintained relations with the regional players that range beyond the economic realm. This relationship offers added value to the process as opposed to other important global players such as India or China, whose relations with the Gulf countries are at an early stage and so far limited to the economic field. However, for a number of reasons, ranging from the lack of internal cohesiveness to an ineffective – and at times patronizing – attitude and beyond, the EU has never managed to capitalize on these relations. For the EU to gain a more coherent strategic weight vis-à-vis its Gulf allies, this shortcoming needs to be overcome.

One of the reasons why the EU has not heretofore been able to become a truly strategic partner with Gulf powers has been that all parties have traditionally given priority to their partnerships with the United States, whose previous attitude was to consider its relations with the Gulf exclusive and closed to others. The EU has in the past accepted this secondary role, crippled by its inability to provide the security guarantees that Washington has provided and by a more generalized lack of a clear and shared political strategy. To find a new space in the region, the EU needs first and foremost to exploit its opportunity to adopt a more proactive approach. Any grand strategy will require bold steps and the ability to overcome obstacles in the name of shared challenges and shared opportunities. A necessary first step would be strengthening the EU's relations with all of the regional actors.

The stimulus must come from the European Council along with the European Commission, the European Union External Action Service and the European Parliament. These and other institutions have a key role to play according to their specific areas of competence.[21]

To begin with, the EU needs sufficient political will to overcome the obstacles hindering EU-GCC relations.[22] It is encouraging that the EU has shown the willingness to overcome the so-called "strategic neglect" vis-à-vis the GCC. Often, individual European countries have pursued competing economic interests with the Gulf monarchies in the region that led them to favor a bilateral approach. More recently, some of these EU member states, especially France and the United Kingdom, have expressed a strong intention to further boost relations with the Gulf countries.[23] However, these states have been hobbled in recent years by severe financial crises and political headaches of various kinds. They have consequently become unable to invest the necessary economic and political resources to assume a leadership position separately.

The smartest choice now would be to pool and share the resources within the EU institutions as to make them complementary. Clearly, the way forward is for EU states to deal with their conflicting interests in Brussels and present a united front to their international partners. Injecting new stimulus into the EU relations with the GCC countries might also create the new disposition needed to confront the crucial misunderstandings that have been halting progress in the political-strategic dialogue. The same paralysis has stalled regional negotiations on a Free Trade Agreement despite the prospects of flourishing economic cooperation that would be generated by enhanced financial and commercial flows and productive business relations. Formal FTA negotiations were suspended by the GCC in 2008, due to disagreements including the insistence of the EU to include a human rights clause and tariffs to be mantained in strategic sectors. While informal talks have since taken place, progress has been slow at best.

The Arab uprisings of 2011 further strained EU-GCC relations: the European response oscillated between indecisiveness and a tentative support for popular grievances and democratic development, in sharp contrast with the GCC's strategic interests from North Africa to Bahrain. However, soon stability emerged as the key European priority, and on this basis is clearly easier to soften divergences regarding regional strategies. A telling example is found in Egypt where the EU initially supported the democratically elected Muslim Brotherhood's government only to then endorse the military government of Abdel Fattah Al-Sisi that ousted it, as soon as the security outlook deteriorated. What is harder to overcome are deep-seated misunderstandings on internal political structures and issues. These misunderstandings have been based on the inability of the EU, in particular the European Parliament (EP), to understand the legitimacy and functionality of the Gulf's autocratic systems, and the inability of the GCC to understand the multi-layered, bottom-up functioning of the EU and all of the interests it has to take into account.[24] As a basic principle for a more promising future, both actors must reorient their aspirations toward the politically achievable and less toward the politically desirable. For their part, the GCC countries must make a more robust effort to understand what the EU really is and what it is not.

With regards to relations with Iraq, it is worth underlining that since 2003, the EU has invested over €1 billion in the country and pledged €75 million for the period 2014-2020 in reconstruction and development aid.[25] This support, later framed in the Partnership and Cooperation Agreement signed of May 2012, included measures to enhance cooperation on good governance, the rule of law, education, poverty reduction, trade, energy, security, and migration. The development of these political relations, declaredly aimed at supporting Iraq's integration within the region and into the international community, took shape in periodic high-level meetings to discuss internal and regional issues, including the Syrian conflict and negotiations with Iran.

The results of these efforts have been quite positive. The trust translated into encouraging declarations by several Iraqi political figures including former Prime Minister Nouri Al-Maliki, who highlighted Iraq's determination to develop relations with Europe to a larger extent.[26] Kurdish Prime Minister Barzani also played a role by asking the EU's Representative for Foreign Policy to facilitate political developments in the relations between the Kurdish Regional Government and the Iraqi federal government in Baghdad.[27] The EC stood ready to support Iraq also following the early ISIS' attacks by allocating a €17 million-package of humanitarian aid, endorsing the decision of some member states to provide military aid to the Kurdish Regional Government forces which were on the front-line of the conflict, and politically supporting the formation of a new and inclusive government. However, fighting a jihadist group that tried to disintegrate a Gulf state from within through military, political, ideological and socio-economic weapons is a mission that cannot succeed without the cooperation of all the regional actors.

One actor whose cooperation under a similar scenario is instrumental is Iran, with which the EU is quickly re-building trust. The European External Action Service's (EEAS) role in the first-ever breakthrough regarding the nuclear negotiations within the P5+1 framework in November 2013 was facilitated by the diplomatic skills of the then High Representative Baroness Ashton, who earned her the respect and trust of Iran's minister of foreign affairs. This laid the groundwork for long-term normalized relations between the EU and Iran. The broader objective was to build upon existing areas of mutual cooperation, such as in the energy sector, and expand them to include political discussions, that were left on hold due to the lingering nuclear dispute.[28] As a matter of fact, re-launching a more political dialogue might help creating a momentous occasion to start involving other regional powers in the discussion on cooperative security

4. Relaunching the Security Framework

Establishing a regional system of cooperative security in the Gulf region has the long-term potential to ease tensions between Iran and Saudi Arabia and other members of the

GCC. The same could be harnessed to manage, if not resolve, the rivalries in other regional hotspots where opportunities exist to tackle collectively any number of common challenges. Regional as well as international interests are likely to converge on issues such as counter-terrorism, piracy, drug trafficking, and illegal migration. Moreover, all these parties share ownership of critical resources, not only oil and natural gas, but also water resources, whose rational management would be pivotal in a broadened interpretation of cooperative security.

In addition it is undeniable that economic cooperation with Tehran would offer fruitful opportunities in terms of trade as well as joint investment. Member states such as Qatar, Oman and even the United Arab Emirates have already explored those opportunities, which could potentially serve as significant incentives toward normalization. Finally, on the socio-political front, only a regional dialogue has the potential to alter the sectarian narrative that has done significant harm to the region. This de-escalation has become a shared priority to defuse extremism and reduce the risk of spillovers from Syria, Yemen and Iraq to the broader region. Aware of its potential, this initiative for regional dialogue has been repeatedly, yet unsuccessfully, proposed.[29]

Arguably, all of the involved actors had to muster the political will needed to overcome the powerful countervailing forces of distrust and suspicion. To begin with, in the first discussions on this framework, Iran had set as precondition the retreat of the United States from the waters of the Gulf, which clearly is a stance that neither the GCC states nor the US can accept. Indeed no security framework can succeed without the participation of United States or, broadly speaking, in the absence of significant security guarantees. On the other hand, it is obvious that any *détente* between Iran and the United States, no matter how tentative, can provide the needed impetus to re-open the discussion. American leaders will need to take such a leap of faith by adopting a posture of enhanced diplomacy and multilateralism rather than unilateralism and hard power. President Obama hinted at this approach by reaching out to Iranian clerics who are in a position to make or break the prospects for political cooperation.

The many barriers to diplomatic success included a case of unfortunate political timing. The idea of a regional security framework was first advanced in 2005 by Hassan Rouhani, the current President of Iran and then Secretary of the National Security Council, during a trip to all GCC states. He returned two years later in Doha and stressed Iran's readiness to remove all concerns the GCC might have about their large neighbor.[30] The project was wrecked, however, by President Mahmoud Ahmadinejad and the profound tensions caused by his hostile rhetoric toward Israel and the West. In this context, his departure and replacement by a moderate leader has the potential to facilitate the confidence-building project. Most importantly, better regional ties are also supported, at least rhetorically, by Iran's supreme leader, Ayatollah Ali Khamenei, who has the final say on all State matters. The main oppositions could be encountered on the opposite shores of the Gulf and, specifically, in Saudi Arabia. The main fear is that a strengthened Iran would work to fuel instability within the GCC countries by playing the Shi'a communities against the Sunni rulers, especially in Bahrain and Saudi Arabia itself. Arguably, however, critical engagement rather than classic deterrence would be the most effective approach to prevent this kind of behavior.

Rouhani gained popular support as the right interlocutor for this dialogue. As an intelligence chief in the 1990s, he signed a security agreement with Interior Minister Prince Nayef Bin Abdelaziz in which Iran's government pledged not to interfere in the domestic affairs of Gulf countries, to hand over Saudis accused in terrorism cases, and suspend support to foreign groups hostile to Gulf countries.[31] These initiatives, together with a similar plan launched by former President Akbar Hashemi Rafsanjani, provide a modest hope for an uneasy yet necessary path toward cooperation and away from the state of rivalry and proxy wars which dominated most of Ahmedinejad's years in power.[32]

Another obstacle worth addressing is the latent conflict among Saudi Arabia, Iraq and Iran on the energy market. As a way to spur economic recovery, Iraq and Iran have pushed to boost their production output and lobbied for higher prices, something that would potentially pose a challenge to Saudi Arabia's status of "swing producer" within the quota-based system of the Organization of Petroleum Exporting Countries (OPEC).[33] The main risk is that accommodating Iraq and Iran's aspirations would threaten the stability of oil prices, unless Saudi Arabia – which covered for their production quota - reduces its output. As these countries' economies are almost completely dependent on oil revenues, it is clear how any destabilization could have a substantial impact on the broader socio-economic environment. However, these disputes are not irreconcilable and can be settled through all-encompassing negotiations within OPEC. All that is needed is a cooperative attitude, the acknowledgement of legitimate developmental goals, and the realization that any confrontational stance could spark price wars and major disruptions to the oil market.

These concerns need to be taken into consideration in the drafting of a plan for the proposed regional framework, keeping in mind that, as brilliantly suggested elsewhere, "the institutional questions should not be the starting point of this process, but rather its result."[34] First off, it would be necessary to prepare the ground by disseminating the idea of the "indivisibility of security" in the Gulf. European and American diplomats would be wise to bring up the concept in bilateral and multilateral meetings that security is not a zero-sum game and must provide collective benefits for all involved. The EU Embassies in Riyadh and Abu Dhabi can be effective focal points from which to disseminate such ideas, but it is particularly important that EU diplomats are aided in this by member states' diplomats.

A truly effective security community in the Gulf needs active participation from the parties, especially from Saudi Arabia, and cannot be built without or in spite of Iran and Iraq. In essence, participation terms should be flexible but inclusive. This idea of active coexistence was a cornerstone of the endeavor of creating the Organization for Security and Cooperation in Europe (OSCE). Formed in spite of deep-seated mistrust and perceptions of existential threats and hegemonic aspirations that remind of those in the Gulf, that experience can teach many lessons, including that collective security should not be primarily defined in military terms but rather as a comprehensive concept including soft and hard security threats. Accordingly, the approach in the Gulf should be multi-level and multi-topical, establishing first issue-oriented and limited cooperation between the regional actors on practical matters, not directly related to high-politics and hard security, in an incremental process of confidence-building.

The first phase of a Gulf-wide framework on security might consist of, for example, of the EC setting up technical working groups, with experts from the Gulf countries engaged in discourse on environmental challenges and related issues such as water and food security. Subject to extreme aridity, the countries of the Gulf are unable to attain food self-sufficiency and thus are highly dependent on imports and highly exposed to price volatility and the risks of supply disruptions.[35] With rising populations and a deteriorating climate, food and water security have become full-fledged national security threats. The countries of the GCC have tried to tackle the challenge first by buying underdeveloped farmlands in Africa and Asia and later, having suffered severe setbacks due to political issues and poor rural infrastructures, by investing in existing farming operations in Europe.

While this solution is viable and functional, and its scope should be broadened by including food security in dialogue with the EC, international solutions should be complemented by a regional strategy. Iran has, for example, large amounts of arable land that remains underexploited due to the lack of sustained investments in the agricultural sector: raising the productivity level of the close-by Iranian land might be beneficial for Iraq and for the GCC countries, other than for Iran itself. The parties should also consider joining efforts and sharing their know-how to work out innovative technological solutions to tackle water scarcity: research and development in renewable and even nuclear technology for desalinization may provide sustainable fixes and give the opportunity to deal with Tehran's nuclear aspiration in a non-confrontational context. Several initiatives can be carried on to enhance the level of technical cooperation among the regional actors in other low-politics fields. Thanks to its long-lasting experience in "soft security" issues and policies, and to its vast technical know-how, the Europeans can give a very meaningful and unique contribution to each one of these initiatives.

A second phase of the normalization of regional relations may encompass fighting the transnational criminal networks that transit through regional waters to engage in illicit trafficking and piracy. Shipping lanes in the Indian Ocean are currently patrolled by a coalition of European naval forces and the US Fifth Fleet, but many countries have also joined the patrolling, including Iran. Iranian expertise and law enforcement forces can provide a boost, as in the past, to the dismantling of drug network. Iran is already coordinating counter-piracy efforts with Oman, a country labeled a high-risk zone of pirate activity.[36] This limited cooperation might be expanded with the support of relevant bodies within the EU's External Action Service and through the creation of a common legal framework to be used as a basis for establishing operational synergies in maritime activities. This would also be a way to create a sense of shared responsibility in the maritime security of the Gulf. Clearly, until EU states are ready to fully integrate defense at the EU-level, thus ending unnecessary costs and short-sighted national competition, they will also have to manage their conflicting interests carefully. At least bilateral partnerships can be beneficial not only for the single defense industries, but also – due to the path dependency of security-political arrangements in the regional strategic culture – to the reinforcement of the political relations.

Finally, a third phase of this regional security dialogue, should confront the most decisive, core issue of sectarianism. Due to the sensitivity of the issue, it is paramount that the European Union is firmly committed to encourage regional actors to constrain sectarian divisions. Member states that have long-standing relations with the countries of the Gulf – especially France, the United Kingdom, Germany and Italy – should flank the EU, which has the necessary authority to take the lead in the matter. Refraining from pushing excessively, the EC is in the position to support existing *fora* of inter-sectarian dialogue and endorse open communications and educational programs regarding the consequences of radicalism in a variety of venues, include international development.

The issue is made more sensitive by the fact that the sectarian discourse has both a regional and a national dimension, and that the two, despite having very different driving forces, are increasingly intertwined. In Saudi Arabia for instance, the Shi'a citizens protesting in the Eastern Province have been accused of being influenced by Iranian agents, and many Sunni citizens have been radicalized by the extremist rhetoric of Salafist clerics and moved into taking part to the sectarian conflicts in Iraq and Syria. The risks of jihadists returning from those conflicts turning against the monarchy are very concrete. These risks are increasingly clear to the Saudi monarchy, which has long ago categorized jihadism as a national security threat. Riyadh has cracked down heavily on Saudis who travel abroad to fight and who "provide terrorist organizations with any form of material or moral support.[37] It is not as clear-cut if the risks of alienating the Saudi Shi'a communities are unanimously recognized, even if by early 2013 there were some encouraging signs. The government, for example, shut down news media that fueled anti-Shi'a rhetoric and built an interfaith dialogue center. At the same time, some Shi'a clerics of Qatif and Al-Ansa - in the Eastern Province – released a statement rejecting armed violence against the state and the politicization of religion.

Similar initiatives should be increasingly supported by international players and scaled up to a regional level. Creating occasions of dialogue among Sunni and Shi'a clerics from all over the Gulf could help in delegitimizing the extremist views. An interesting role might be played by Oman, which has excellent political relations with Iran and whose official doctrine, Ibadism, is characterized by openness to engaging with other schools of thought within Islam. However, as a number of studies have recently exposed, sectarianism is primarily rooted in the discrimination to which minorities are often subject: addressing these basic grievances is a difficult but necessary task for the long-term social stability.[38]

Sectarianism in the Middle East reached new ferocity with civil wars in Iraq and Syria rendering them "failed states" that could not provide basic services or protect their citizens. The deep grievances, rooted in the Shi'a discrimination against the Sunni citizens, fueled popular support for the group named Islamic State of Iraq and Syria (ISIS).[39] The quick advancement of ISIS fighters, who in the summer of 2014 easily defeated the Iraqi army in the center of the country and then fought the Kurdish Regional Government forces in the north, persuaded American leaders to join the fight against the group. The Obama administration subsequently formed a broad international coalition, including several countries from the MENA region, whose aim was to defeat the terrorist group militarily in the absence of a negotiated settlement. The US commitment was limited, however, restricting "boots on the ground" to logistics, training exercises, and humanitarian missions.

This US resolve to join the fight against ISIS has shown that the United States was not going to ignore its security responsibilities in the Gulf. On the other hand, the insistence on maintaining a low profile by focusing on intelligence sharing and material support, would carry out Obama's intention to "lead from behind." Given the unreliability and, to some extents, the weakness of the Iraqi army, support from America and other international partners would be necessary to defeat ISIS and dismantle the so-called "Islamic Caliphate" it declared in 2014. But this would certainly not be enough to eradicate jihadism from the country. Indeed, at a domestic level, it is paramount that the Iraqi government strives to answer to an inclusive logic, addressing the popular grievances among its Sunni citizens that provided the fertile ground for insurgency and defending the rights of its Kurdish population. Good governance is key to the process of re-building the Iraqi state and nation. The government should commit to address its dysfunctional administration; tackle corruption and clientelism, especially in the judicial and security sectors; implement a national law on oil exploitation; and fight the residuals of the de-ba'athification mentality and its consequences.

At the regional level, ISIS – targeting internationally strategic interests as much as the security and political stability of all bordering countries – could represent the common threat unifying regional actors. On the economic side, external actors could achieve much in providing short-term relief to Iraq's disastrous economy, for example by investing in key infrastructure to provide basic services (water, electricity). The effort could also entail broadening the scope and intensity of existing aid and development programmes. Of greatest urgency is easing the refugee crisis and activating de-radicalization programs within the refugee camps.

On the political side, all regional actors in the Persian Gulf, with the support of the EU and the United States, should prioritize the facilitation of a national reconciliation process in Iraq. Given its own history and tradition of diplomacy, the EU is well placed to facilitate the dialogue among the country's ethno-religious constituencies. The United States should keep pressuring the country's leadership to give up the sectarian logic. Finally, regional players can give a much-needed contribution. Saudi Arabia and the other Gulf monarchies could use tribal and religious links to pressure the Sunni tribal leaders in Iraq to engage in a national dialogue, while Iran could use its significant influence on the Shi'a ruling parties to the same end. In fact, only when Iran will be willing and able of playing a constructive role in the sectarian conflicts across the region, from Syria to Yemen, its re-integration in the international community and in its region will be fulfilled and the Gulf-wide security framework will have achieved its greatest accomplishment.

5. Conclusions

As the world's demands for energy are bound to steadily increase, the global economy will become even more interconnected and societies will become hungrier for security. In this context, the Gulf is set to remain a geo-strategically relevant region, both in absolute terms than to the United States and, especially, to Europe. Regional countries in the Gulf will have to confront many challenges, ranging from failed states and sectarian bloodshed to transnational terrorism. By neglecting this mandate, and allowing threats to escalate, both regional actors and their international partners would put international strategic interests at great risk.

In order to address these challenges, all players involved should find ways to adapt quickly to a changing global order, also reflected in a renewed, politically less pervasive, US presence in the region. The EU should commit to a long-term vision that, based on shared challenges and shared opportunities, has the potential to become an effective strategy to facilitate regional integration and trigger a virtuous cycle to advance its own position in the Gulf. If Brussels will be up to the challenges, it will depend chiefly upon the realization in the European capitals that a more successful, more united international presence is also among Europe's best chances to overcome its own woes.

Notes

1 "An Interview with Gregory Gause: Gulf Security and the US-Gulf Relationship", Brookings Institutions website, October 3, 2013 http://www.brookings.edu/research/interviews/2013/10/03-Gulf-security-gause.

2 Gerges Fawaz A, "The Obama Approach to the Middle East: The End of America's Moment?" *International Affairs* 89, no. 2 (2013): 299-323.

3 The P5+1 is a group of six world powers which in 2006 joined the negotiations with Iran on its nuclear programme. The term refers to the five permanent members of the UN Security Council, namely United States, Russia, China, United Kingdom, and France, plus Germany.

4 United States Department of Defense, *Sustaining US Global Leadership: Priorities for 21st Century Defense*, (Washington D.C.: Defense Strategic Guidance, 2011), 2.

5 Anthony Cordesman, "The United States, the Indian Ocean Region, and the Gulf", Commentary, Center for Strategic and International Studies, December 16, 2013, http://csis.org/publication/us-indian-ocean-region-and-Gulf.

6 United States Energy Information Administration (USEIA), *International Energy Statistics* http://www.eia.gov/cfapps/ipdbproject/IEDIndex3.cfm?tid=5&pid=57&aid=6.

7   Manuel Zamora, and Linda Zamora, "The Strait of Hormuz as a Global and US Security Concern: A Transportation and Maritime Security Case Illustration." *Journal of Homeland and National Security Perspectives* 1, no. 1 (2014), 65-78.

8   United States Department of Defense, *US Security Strategy for the Middle East*, (Washington, D.C.: US Department of Defense, 1995), 48

9   USEIA, *International Energy Outlook 2013* (Washington, D.C.: Energy Information Administration, 2013), 23-24.

10 *Ibid.*

11 This and related data can be found in Gawdat Bahgat, "Sovereign Wealth Funds in the Gulf - An Assessment." *Kuwait Program on Development, Governance and Globalisation in the Gulf States* 16 (2011). London: London School of Economics and Political Science, http://www.lse.ac.uk/middleEastCentre/kuwait/documents/Bahgat%20paper.pdf.

12 USEIA, *International Energy Outlook 2013*, (Washington D.C.: U.S. Energy Information Administration, 2013), 23-24.

13 US Department of State, Bureau of Counterterrorism, *2013 Country Reports on Terrorism*, April 2014, www.state.gov/documents/organization/225886.pdf.

14 The group is also known as Islamic State of Iraq and the Levant (ISIL) or simply Islamic State (IS).

15 USEIA, *International Energy Outlook 2013*, (Washington D.C.: U.S. Energy Information Administration, 2013), 23-24.

16 "Sunni Rebels Declare New 'Islamic caliphate,'" *Al Jazeera*, June 20, 2014, http://www.aljazeera.com/news/middleeast/2014/06/isil-declares-new-islamic-caliphate-201462917326669749.html.

17 Kenneth Katzman, "US-Gulf Cooperation in the Global War on Terrorism, The Future of GCC-US Relations: Post-US Presidential Elections," paper presented at conference sponsored by Gulf Research Center, Dubai, 5-6 January, 2005.

18 Joshi Shashank, "Iran Nuclear Deal Triggers Anxiety for Israel and Gulf," *BBC News*, November 25, 2013, http://www.bbc.com/news/world-middle-east-25083894.

19 Molly McCluskey, "US Congress Wary of Iran Nuclear Deal," *Al Jazeera*, November 29, 2013, http://www.aljazeera.com/indepth/features/2013/11/us-congress-wary-iran-nuclear-deal-2013112971930874727.html.

20 Data on the US military posture in the Gulf were taken from "Global Security Priorities for the United States," speech by former US Secretary of Defense Chuck Hagel, at the 9th IISS Regional Security Summit Manama Dialogue 2013, First Plenary Session, 7 December 2013, Manama.) Full transcript of the speech available at http://www.iiss.org/en/events/manama%20dialogue/archive/manama-dialogue-2013-4e92/plenary-1-a895/chuck-hagel-80d9.

21 References to the EU indicates most or all of the EU institutions. Otherwise the paper refers to specific institutions via their specific names and acronyms.

22 Christian Koch, *Unfulfilled Potential: Exploring the GCC-EU Relationship*, (Dubai: Gulf Research Centre, 2005).

23 Interviews of the author with NATO officials, Rome, 2014.

24 Thomas Demmelhuber, and Christian Kaunert, "The EU and the Gulf Monarchies: Normative Power Europe in Search of a Srategy for Engagement," *Cambridge Review of International Affairs*, 27, no. 3 (2014).

25 "EU-Iraq relations" on the European External Action Service website, last update April 2014, http://eeas.europa.eu/iraq/index_en.htm.

26 "رئيس الوزراء السيد نوري كامل المالكي: علاقاتنا مع دول الاتحاد الأوربي عريقة ونحن عازمون على تطويرها", Press Release, June 17, 2013, Iraqi Prime Minister Office official website, www.pmo.iq.

27 "EU delegation discusses strategic issues, establishment of permanent representation with Kurdish leadership,"press release, May 10, 2014, Kurdistan Regional Government official website, www.KRG.org.

28 Peter Spiegel, "EU Foreign Policy Chief Lady Ashton Comes of Age in Iran Talks," *Financial Times*, November 26, 2013.

29 More about this in Mehran Kamrava, "The Changing International Relations of the Persian Gulf" in *International Politics of the Persian Gulf*, ed. Mehran Kamrava (New York: Syracuse University Press, 2011), 94-120.

30 "10-Point Plan to Promote "Cooperation, Security, and Development in Persian Gulf," speech by Hassan Rowhani at the World Economic Forum, Doha; April 9-10, 2007, Center for Strategic Research website, http://www.csr.ir/departments.aspx?lng=en&abtid=00&depid=106&semid=193.

31 Abdulrahman Al-Rashed, "Rowhani's Election: Welcoming an Old Friend,"*Al-Arabiya News*, June 17, 2013   http://english.alarabiya.net/en/views/2013/06/17/Rowhani-s-election-Welcoming-an-old-friend.html.

32 Ali Hashem, "Rafsanjani offers road map for Iran-Saudi ties" *Al Monitor*, May 21, 2014, http://www.al-monitor.com/pulse/originals/2014/05/iran-saudi-arabia-relations-road-map-rafsanjani-regional.html.

33 Andrew Critchlow, "Iraq and Iran Plot Oil Revolution in Challenge to Saudi Arabia," *The Telegraph*, January 28, 2014, http://www.telegraph.co.uk/finance/newsbysector/energy/10601899/Iraq-and-Iran-plot-oil-revolution-in-challenge-to-Saudi-Arabia.html.

34 Bauer Michael, Christian-Peter Hanelt and Christian Koch, "The EU-GCC Partnership: Security and Policy Challenges," *Al Jisr Project Policy Brief*, (2010), Gulf Research Center, p.6.

35 The amount of food imports on the total food consumption accounts for 80-90% in the GCC countries, 50% in Iran and more of 80% in Iraq. For more see Rob Bailey and Robin Willoughby, "Edible Oil: Food Security in the Gulf,"*Briefing Paper* (2013), London: Chatham House.

36 Sigurd Neubauer, "Oman's Neutral Approach to Maritime Security" June 18, 2013, Middle East Institute website, http://www.mei.edu/content/omans-neutral-approach-maritime-security.

37 Badr Al-Qahtani and Obaid Al-Suhaymi "Saudi King Issues Royal Decree Cracking Down on Terrorism," *Asharq al-Awsat*, February 4, 2014, http://www.aawsat.net/2014/02/article55328501.

38 See for example Frederick Wehrey, *Sectarian Politics in the Gulf: From the Iraq War to the Arab Uprisings*. (New York: Columbia University Press, 2013).

39 Myriam Benraad, "Iraq's Long Road to National Reconciliation," *The International Spectator* 46, no. 3 (2011), 25-33.

Bibliography

Alcaro, Riccardo and Andrea Dessì, eds. *The Uneasy Balance. Potential and Challenges of the West's Relations with the Gulf States,* IAI Research Papers no. 8, Roma: Nuova Cultura, 2013.

Bauer, Michael, Christian-Peter Hanelt, and Christian Koch. "The EU-GCC Partnership: Security and Policy Challenges", *Al Jisr Project Policy Brief*, (2010), Gulf Research Center.

Demmelhuber, Thomas, and Christian Kaunert. "The EU and the Gulf Monarchies: Normative Power Europe in Search of a Strategy for Engagement," *Cambridge Review of International Affairs* 27, no. 3, 2014.

Gause III, F. Gregory. *The International Relations of the Persian Gulf*. Cambridge: Cambridge University Press, 2011.

Gerges, Fawaz A. "The Obama Approach to the Middle East: The End of America's Moment?" *International Affairs* 89, no. 2, 2013.

Kamrava, Mehran. *International Politics of the Persian Gulf*. New York: Syracuse University Press, 2011.

Koch, Christian, *Unfulfilled Potential: Exploring the GCC-EU Relationship*. Dubai: Gulf Research Centre, 2005.

Wehrey, Frederick. *Sectarian Politics in the Gulf: From the Iraq War to the Arab Uprisings*. New York: Columbia University Press, 2013.

10

On the Right Side of History?
US Transitions and the Possibilities
of a British Strategic Role in the Gulf

Saul Kelly and Gareth Stansfield

1. Introduction

The debate concerning the intentions of the US government towards the Gulf, particularly in the realm of security provision and the maintaining of defence arrangements with key Gulf allies, has received considerable attention from academics. Some view the US 'pivot to Asia', which was referred to by President Barak Obama as a 'rebalancing', as a strategy that will see the US security footprint in the Gulf diminish. Others have contended the very opposite – that the rebalancing of US attention to the Far East will actually strengthen the US commitment to securing the Gulf, because of the inherent geopolitical value of the region in terms of its location and the dependence of Far Eastern countries on its hydrocarbons reserves.[1]

Whatever the reality or 'rebalancing' actually is, the UK has moved to reposition itself as a more significant actor in the security of the Gulf – perhaps in a way that is deemed supportive of US plans, or perhaps in a more self-interested fashion, or perhaps with elements of both agendas being apparent. The most obvious example of this repositioning occurred in December 2014 with the announcement that Britain will establish a permanent military base in Bahrain focused upon the Mina Salman port. The facility will be able to operate Royal Navy aircraft carriers and destroyers, giving the British an immediate force-projection capability that they have not had in the region since the early 1970s. Clearly presenting this initiative in the context of Britain supporting the US 'rebalancing' strategy, Foreign Secretary Philip Hammond noted that '[c]learly as the US focuses more of its effort on the Asia Pacific region, we and our European partners will be expected to take a greater share of the burden in the Gulf'.[2] The move, however, came at a time when Bahrain had been heavily criticized for human rights abuses against pro-democracy demonstrators, with campaigners noting that the base – the £15 million construction costs of which will be met mainly by

Bahrain – was a 'reward' for the British government's silence over Manama's treatment of protestors.[3] The basing announcement came following a longer period of enhanced UK engagement with Gulf states, which had steadily brought into focus the inherent tension between national interests and normative values – or material interests and human rights – in UK foreign policy. This chapter investigates this tension and presents it is as a constant in the UK policy debate concerning the Gulf, but one in which tangible national interests consistently reassert themselves over the intangible values of human rights.

2. The UK and the Arab Spring: The Dilemma Exposed

Ever since the Arab Spring burst upon an unsuspecting world in 2011, sweeping away sclerotic nationalist dictators in North Africa and the Yemen, rocking the last tyrant standing in Syria, and causing consternation among the assorted autocrats of the Gulf, the UK foreign policy community[4] has been engaged in a prolonged navel-gazing exercise with regard to the nature, effectiveness, and even virtue of Britain's engagement with the Middle East.[5] There seems to be an overweening concern that the United Kingdom, to quote U.S. President Barack Obama, should be 'on the right side of history' in the region.[6] Passing from the Foreign and Commonwealth Office's unpreparedness for the Arab Spring to the UK's relations with Saudi Arabia and Bahrain, one investigative body in particular, the Foreign Affairs Committee of the House of Commons, has focused the attention of the Government and the interested public on the dilemmas of British policy in the Middle East, and especially towards the Arab states of the Gulf.[7] The obvious geo-strategic importance of these states to Britain, whether in energy supplies, defence sales, trade links, or security and counter-terrorism co-operation, has to be balanced against the increasing emphasis in British foreign policy on human rights. This poses a critical dilemma for British policy-makers, trying to appease shrill voices at home and at the same time trying to smooth ruffled feathers among Gulf Rulers, while preserving and promoting British interests in the area. This article will seek to tease out the tangled threads of British policy towards the Gulf Arab states, examine whether the knotted dilemma at the heart of Britain's position in the Gulf can be resolved.

It has been an axiom of British foreign policy for many decades now that the United Kingdom should stay in lock-step with the United States in the Middle East, in order to safeguard their perceived common interests in the region. Yet, there are differences of emphasis, not only over Israel-Palestine, but in the very language used to explain and justify policy. The current crop of British politicians, unlike their American contemporaries, are not given to soaring flights of rhetoric in their speeches. There is no taste for the rallying cry, vibrating with moral indignation that stirred their nineteenth century predecessors, such as William Wilberforce and Viscount Palmerston seeking to abolish the slave trade and slavery.[8] The mundane and imprecise moral desire to be 'a force for good' in the world, and to take a 'values-based approach', seems to inform British foreign policy when it comes to promoting the cause of human rights abroad. This odd fusion of the feel-good with the technocratic is expressed in the moderate tones of the Foreign Secretary, William Hague, who shortly after taking office in the coalition government in 2010 declared that: 'Our foreign policy should always have consistent support for human rights and poverty reduction at its irreducible core and we should always strive to act with moral authority, recognising that once that is damaged it is hard to restore.'[9]

Having erected human rights as a 'pillar' of his foreign policy, Hague and the Foreign and Commonwealth Office (FCO) were forced to take the strain of a 'values-based approach' to the events of the Arab Spring in North Africa and the Middle East in 2011, which swept the likes of Ben Ali, Mubarak and Qadhafi from power. It was in this heady atmosphere that the British Prime Minister, David Cameron, found himself in February 2011 addressing the Kuwait National Assembly, the oldest and arguably, along with the Bahrain National Assembly, most disputatious popular assembly in the Gulf. Cameron entered into the spirit of the occasion, declaring that:

> For decades, some have argued that stability required highly controlling regimes, and that reform and openness would put that stability at risk. So, the argument went, countries like Britain faced a choice between our interests and our values. And, to be honest, we should acknowledge that sometimes we have made such calculations in the past. But I say this is a false choice.
>
> As recent events have confirmed, denying people their basic rights does not preserve stability, rather the reverse. Our interests lie in upholding our values – in insisting on the right to peaceful protest, in freedom of speech and the internet, in freedom of assembly and the rule of law. But these are not just our values, but the entitlement of people everywhere; of people in Tahrir Square as much as Trafalgar Square.[10]

Cameron went on to offer 'a new chapter in Britain's long partnership with our friends in this region'.[11] Three years on, it is pertinent to ask how this new chapter has fared in the face of the political gusts and tempests which have swept the Middle East since 2011, and in particular how it has affected the UK's relations with its traditional friends, the Gulf Arab states. Has Cameron's government managed to solve the stated dilemma between the UK's 'interests' and 'values' by making the latter an interest as well? Or has the renewed emphasis by his government on 'values', or human rights, complicated the protection of other, more traditional, British interests, such as energy supplies, defence sales, trade links, security and counter-terrorism co-operation? To what extent has the Cameron government been held captive by its own rhetoric on human rights? In order to answer these questions, and to assess whether the UK has been 'on the right side of history' in the Gulf, or has simply got its history, and therefore policy, wrong, we have the advantage of being able to consult a reasonably reliable up-to-date source, namely the two reports by the House of Commons

Foreign Affairs Committee (FAC) on 'British foreign policy and the "Arab Spring"', published in July 2012, and 'The UK's relations with Saudi Arabia and Bahrain', released in November 2013. These documents show, in considerable detail, as a result of consultations with ministers, diplomats, pressure-groups, businessmen and trusted academics, the views, debates and thrust of thinking of that small group of people who constitute the British 'official mind' on the Middle East and the Gulf. That 'mind', reflected in, and illuminated by, these parliamentary reports will be scrutinised, and assessed, through the use of other sources, mainly historical, which chronicle British policy towards the Gulf in the past, and which help divine the true nature of the UK's traditional engagement with the Gulf Arab states. In so doing, these documents help locate current policy within a longer-range perspective, the character of which has tended to endure rather than fundamentally alter over the years.

In assessing the UK's policies towards the North African countries of Tunisia, Egypt and Libya in 2011, the FAC was critical not only of the quality of the FCO's political reporting and information-gathering capability before the uprisings, but of the seemingly clumsy way in which the British government handled the emerging crisis.[12] In particular, the FAC referred directly to Cameron's speech in Kuwait:

> We conclude that the goodwill that could have been generated by a Prime Ministerial visit to the region [Cameron stopped off in Cairo en route to the Gulf] at such a critical time was somewhat squandered by the Government's misjudgement in including members of the British arms trade in the delegation to the Gulf, as indeed it has been damaged by decades of arms sales to repressive governments. Regardless of the legality, it was a mistake for the Prime Minister to be seen to be promoting the UK's arms trade on a visit to a region undergoing uprisings in which some authoritarian regimes had used force against their own people.[13]

The FAC was seemingly aggravated by the tension between the UK selling arms sales to Middle Eastern states, while seemingly remaining uncritical of the repression of pro-democracy demonstrators. Witnesses before the FAC, ranging from the Henry Jackson Society to Amnesty International, both of which have their own agendas to forward, highlighted the contradiction between the UK government's 'stated aim of upholding human rights' and the sale of arms to 'undemocratic regimes'.[14] The FAC pointed out, on the basis of evidence from Amnesty, that:

> The issue of British arms sales became particularly controversial during the Arab Spring. The Government revoked a number of export licenses to Libya and Bahrain, and allegations were made that equipment sold by the UK was used by Saudi Arabia in dealing with protests in Bahrain.[15]

Alistair Burt (Parliamentary Under-Secretary of State for the Middle East and North Africa) disputed the latter allegation, as did William Hague.[16] This was too much for Sir John Stanley, MP, a long-serving member of FAC as well as chairman of the parliamentary committee on Arms Export Controls (CAEC), who observed:

> Given that there has been, understandably, an almost total absence of official observers in close proximity to the violent repression that has been taking place, and given also the fact that the UK government approved arms exports including machine guns, sniper rifles, combat shotguns and ammunition were not emblazoned with union jacks, it is hardly surprising that the [FCO] could safely conclude "there was no evidence of any misuse of controlled military goods exported from the United Kingdom."

He pointed out that the government's revocation of 157 arms export licenses to MENA following the Arab Spring was 'the clearest evidence of the scale of the misjudgement of the risk that arms approved for export to certain authoritarian countries in North Africa and the Middle East might be used for internal repression, a misjudgement by the government and its predecessor.'[17]

The FAC supported the CAEC in its recommendation that

> the Government state whether it remains satisfied that none of the extant UK arms export licenses to states in the region, including Bahrain, Egypt, Libya, Saudi Arabia and Tunisia (among others) contravenes the Government's stated policy not to issue licenses where it judges that there is a clear risk that the proposed export might provoke or prolong regional conflicts, or which might be used to facilitate internal repression.[18]

Both the CAEC and the FAC had pinpointed the need for the government to say 'how it intends to reconcile the potential conflict of interest between increased emphasis on promoting arms exports with the staunch upholding of human rights.'[19] The FAC recommended that the government be 'sensitive' to this feeling and 'avoid discrediting its "values-based" approach by promising more than it can deliver.' This qualified assessment elided with its sober conclusion that 'while the Government is right to consider interests and values as connected…we share our witnesses' doubts that they will always be in such clear alignment.'[20] Given these criticisms, it was surprising that the FAC pulled its punches in the final section of its report, opining that the government had coped with the challenge posed by the Arab Spring 'reasonably well', though chiding it for not showing any sign of grasping the apparent opportunities on offer for the UK. The latter was 'still struggling to create a compelling and – most importantly – consistent narrative for its approach to the region.' The FAC called upon the government to learn the lessons from the 'revolutions' and apply them to 'its relations with other Arab and Gulf states, and more widely, whose governments as yet show no sign of reforming, or that are actively resisting reform. In this regard the greatest challenges of the Arab Spring may still lie ahead.'[21]

Now that the FAC had the spring of revolution in its step, there was no holding it back. In the autumn of 2012 it announced that it was launching an enquiry into the UK's relations with Saudi Arabia and Bahrain and 'how the UK can encourage democratic and liberalising reforms' in those countries. This was followed by the release of a report into human rights, which criticised the UK government for its reaction to the 'Bahraini authorities' brutal repression of human rights in February and March 2011.' The FAC believed that 'Bahrain should have been designated as a country of concern in the [FCO's] 2011 report on human rights and democracy' and accused the government of a double-standard in not boycotting the Bahrain Grand Prix but doing so with regard to the football European Championship in the Ukraine.[22] The FAC recommended that 'the criteria for designation should be based purely on assessments of human rights standards and should not be coloured by strategic or other considerations.' Yet earlier in its 2011 report, the FAC recognised that the UK had 'strategic, commercial or security-related interests overseas which have the potential to conflict with its human rights work...The Government should not be trying to assert that the two can co-exist freely: it should instead be explaining publicly its judgements on how to balance them in particular cases.'[23] One would have thought that Bahrain was such a case, given its strategic importance as a base for US and UK naval forces in the Gulf. Apparently not in the view of the FAC. Human rights considerations were paramount. This did not impress the governments of Bahrain and Saudi Arabia. The Saudi ambassador in London, Prince Mohammed bin Nawaf Al Saud informed the BBC that his government was 'insulted' at FAC's temerity in looking into his country's relations with the UK, and threatened to re-evaluate them.[24] One member of the FAC, Mike Gapes, M.P, expressed surprise at the Saudis' 'prickly' and 'vehement' reaction to the projected enquiry, suggesting that '[e]ither they have misunderstood the role of the committee or there is some other agenda I don't know about. We're not picking on the Saudis...since our closest relationship is with the Saudi Arabia and Bahrain, we felt it appropriate to concentrate on those countries.' He seems to have been unaware of the Saudi conviction that Iranian-sponsored Shia human rights activists in Bahrain were exerting undue influence on FAC's deliberations and thus facilitating interference in the internal affairs of a Gulf Co-operation Council (GCC) country. As one observer noted:

> The [committee] will have a lot of awkward questions for the UK government and its partners in the region. It will be a major embarrassment...The British government is in a lose-lose situation because it is under a great deal of pressure to make declarations about human rights but then fails to act on them. Its long history with Saudi Arabia and Bahrain mean it is loath to intervene too directly...But the government may put pressure on the committee to limit its

criticism. Saudi Arabia knows the balance of power between an oil-rich Gulf and a resource-poor Europe and can tell Britain that it must engage on its terms or not at all. [25]

Clearly, for both London and Riyadh, the relationship was important enough to allow for a FAC report on the one side and to generate on the other side a response that suggested the betrayal of a close friendship. For political leaders in both countries, the unfolding of the Arab spring events in Bahrain would provide a very unwelcome headache, and not least because the interests versus values dilemma stalking Whitehall would now emerge in the open as Saudi military forces assisted Bahrain's security organizations in the repression of demonstrations in the capital of a long-standing ally.

3. UK Relations with Bahrain and Saudi Arabia

They say that a week is a long time in politics, but a year and a half is even longer. It is interesting to contrast the overall tone of the FAC's report on 'The UK's relations with Saudi Arabia and Bahrain', published on 22 November 2013, with that of its previous report on 'British Foreign Policy and the Arab Spring', released on 19 July 2012.[26] Whereas the earlier effort took the government to task about the need to live up to its declared policy of promoting human rights, in North Africa as elsewhere, the later assessment seems keen to portray its understanding of the dilemma the government faces in trying to balance its commitment to human rights with the protection of its strategic interests (in defence, security and commerce) in the Gulf, which affect Britain's relations with two key allies, Bahrain and Saudi Arabia. Given the importance of the latter, the FAC thought that 'the Government's emphasis on gradual [political] reform based on participation and consent is a realistic approach.'[27] In an interview with the BBC, the FAC's chairman, Richard Ottaway, MP, put it more starkly: 'We have to weigh up on the one hand our concerns about the human rights situation in the Gulf, but balance it against our interests and the only way to do this is to be open and honest and to recognise that it's not a perfect world and sometimes interests clash with values.'[28] This is a far, and even faint, cry from the earnest entreaties of the earlier FAC reports in 2012 on the Arab Spring and Human Rights, and from the CAEC's 2012 report on the arms trade. Both had called for a rebalancing of the UK's priorities in the Middle East, including in the Gulf, as David Cameron had promised in Kuwait, in order to make the promotion of human rights (in the shape of political reform) a British interest, on a par with more traditional defence, security and commercial considerations.

Why the change of tone in the space of a year and a half? Judging from the evidence contained in the latest FAC report, this has been due to a realisation by the committee that its earlier enthusiastic advocacy of human rights in the Middle East had not gone down well in the Gulf, especially with the ruling families in Bahrain and Saudi Arabia, who saw it as hectoring and unwarranted criticism of their internal affairs by their old ally Britain. Moreover, it was seen as serving the interest of their mutual enemy, Iran. In realising this, and adjusting its assessment accordingly, the FAC seems to have followed the lead of the FCO which has been engaged in an assiduous damage-limitation exercise to the UK's relations with Bahrain and Saudi Arabia since mid-2011, following the over-enthusiastic endorsement by British politicians and even diplomats of the opposition forces which emerged from the Arab Spring. The basic pattern thus seems to have been one of the policy-making system reverting to an 'interests'-dominated agenda, rather than one that placed 'values' as a higher aim. From the perspective of Gulf states, this reverting to an established pattern would ultimately be viewed as being a positive development.

4. The UK's Relations with Bahrain

The FCO-led policy seems to have been relatively successful in Bahrain, where both the FAC and the FCO must have breathed a sigh of collective relief when, at the resumption of the annual ISS Manama Dialogue in December 2012 (suspended in 2011), the Bahraini Crown Prince Salman singled out UK 'diplomats, the leadership and the government' for having

> stood head and shoulders above others. You have engaged all stakeholders. You have kept the door open to all sides in what was sometimes a very difficult and sometimes unclear situation. Your engagement and your help in police reform and judicial reform, and your direct engagement with the leadership of Bahrain and with members of the opposition, has saved lives, and for that I will be personally eternally grateful. Thank you.[29]

Clearly a positive nod to the British, the statement has also been interpreted as a reproach to the U.S. government, which was represented at the conference by Secretary for Defense Chuck Hagel, for its apparent meddling in Bahraini politics in 2011.[30] However, given that the US had identified the Crown Prince as the future leader of political reform in Bahrain (perhaps because he declared early on that he wanted to be 'on the right side of history'), and backed his abortive negotiations with the opposition in 2011, it is possible that the Crown Prince was signalling to Washington that it should adopt the British 'way' in engagement, which is preferred by Bahrain, to the more forthright American approach. Certainly, as Chuck Hagel's successor contemplates the possible sale of an anti-missile defence system to the GCC countries, he might look to the British 'way' which seems to have proved relatively successful. Apparently, Bahrain threatened to withdraw defence co-operation with the UK in 2011 as retaliation for British criticism of its handling of the political protests. But by October 2012 the UK government had signed a Defence Co-operation Accord (DCA) with Bahrain which, according to William Hague, 'complements existing agreements':

It provides a framework for current and future defence activity with Bahrain, including training and capacity-building, partly in order to enhance the stability of the whole region.[…] we have defence assets of our own stationed in Bahrain, our minesweepers in particular, which are responsible in any crisis for maintaining freedom of navigation in the Gulf…'[31]

Hague even argued that this updating and amendment of the UK's pre-existing DCA with Bahrain, which did not 'change our approach to export licensing [of weapons systems] in any way', 'might have benefits in the human rights area. After all, it is often argued by those in authority in Bahrain that what they need is their security forces to know what to do, to be trained in how to handle civil disorder.'[32] Although the British government is not in the habit of releasing the actual texts of its DCAs, it seems that Hague was heavily hinting that the DCA with Bahrain concerned British training of their police in riot control. The FAC commended the UK government for this but asked for details of 'the elements included in each of the training programmes provided to Bahrain that cover rights, the rule of law and the correct use of force.'[33]

It is instructive to compare the active, behind-the-scenes approach adopted by the FCO and the British government with Bahrain since mid-2011 (detailed in the FAC report), with their approach sixty years earlier to similar internal political turmoil on the islands. Then, events in Egypt, Iraq and Syria, in an earlier 'Arab Spring', had inspired nationalist and republican sympathies among the crowds who thronged the streets of Manamah and Muharraq to protest against the autocratic rule of the Al Khalifah and Britain, as the protecting power in the Gulf.[34] The British had a marked presence in Bahrain, with their political residency for the Gulf, their naval base at Ras Jufair and RAF base on Muharraq island. It was the British who assisted the Shaikh of Bahrain, and his adviser Sir Charles Belgrave, to suppress the protests against the Baghdad Pact and the Suez Crisis, imprisoning the ringleaders or exiling them, *a la Napoleon*, on St. Helena. The young Bahraini nationalists may have cried out against British perfidy, but they were careful in the 1960's to confine their protests to union strikes rather than revolt. The point about this is that the Al Khalifah have long had to contend with manifestations of political and economic discontent and the resentment of successive generations of the young, weaned on radical political theories, at being excluded from a decisive voice in the government of Bahrain. As the political pendulum has swung over the decades from a nationalist to an Islamist direction, the expectations of the young have grown markedly. Successive Al Khalifah rulers have made considerable efforts to conciliate the Shi'a, being careful to consult both the Shi'a mullahs and the Sunni divines, as authoritative representatives of their respective communities, on sensitive political issues. Despite this, they have always been an unpredictable force in Bahraini politics, tending towards promoting democracy or pursuing a Shi'a agenda – depending upon your point of view – but with the Bahrain government employing increasingly oppressive tactics against them in either case. Bahrain's experiment in representative government, initiated by the ruler, Shaikh Isa bin Salman, between 1972 and 1975, ended in farce, when the national assembly failed to pass one piece of legislation, spending its time in personal vendettas and religious and political polemics. After the assembly, in the wake of violence instigated by Marxist and Baathist cells, refused to pass a draft internal security law Shaikh Isa suspended the constitution and dissolved the assembly. Attempts by successive rulers in the 1990s and in the last decade to establish a constitutional monarchy have been derailed by the political opposition (since 2005 the *Al Wifaq* bloc in the National Assembly), inevitably followed by violent street disturbances and a crackdown by the security forces. This is the established rhythm of Bahraini politics and was seen, in its latest iteration, in the Arab Spring protests at the 'Pearl roundabout' in Manama in February and March 2011.[35] What was new was the attention of the world's media, excited as it was by the prospect of further revolt, and even revolution, in the Middle East, following events in North Africa and the Yemen, and the intervention of a Saudi-led GCC force to demonstrate its support for the Al Khalifah. As the FAC report noted: 'There was outrage within and outside Bahrain at allegations of widespread human rights abuses that took place during the crackdown perpetrated by Bahraini security officials.'[36] The FAC went on to note that:

> Although it has accepted many of the criticisms about its response to the protests in 2011[37], Bahrain has complained that the international community has misunderstood the situation in Bahrain. It argues that the opposition is not pro-democracy but is motivated by a sectarian agenda, and that the illegal demonstrations are inhibiting – and sometimes endangering – the lives of the ordinary public. Some opposition protests have turned violent and there have even been bombings in Manama, for which the government has blamed Hezbollah. Opposition groups claim they are a democratic movement and street protests are responding to state-sponsored police violence and repression. As the situation has developed, more nuanced differences between groups have emerged, including Islamist and secular groups, violent and non-violent, domestic or connected to expatriates or other groups abroad. The longer the conflict continues, the greater the likelihood that groups move to polarised extremes.

One recent observer has concluded that, on the contrary, the Al Khalifah, like other ruling families and elites in the Gulf, is actively encouraging such 'sectarian identity politics', tacitly backed by the UK and other Western states, in order 'to weather the storm of the Arab Spring and to further isolate Iran.'[38] Yet the same commentator has provided some interesting detail on the growing sectarian impulse within opposition politics. He notes, using suitably revolutionary terms, that up to a half of the 'cadres and supporters' of the main opposition bloc, *Al Wifaq*, are Hezbollah, while the other half are from *Al Dawa* (the party of the Iraqi PM Nuri al Maliki). Nevertheless, he assures us 'that does not mean that *Al Wifaq's* agenda is firmly in line with Iranian regional ambitions, or that all of *Al Wifaq* are Hezbollah.' And as long as the protests do not cross the sectarian divide, to the various Sunni constituencies supporting the regime, he surmises that the Al Khalifah will survive. This may be so, though it is legitimate to believe that the apparent growing sectarian divide, not only in the Gulf but throughout the Middle East, fuelled by the war in Syria, is continuing to have a destabilising effect on Bahraini politics. As for Iran, which still seems to regard Bahrain as part of its territory[39], the BICI report found no evidence that it had been behind the February 2011 protests. But witnesses before the FAC noted that the Iranian government had exploited the situation through propaganda broadcasts to Bahrain aimed at '"stirring up" the discontented Shia population'. The minister from the FCO, Alistair Burt, intriguingly referred to recent evidence 'of some more active involvement on the ground. Alas I am not able to share that evidence.' But the British Ambassador to Bahrain, Iain Lindsay, was more forthcoming to the local press in Bahrain, referring to those behind a recent spate of bombings in Bahrain as 'terrorists' and saying that 'there was "increasing evidence" that Iran was "providing support to people here who are bent on violence"'. Burt regards the implementation of a political reform programme by the Bahrain government as 'the most likely counterbalance to anything the Iranians might wish to do.'[40] The FAC goes further, urging the government to involve regional players, by which it must mean Iran, Saudi Arabia and perhaps Iraq, 'in the reform and reconciliation process if it is to have any chance to succeed.'[41] While eminently sensible, such an approach would be running contrary to the historical record that has seen Bahrain protected and nurtured by Britain. As one authority has pointed out, it was British protection from 1861 which freed Bahrain from having 'to make the kind of humiliating submission to her larger neighbours that she had been earlier forced to make to keep out of their clutches.'[42] It also helped to enforce the maritime peace, and thus trade, in the Gulf, the main reason for Britain's presence. Since 1971, when Britain ended her formal protection of Bahrain, Bahraini independence against Iranian or Iraqi claims has been underwritten by Saudi Arabia, and American and British military power since the end of the Kuwait War in 1991. This received its most tangible expression when a Saudi-led GCC force crossed the causeway between the mainland and the islands in March 2011 in order to support the Bahraini security authorities in their suppression of the unrest.

5. The UK's Relations with Saudi Arabia

There is a tone of puzzlement and regret pervading the pages of the FAC report dealing with the UK's relations with Saudi Arabia. The FAC noted that, despite the best efforts of British diplomats and ministers (including two visits by David Cameron in 2012), the Saudis seem unwilling to revive the annual 'Two Kingdoms Dialogue', which lapsed in 2011, let alone to upgrade it to the sort of 'Strategic Partnership' that the UK has with some other Gulf Arab states. This is put down to 'reasons largely outside the [UK] Government's control', including 'illnesses and ill-health in Saudi Arabia', not to any deterioration in the

Anglo-Saudi relationship.[43] The FAC thought this was 'regrettable' and urged the FCO to redouble its efforts to restore 'the talks via a strategic partnership'.[44] It does not seem to have occurred to either the FAC or the FCO, or if it has they are not saying so publicly, that the Saudi reluctance to re-engage in a dialogue with the UK may well be due to displeasure at the UK's stance on human rights in the Arab Spring, whether with regard to Egypt, Bahrain, Syria or even Saudi Arabia. According to one commentator: 'Since 2011, Saudi Arabia has seen the largest street protests the country has ever known.'[45] These have been largely among the Shi'a in Hasa, or the Eastern Province, centred on Awwamiyya and Qatif and inspired by the example of their co-sectarians across the causeway in Bahrain. On 23 November 2011, 'tens of thousands', shouting 'Death to the Al Saud' took to the streets of Qatif for the funerals of two youths who had been shot dead by Saudi security forces (two more were shot dead during the actual demonstration).[46] The Al-Saud have managed, through a combination of repression, disbursement of funds and sectarian propaganda, to ride out the Shi'a protests, which they attribute to Iranian meddling. But they have not addressed the fundamental problems which lie at the heart of this discontent, namely the Sunni regime's long sectarian discrimination, manifested through political and economic means, against the Shi'a community in Hasa, which makes them second-class subjects in the oil-rich Eastern Province. Relations between the Saudi Shia and the state have not been this bad since the Iranian Revolution in 1979, and future protests and their inevitable suppression by the security forces will make them even worse. When combined with Sunni protests in Buraida and Riyadh, the heartland of the Saudi state, demanding political reforms and the release of political prisoners, one can see why the Al Saud may have other matters on their minds than upgrading the strategic partnership with the UK, and that they might resent preaching on human rights from the British government.[47]

The FAC report is replete with references to the 'long history of friendship and co-operation between the UK and Saudi Arabia' and 'shared' or 'common' interests in defence, security and trade, all of which underlies the current Anglo-Saudi relationship.[48] It is based on a reading of the history of those relations which does not accord with the historical record. It is worth scrutinising the latter for it casts a different light on the nature of, and problems with, Anglo-Saudi relations which the FAC and the FCO seem to be at a loss to understand or desire to skate over. It became a governing principle of British policy in the Gulf from the early nineteenth century to watch and prevent the growth of Al Saud and Wahhabi power and influence over the smaller Gulf sheikhdoms (especially in the strategically important al-Buraimi oasis[49]) since it destabilised the latter, with concomitant effects at sea, where it often led to piracy and the undermining of the maritime truce, which was policed by the Royal Navy and the British Bombay Marine. By guaranteeing the sheihkdoms' independence, Britain set herself in opposition to the expansion of Wahhabi dominion in eastern Arabia beyond Nejd and Hasa. For some eighty-three years after the expulsion in 1869 of the Wahhabis from the al-Buraimi oasis by the Omanis, they made no attempt to venture there again, nor were they in a position to do so. It was not until after the establishment of the Kingdom of Saudi Arabia in 1932 that Abdul Aziz ibn Saud felt able to direct Saudi eyes again towards the Gulf sheikhdoms. His award of an oil concession to Standard Oil of California (SOCAL) in 1933 raised the question of the eastern boundaries of the new Saudi kingdom and he was quick to lay claim to large tracts of Qatar, Abu Dhabi and Oman. The British Foreign Office, in line with the prevailing spirit of appeasement in British foreign policy at the time, was prepared to give away part of the sheikhdom of Abu Dhabi in the hope of winning over Ibn Saud as an ally in the Middle East, and especially in Palestine, where the Arab population was in revolt against British mandatory rule. The Foreign Office was only prevented from doing so by the British Government of India, and its representative department in Whitehall, the India Office, on the grounds of principle and policy. However, the spirit of appeasement lingered on in the Foreign Office and, after inheriting responsibility for the Gulf, from the India Office after the demise of British power in India in 1947, it manifested itself in the mistaken, and frankly craven, British response to a renewed frontier claim by the Saudis in 1949. The latter now demanded four-fifths of the sheikhdom of Abu Dhabi, where Petroleum Concessions Ltd. (a subsidiary of British-run Iraq Petroleum Company, IPC) had the concession to prospect for oil. In order to placate the Saudis, and particularly the Emir (later King) Faisal ibn Abdul Aziz, the Foreign Office in August 1951 accepted the Saudi proposal for a ban on all oil-prospecting and policing activities while a commission determined the frontiers. This was tantamount to admitting that California Arabian Standard Oil Company (CASOC) and Saudi Arabia had concessionary and territorial rights in the area and that IPC's rights were invalid. Whereas the British honoured their side of the standstill agreement, the Saudis illegally occupied the al-Buraimi oasis in August 1952 and engaged in wholesale bribery of tribal leaders in order to have them declare their allegiance to Saudi Arabia and bolster Saudi claims to the western areas of Abu Dhabi and inner Oman. It was only when the Saudis tried to ensure a sympathetic finding by the international tribunal sitting in Geneva through bribery that even the Foreign Office decided it had had enough. It not only ended the arbitration but sanctioned the ejection of the Saudi force from al-Buraimi by the Trucial Oman Scouts in October 1955, much to the disquiet of the Saudis, ARAMCO (Arabian-American Oil Company), and the U.S. Government. After the Suez Crisis in 1956, and the severing of diplomatic relations by the Saudis, the Foreign Office returned to its former defensive and apologetic approach to such an extent that by 1970 it was prepared to facilitate Saudi claims on Abu Dhabi-held territory in order to ease Britain's passage out of the Gulf the following year.[50]

This is a very different version of the history of Anglo-Saudi relations up to 1971 than that presented by the FAC. But it is critical to understanding why the relationship has not, as the FAC and the FCO would have it, been 'a long history of friendship and co-operation', nor has it been one of 'shared' or 'common' interests. On the contrary, British and Saudi interests were fundamentally opposed to each other, no matter how hard the Foreign Office has tried to disguise the fact. The latter has been assiduous since 1971, in its adoption of the American policy of recycling petrodollars through arms sales to Saudi Arabia and other Gulf Arab states (and Iran before the fall of the Shah in 1979), and in its successive attempts to forge a special or 'strategic' relationship between The Two Kingdoms. This has involved rewriting history. Thus, the FAC report, repeating the FCO line, remarked with seeming regret that the relationship 'suffered under a 1973 oil embargo imposed by Saudi Arabia and other OPEC members … on the UK and Western states following their support for Israel in the October War [of] 1973.'[51] Irrespective of the FCO's reading of history – with an argument being that Western oil companies had exploited the Middle Eastern oil producers mercilessly over the whole period since 1972, thus forcing the oil price down to very low levels being particularly persuasive – the British government still chose to forget its previous disputes with Riyadh and instead praised the Saudis for their moderation. The FAC report notes that the '1980s saw warmer relations and a major defence agreement…'[52] This is a reference to the two Al Yamamah agreements from 1985 which provided for the supply by the UK of Tornado and Hawk jets, and other military equipment, to Saudi Arabia. According to the FAC report, 'it was worth over £43 billion by 2004.' However, after 'allegations of corruption and a Serious Fraud Office [SFO]investigation, Al Yamamah was officially closed in 2006.'[53] There is nothing here about successive price rises orchestrated by the Saudi oil minister, Zaki Yamani, throughout the 1970s, which brought the economies of not only Britain, Western Europe and the United States, but Latin America and Africa, to their knees. Instead of condemning these threats to British interests, the FCO praised the Saudis for their moderation.[54] The SFO investigation 'into alleged bribes paid as part of the al Yamamah deal was controversially halted after it was advised that Saudi Arabia might withdraw intelligence cooperation.'[55] This demonstrates FAC's point about the Saudis being a 'complicated counter-terrorism partner for the UK and the wider international community' and as being 'part of the problem as well as part of the solution.'[56] The sharing of intelligence has to be balanced against the flow of funds and Wahhabi ideology by way of support to extremist groups in Syria, North Africa, Pakistan, Bangladesh and Indonesia. These two problems – of the Al-Yamamah deal and issues relating to counter-terrorism – are not in themselves linked, apart from in the way that Riyadh and London then contained them, indicating perhaps more clearly than any obvious statement of cooperation just how strong the relationship was.

In 2007 two new defence agreements were concluded. The Saudi-British Defence Cooperation Programme provided upgrades and servicing to the Tornado fleet and associated equipment. The Salem ('Peace') Project was for the supply of 72 Eurofighter Typhoon aircraft: 24 were delivered in 2009, but there were 'continued delays and price "issues" relating to the remaining Typhoons', until a deal was finalised in February 2014. Although the initial contract was for £4.4 billion, some estimates suggest it could be worth in the region of £20 billion. Both programmes are overseen by the UK Ministry of Defence Saudi Armed Forces Project (MODSAP). The other MOD oversight body, the Saudi Arabia National Guard Communications Project (SANGCOM) has had recently to deal with an

SFO investigation into GPT, a subsidiary of EADS, the pan-European defence contractor that has supplied the Saudi National Guard with communications equipment, 'in light of further bribery allegations.' According to FAC, the 'Government has thus far declined to give further information about the case.'[57] Although the FAC expressed gratitude to the Saudis at having 'hosted British Tornados' during the 1990-91 Kuwait War and 'providing support and bases for the allies' during the Iraq War, it has to be remembered that in both cases the wars were fought in defence of British interests, alongside those of Saudi Arabia and other Gulf Arab states against the perceived threat posed to all interested parties by Saddam Hussein's regional ambitions.[58] As the FAC reminds us, British defence sales to Saudi Arabia constitute a large portion of the UK's total trade with that country. 'Saudi Arabia is one of the British defence industry's largest markets.' But it is 'hard to obtain exact figures as to the volume of defence trade as the Government restricts the supply of some information; however, the UK has granted export licenses for almost £4 billion worth of defence equipment over the last five years.'[59]

British defence sales to Saudi Arabia are controversial and have come in for criticism on three main grounds: corruption, human rights and leverage. The question of corruption has already been touched upon, and the FAC seems to think that the 2010 UK Bribery Act and an improvement in Saudi Arabia's mid-range rating on Transparency International's Corruption Perceptions Index demonstrates hope on this score for the future.[60] With regard to human rights, and concerns that British-supplied military equipment might have been used for purposes of internal repression in Hasa, or the external interventions in Yemen in 2009 and Bahrain in 2011, the FAC simply repeated the UK Government's line 'that none of the extant licenses for Saudi Arabia contravene its stated policy.'[61] As to the possible 'leverage' exerted by Saudi Arabia or other Gulf Arab states on Britain, provided by British dependence on arms sales to these countries, the FAC seemed to discount this for lack of evidence. Yet, the view was expressed to them 'that when Gulf rulers are upset about something (such as the above-mentioned SFO investigation) the message comes out, "We don't actually have to buy your Typhoons. We can always buy from someone else."'[62]

6. Spurned by the United Arab Emirates

The above perceptive remark seems to have been borne out by recent developments, namely the decision by the UAE not to buy Typhoons, despite a hard sell campaign by the British government led by David Cameron, and the fact that for three years BAE Systems has failed to agree a final price for the sale of Typhoons to Saudi Arabia. The observation was made in late 2013 that:

> The UAE's decision to reject the fighter [Typhoon] perhaps in favour of Rafale
> [the French Dassault jet] could complicate negotiations further by giving the

Saudis even more leverage to haggle over the "Salam" deal that was first brokered in 2007...In this regard BAE's task has been complicated exponentially by a breakdown in goodwill between Riyadh and Westminister since possible British military intervention in Syria was rejected. Removing the Iranian-backed regime of Bashar al-Assad from power in Damascus is a stated goal of King Abdullah's government and the failure to support this objective has opened up a deep rift with western allies. The UK has also strongly supported the US-led initiative to partially lift economic sanctions once aimed at stopping Iran's nuclear programme, which has rubbed further salt into the wounds of Saudi's tetchy Sunni-Muslim rulers. Saudi Arabia's Ambassador to Britain Prince Mohammed bin Nawaf recently branded the reprochment with Iran as a "dangerous gamble".[63]

There is evidence to suggest that 'the UAE was also disturbed by Britain's uncritical acceptance of the Geneva agreement on Iran's nuclear ambitions. France, in contrast, rejected the first draft and ensured that the final deal was significantly tougher on Iran.'[64] France was also prepared to use force against Syria and has a permanent military base in the UAE. In other words, France is seen as a more reliable guarantor of UAE security than Britain. Although a UK Government spokesman attributed the loss of the Typhoon deal to 'a commercial decision'[65], a UAE source close to the negotiations said, no doubt tongue in cheek, that 'the interim deal with Iran along with direct diplomatic engagements the UAE has conducted have relaxed tensions between the Gulf neighbours and contributed to the deal's breakdown. "At this point there is no need to acquire weapons as our diplomatic efforts have succeeded."[66] It will be interesting to see how a possible Rafale deal fares.

The UAE's position towards Iran is complex and reflects the range of interests of the constituent emirates. As an important trading and investment partner for Dubai, Iran enjoys a privileged position. Despite what the UAE spokesman says, however, Abu Dhabi, as well as Sharjah and Ras al-Khaimah have had tense relations with their neighbour across the water. One of the eternal bones of contention has been the illegal annexation in 1971 by Iran, as Britain moved out of the Gulf, of the islands of Abu Musa and the Tunbs, near the shipping lanes in the lower Gulf. Anxious to make amends for its original mistake in not preventing Iran's original seizure of these islands, and as part of its revival of defence co-operation with the UAE (under the original 1996 DCA), the British government, in the form of the Defence Secretary, Philip Hammond, expressed its support in March 2012 for 'the UAE against any threat by Iran'.[67] The FCO was also trenchant in its criticism of Iranian President Ahmadinejad's visit to Abu Musa in April 2012, saying that it was 'highly unfortunate and only serves to make matters worse.' It went on: 'The United Kingdom supports a peaceful settlement to the dispute...acceptable to both parties... [t]he UK values the reasoned approach taken by the UAE over the issue.'[68] In view of such strong statements of support for the UAE against Iran, the UAE must have wondered at the UK's 'uncritical acceptance' of the Geneva interim agreement on Iran's nuclear programme. It is unclear whether this and the carping criticism of the liberal media in Britain of the prosecution and imprisonment of Muslim Brotherhood activists (from *al-Islah*) in the UAE, led to the collapse of the Typhoon deal (presaged in 2012 by the refusal to allow BP to tender for a new oil concession). There is no doubt, however, that this has been a setback for the UK coalition government's concerted attempt since 2010 to bolster the UK's military presence in the UAE to offset possible waning interest by the United States and to protect the UK's considerable interests in the UAE and other Gulf Arab states.[69] The setback is directly due to the essential dilemma at the heart of British policy in the Gulf since at least 1971 (greater, indeed, than the clash between human rights and arms sales), namely the FCO's instinctive preference to giving greater weight to the UK's relations with the larger regional powers, Saudi Arabia, Iran and Iraq, yet trying at the same time to allay the competing concerns of the smaller Gulf Arab states. The State Visit of the President of the UAE, His Highness Sheikh Khalifa bin Zayed Al Nahyan, to Britain in May 2013 would have signalled to the UAE that the UK was returning, whether the coalition government was aware of it or not, to a much older relationship that prevailed in the years before 1971, whereby the UK guaranteed the defence of Abu Dhabi, Dubai, and the other sheikhdoms of the Trucial Coast, as well as Oman, Qatar, Bahrain and Kuwait, against the depredations of their larger and more aggressive neighbours – this time, though, in the isolated form of Iran.[70] In taking this course, the UK seemed to be righting the historical wrong perpetrated when in 1971 it simply abandoned the Sheikh of Abu Dhabi, Zayed bin Sultan, and his fellow rulers on the Trucial Coast to their fate as it pulled out east of Suez. But Britain's 'uncritical acceptance' of the Geneva interim agreement on Iran seems to have cast doubt on the degree and seriousness of the UK's defence commitment to the UAE, hence the latter's tilt back towards France. This doubt will only increase unless the UK returns to a more traditional and logical policy, *a la Francaise*, commensurate with British interests in the Gulf. Ultimately, managing this issue in British policy towards the Gulf Arab states presents a greater dilemma for the UK than the clash between 'values' and 'interests'.

7. The Triumph of 'Interests' over 'Values'

The chairman of the FAC admitted that British 'values' sometimes clash with the UK's 'interests', and that this is especially the case in the Gulf. It recognises that the UK Government has 'a credibility problem' with regard to the extent to which its private and public pressure upon the Saudi government to engage in political reform has actually produced any results. The FAC seems to have no remedy for this beyond suggesting that the UK Government 'do more to explain its policies' and engage in more public diplomacy from its Embassy in Riyadh, in an attempt to improve the poor mutual perception among the public, especially the young, in both countries – a perception that relates as much to British subservience to US agendas as it does to notions of Britain failing to defend human rights. At the end of the day, however, the FAC regards British interests as being of paramount importance:

> Saudi Arabia is a large and growing market for the UK, and the Saudi government's large-scale spending programmes offer huge opportunities for British businesses. Saudi Arabia is also an important if controversial buyer for the UK defence industry. We have seen no conclusive proof that Saudi Arabia has misused the equipment sold by the UK, and the UK provides training alongside its sales programmes which enhances the UK-Saudi defence relationship and benefits Saudi forces' training. Ending defence sales would have significant costs for the UK-Saudi relationship and there is little evidence that it would have any positive effect, particularly given the presence of other sellers in the market.[71]

The evidence therefore culminates in the uncomfortable finding that, ultimately, British 'interests', by which is meant defence sales to Saudi Arabia and Bahrain, as well as other Gulf Arab states, and military basing requirements, triumph over British 'values', in terms of the promotion of human rights, when it comes to British policy towards Bahrain and Saudi Arabia. But was this not always going to be the case? The association of 'interests' and 'values', and the viewing of weapons sales as policy aims (that is, as part of a strategy by which to curry strategic influence with partners and allies) ignores the simple economic imperative that also underpins the UK's policy of selling weapons to the Gulf states. This economic imperative is critical to understand – in brief, weapons systems are extremely costly to develop, with very high research and developments costs that need to be recouped, particularly when the 'home' forces are small and require few units. Regardless of any other policy calculation that may be considered across UK government departments, the strong economic incentive to export arms to customers with significant resources to allocate will rank very highly in UK policymakers' minds. Indeed, Whitehall and Westminster have attempted to resolve this particular dilemma in British policy by quietly dropping the rhetoric in 2011-12 about human rights in favour of a more hard-headed emphasis on arms sales and general trade to the Gulf Arab states. In other words, more of the same: the 'mercenary' rather than the 'gamekeeper' approach to security in the Gulf.[72] There is no sign here of a recognition that relations with these states cannot progress further until there is a fundamental reappraisal of British policy which seeks to identify the UK's real strategic interests and her true friends in the Gulf.

The need for such a recalibration is shown clearly by an assessment of the existing policy. As has been pointed out: 'In the last three years, British ministers have made over 230 visits to the Gulf states, reflecting the fact that 160,000 British citizens live in this region. Bilateral trade between the Gulf and the UK, meanwhile, has grown by almost 40 per cent since 2011 to reach £30 billion.'[73] This is the result of a concerted effort since 2010 by the Foreign Secretary and the UK Government, under their 'Gulf Initiative' to strengthen bi-lateral relations with all Gulf Arab countries and to expand co-operation 'across the board, in culture, education, defence, security, trade and investment, and foreign policy.'[74] If the UAE had bought Typhoon, defence sales would have been boosted by another £6 billion. There is reason to believe that Britain lost this sale, and that negotiations over Typhoon with Saudi Arabia were stalled for three years, because of the earlier emphasis on human rights during the Arab Spring by the UK Government and the latter's policy towards Egypt, Syria and Iran. There are indications that the Gulf Arab states feel that their concerns about Iran have not been addressed by either the UK or the USA, not only on the nuclear issue, but on Iran's 'continued involvement in state-sponsored terrorism'. At the ISS Manama Dialogue in December 2013, the Crown Prince of Bahrain, Shaikh Salman, articulated the doubt of Gulf Arab states that 'they could rely on the West to protect their interests.' He said that, in the light of the coup by the Russian President, Vladimir Putin, in seizing the initiative from President Obama, during the crisis over Syria's chemical weapons crisis, 'some states were now seriously reviewing their relations with the US'. 'The Russians have proved they are reliable friends.'[75] The prospect of Russia increasing its influence over countries, such as Egypt and the GCC, controlling the great strategic pinch-points of the world, Suez and the Strait of Hormuz, should sound the alarm in the corridors of Whitehall and Westminster, let alone Foggy Bottom and on Capitol Hill. William Hague seems to be aware of the threat, speaking in Bahrain about his desire to deepen Britain's ties with the Gulf on the basis of 'mutual understanding'.[76] But the UK Government's determination to revive Britain's military presence east of Suez has been set back by problems over the Typhoon sales to the UAE and Saudi Arabia, which are the result not only of the rhetoric about human rights but of a perception by these countries, and Bahrain, that the UK, in contrast to France, is not a reliable defence partner.[77] It would be a historical irony if another power replaced both the USA and the UK as guarantors of the security of the Gulf Arab states. It is very unlikely to imagine right now, but other countries do have interests in the Gulf – China, India, and Russia, for example – that may in future decades pursue a more muscular security policy. For two centuries, British and later American policy aimed, on the whole successfully, at keeping Russia out of the Gulf. But the last laugh might lie with Russia. In a speech on 16 June 2012, concerning defending Russia's stance on Syria, the Russian Foreign Minister, Sergey Lavrov, talked of Russia being 'on the right side of history'.[78] It remains to be seen who will be on right side of history in the Gulf. There is even talk of 'China's historic return to the Gulf'. [79] But if the UK and the US governments, in their pursuit of defence sales and advocacy of human rights, forget the lessons of their own history in the Gulf, and where their true interests and friends lie, they may well find themselves on the wrong side of history.

8. Conclusion

The return of Britain to the Gulf, in the form of a new military base in Bahrain, presents a range of vantage-points to consider questions relating to Gulf security, international politics, and the importance of so-called international norms in maintaining the order to the state system. Few of these developments and issues are new, however. Indeed, they all have historical roots that run deep – whether in terms of the continued UK defence relationships with Arab Gulf states following Britain's public withdrawal 'east of Suez' in 1971, or through to the unpalatable fact that British foreign policies – in keeping with other countries' policies' – are nearly always dictated by national, material, interests rather than other intangible values and norms. A further reality to perhaps acknowledge here at this late point is that it would be remarkable indeed if the US were indeed rebalancing to Asia in such a way as to see their footprint in the Gulf diminish. The footprint may alter in terms of shape of forces, their capabilities, and their locations, but the ability of the US to project force in the Gulf, and to defend their allies, will probably remain as potent, if not more so, in the years ahead. It is in this rebalanced framework that Britain is once again seeking to re-establish its role, but by enhancing the enduring legacies of her relationship with Gulf states, rather than creating anything particularly new. And, in this re-discovered environment, the ties that bind London with the Arab Gulf will remain as strongly focused upon the protection and promotion of 'national interests' rather than the more complex and sensitive notion of values and human rights, as future Foreign Affairs Committee reports may testify.

Notes

1   See, for example, Anoushiravan Ehteshami (2013) *Dynamics of Change in the Persian Gulf: Political Economy, War and Revolution*. London: Routledge.
2   Quoted in Elizabeth Dickinson, 'Bahrain naval base will give UK stronger Gulf presence', *Financial Times*, 7 December 2014.
3   Jamie Merrill, 'British military base in Bahrain is a 'reward' for UK's silence on human rights, say campaigners', *The Independent*, 6 December 2014.
4   It is important to note that this community is not monolithic. We acknowledge that there are different components to this community, from the politicians and policy makers in government, to the legislative 'vetters' and monitors in parliamentary committees – who can comment but not actually determine policy – and outside experts, in universities, think-tanks, NGOs, and the media who can give evidence and attempt to influence policy.
5   There already exists a sizeable literature on the events of the Arab Spring. Of note are Marc Lynch (2012) *The Arab Uprising: the Unfinished Revolutions of the New Middle East* (Washington D.C.: Public Affairs); Tariq Ramadan (2012) *The Arab Awakening: Islam and the New Middle East* (London: Allen Lane); Michael Willis (2012) *Politics and Power in the Maghreb: Algeria, Tunisia, and Morocco from Independence to the Arab Spring* (London: Hurst & Co.); Fawaz Gerges (2013) *The New Middle East: Protest and Revolution in the Arab World* (Cambridge: Cambridge University Press); Toby Matthiesen (2013) *Sectarian Gulf: Bahrain, Saudi Arabia, and the Arab Spring that Wasn't* (Stanford: Stanford University Press).

6   'On the right side of history' is a phrase much favoured and used by President Barack Obama. In his inaugural address to the American people on 29 January 2009, he warned those 'leaders around the globe that cling to power through corruption and deceit and their silencing of dissent, know that you are on the wrong side of history but that we will extend a hand if you unclench your fist'. He also used the phrase with reference to Iran in 2009, Egypt in 2011, and Syria in 2013. See Mir Sadat and Daniel Jones (2009) 'US Foreign Policy Toward Syria: Balancing Ideology and National Interests', *Middle East Policy*, Vol. XVI, No. 2; Hilary Clinton, when U.S. Secretary of State, put it most succinctly when she said: 'There is a phrase that people in the United states invoke when urging others to support human rights. "Be on the right side of history."' www.huffingtonpost.com/2011/12/06Hilary-clinton-gay-rights-speech-geneva.

7   House of Commons Foreign Affairs Committee, 'British foreign policy and the "Arab Spring". Second Report of Session 2012-13, 19 July 2012, and 'The UK's relations with Saudi Arabia and Bahrain'. Fifth Report of Session 2013-14, Vol. 1, 22 November 2013. www.parliament.ul/business/committees-a-z/commons-select/foreign-affairs, accessed 24 January 2014.

8   See William Hague (2007) *William Wilberforce. The Life of the Great Anti-Slave Trade Campaigner* (London: Harper).

9   FAC report, 'The UK's relations with Saudi Arabia and Bahrain', p. 22.

10 See   https://www.gov.uk/government/speeches/prime-ministers-speech-to-the-national-assembly-kuwait.

11 Ibid.

12 The membership of the Foreign Affairs Committee consists of MPs from across the parties represented in parliament. As of January 2015, the the committee comprises: Sir Richard Ottaway (Chair – Conservative); John Baron (Conservative); Sir Menzies Campbell (Liberal Democrat); Ann Clwyd (Labour); Mike Gapes (Labour); Mark Hendrick (Labour); Sandra Osborne (Labour); Andrew Rosindell (Conservative); Frank Roy (Labour); Sir John Stanley (Conservative); and Nadhim Zahawi (Conservative).

13 FAC report, 'BFP and Arab Spring', p. 41.

14 Ibid., p. 40.

15 Ibid.

16 See www.theguardian.com/politics/2011/jul/21/uk-arms-sales-middle-east

17 Ibid.

18 FAC report, 'BFP and Arab Spring', p.40-41; see also Committee on Arms Export Controls, First Joint Report of Session 2012-13, *Scrutiny of Arms Exports (2012): UK Strategic Export Controls Annual Report 2010, Quarterly Reports for July to December 2010 and January to September 2011, the Government's Review of Arms Exports to the Middle East and North Africa, and wider arms control issues*, HC 419, p. 6-7.

19 www.theguardian.com/politics/2011/jul/21/uk-arms-sales-middle-east

20 FAC report, 'BFP and Arab Spring', p. 40-41.

21 Ibid., p. 75. For the FCO's defence of its conduct during the Arab Spring, see Cm 8436, *Government Response to the House of Commons Foreign Affairs Committee Report of Session 2012-13, 'British Foreign Policy and the "Arab Spring"'. Presented to Parliament by the Secretary of State for Foreign and Commonwealth Affairs by Command of Her Majesty. September 2012.*

22 www.thenational.ae/news/world/middle east/uk-interference-in-gulf. For full report, see House of Commons, Foreign Affairs Committee, 'The FCO's human rights work in 2011.' Third Report of Session 2012-23. HC 11, 17 October 2012. www.parliament.uk/business/committees-a-z/commons-select/foreign-affairs.

23 Ibid.

24 Frank Gardner, 'Saudi Arabia "insulted" by UK inquiry', 15 October 2012. www.bbc.co.uk/news/uk-politics.

25 www.thenational.ae/news/world/middle-east/uk-interference-in-gulf.

26 FAC report, 'The UK's relations with Saudi Arabia and Bahrain'.

27 Ibid., p. 3.

28 Frank Gardner, 'MPS question UK relations with Saudi Arabia and Bahrain', 22 November 2013, www.bbc.co.uk/news/uk.

29 FAC report, 'The UK's relations with Saudi Arabia and Bahrain', p. 76.

30 Angus McDowall, 'Bahrain Crown Prince calls for talks with opposition', 8 December 2012, www.reuters.com.

31 Ibid, pp. 86-7.

32 Ibid.

33 Ibid., pp. 87-8.

34 Bahrain came under British protection on 31 May 1861, not in 1820 as the FAC report (71) seems to think. See J.B. Kelly, *Arabia, the Gulf and the West* (London,1980), p.179.

35 It is also the warp and weave of Kuwaiti politics, where successive emirs keep disbanding the various parliaments and holding new elections because they cannot obtain the result they desire, namely an assembly not dominated by the Islamist-led opposition, which also comprises nationalist and youth groups. In contrast to the Al Khalifah in Bahrain, however, their 'cousins' the Al-Sabah in Kuwait, are dependent upon the support of the old Shi'a merchant families, which makes for a more complicated political situation in Kuwait.

36 FAC report, 'UK relations with Saudi Arabia and Bahrain', p. 73.

37 Embodied in the report of the Bahrain Independent Commission of Inquiry (BICI) of November 2011 and the Universal Periodic Review of the UN Human Rights Council of September 2012. According to the FAC, the Bahrain government has been slow to implement the recommendations of these two bodies, and urges them to do so.

38 Matthiesen, *Sectarian Gulf.* pp. ix and 127.

39 Iranian maps continue to show Bahrain as part of Iran and the Iranian *majlis*, or parliament, holds seats open for Bahraini M.P.s, which seems to indicate that the Islamic regime has not relinquished the Iranian claim to the islands, as did the Shah in 1970. For the flimsiness of the Iranian claim, see S.B. Kelly. ed., *Fighting the Retreat from Arabia and the Gulf. The Collected Essays and Reviews of J.B Kelly, Vol.1* (New English Review Press, 2013) pp.30-9 and 101-105 and Kelly, *Arabia, the Gulf and the West*, pp. 54-9 and 180.

40 FAC report on 'The UK's relations with Saudi Arabia and Bahrain', pp. 94-5.

41 Ibid., p. 96.

42 Kelly, *Arabia, the Gulf and the West,* p. 181.

43 FAC report 'The UK's relations with Saudi Arabia and Bahrain', pp. 3 and 30.

44 Ibid., p. 7.

45 Matthiesen, *Sectarian Gulf*, p. 73.

46 Ibid., pp. 80-1.

47 It seems, however, that the British government abandoned this approach fairly quickly after 2011 and no longer seems to do it with regard to the Gulf.

48 FAC report on 'The UK's relations with Saudi Arabia and Bahrain', pp. 28-9 and *passim*.

49 The FAC report, citing the former British ambassador to Saudi Arabia, Sir Alun Monro, refers to the 'Bahraini oasis', an unfortunate slip of the tongue which serves to confuse more than edify.

50 See Kelly, *Arabia, the Gulf and the West, passim*; also J.B. Kelly, Eastern Arabian Frontiers (London, 1964), *passim*.

51 FAC report on 'The UK's relations with Saudi Arabia and Bahrain', p. 28.

52 FAC report on 'The UK's relations with Saudi Arabia and Bahrain', p. 28.

53 Ibid., p. 42.

54 It should be noted that the reasoning given by Saudi Arabia for the oil embargo focuses mainly on a view that Western oil companies had exploited the Middle Eastern oil producers mercilessly over the whole period since 1972, thus forcing the oil price down to very low levels.

55 Ibid., p. 44.

56 Ibid., p. 4.

57 Ibid., p.44; Alan Tovey, 'BAE agrees pricing on Typhoon deal with Saudi Arabia', 19 February 2014, www.telegraph.co.uk/fiance/newsbysector/epic/badot/10648144/BAE-agrees

58 Ibid., pp. 28-9.

59 Ibid., p. 40.

60 Ibid., p. 45.

61 Ibid., p. 44.

62 FAC report on 'The UK's relations with Saudi Arabia and Bahrain', p. 45.

63 Andrew Critchlow, 'David Cameron's debacle a sign of Britain's declining Arabian influence', 19 December 2013, www.telegraph.co.uk/finance/newsbysector/industry/defence.

64 David Blair, 'Britain's ambitions in the Gulf suffer blow as UAE rejects Typhoon deal', 20 December 2013, www.telegraph.co.uk/news/worldnews/middleeast.

65 Ibid.

66 Andrew Chuter and Awad Mustafa, 'UAE backs out of Typhoon Discussions', 19 December 2013. www.defencenews.com/article.

67 www.gulfnews.com/news/gulf/uae/government/uae-uk-seek-to-boost-defence-cooperation.

68 www.gov.uk/government/news/foreign-office-commnets-on-highly-unfortunate-visit-by-president-ahmadinejad-to-abu-musa-island.

69 For details see Saul Kelly and Gareth Stansfield, 'Britain, the United Arab Emirates and the defence of the Gulf revisited', *International Affairs*, 89, 5 (2013), pp. 1203-1219.

70 The Trucial Coast was so-named from the series of truces signed with the maritime tribes of the Arabian shore in the nineteenth century to guarantee peace and good order in the lower Gulf.

71 FAC report on 'The UK's relations with Saudi Arabia and Bahrain', p. 4.

72 See Saul Kelly, 'The Gamekeeper versus the Mercenary Spirit: The Pax Britannica in the Gulf', in Macris and Kelly, *Crossroads of Empire*, pp. 49-60.

73 Blair article in Daily Telegraph, 20 December 2013, citing figures from the FAC report.

74 FAC report on 'The UK's relations with Saudi Arabia and Bahrain', p. 15.

75 Con Coughlin, '"Schizophrenic" US foreign policy pushing Arab states toward Russia, Bahrain warns', 8 December 2013, www.telegraph.co.uk/news/worldnews/middleeast

76 Con Coughlin, 'We must look after our allies east of Suez', 10 December 2013, www.telegraph.co.uk/news/worldnews/middleeast.

77 On the British military presence in the Gulf, see Gareth Stansfield and Saul Kelly (2013) 'A return to east of Suez? UK military deployment to the Persian Gulf', RUSI briefing paper (London: RUSI).

78 Sergey Lavrov, 'On the Right Side of History', 16 June 2012, www.voltairenet.org/On-the-Right-Side-of-History.

79 See Ben Simpfendorfer, 'China's historic return to the Gulf', in Jeffrey Macris and Saul Kelly, eds., (2012) *Imperial Crossroads. The Great Powers in the Persian Gulf* (Annapolis: Naval Institute Press), pp. 167-84.

Bibliography

Committee on Arms Export Controls, First Joint Report of Session 2012-13, *Scrutiny of Arms Exports (2012): UK Strategic Export Controls Annual Report 2010, Quarterly Reports for July to December 2010 and January to September 2011, the Government's Review of Arms Exports to the Middle East and North Africa, and Wider Arms Control Issues*, HC 419, p. 6-7.

Ehteshami, Anoushiravan (2013) *Dynamics of Change in the Persian Gulf: Political Economy, War and Revolution.* London: Routledge.

Gerges, Fawaz (2013) *The New Middle East: Protest and Revolution in the Arab World* (Cambridge: Cambridge University Press).

Hague, William (2007) *William Wilberforce. The Life of the Great Anti-Slave Trade Campaigner* (London: Harper).

House of Commons Foreign Affairs Committee, 'British foreign policy and the "Arab Spring". Second Report of Session 2012-13, 19 July 2012.

House of Commons, Foreign Affairs Committee, 'The FCO's human rights work in 2011.' Third Report of Session 2012-23. HC 11, 17 October 2012. www.parliament.uk/business/committees/committees-a-z/commons-select/foreign-affairs

House of Commons Foreign Affairs Committee, 'The UK's relations with Saudi Arabia and Bahrain'. Fifth Report of Session 2013-14, Vol.1, 22 November 2013. www.parliament.ul/business/committees-a-z/commons-select/foreign-affairs, accessed 24 January 2014.

Kelly, J.B., *Arabia, the Gulf and the West* (London, 1980).

Kelly, S.B.. ed., *Fighting the Retreat from Arabia and the Gulf. The Collected Essays and Reviews of J.B Kelly, Vol.1* (New English Review Press, 2013).

Kelly, Saul and Gareth Stansfield, 'Britain, the United Arab Emirates and the defence of the Gulf revisited', *International Affairs*, 89, 5 (2013).

Lynch, Marc (2012) *The Arab Uprising: the Unfinished Revolutions of the New Middle East* (Washington D.C.: Public Affairs).

Matthiesen, Toby (2013) *Sectarian Gulf: Bahrain, Saudi Arabia, and the Arab Spring that Wasn't* (Stanford: Stanford University Press).

Ramadan, Tariq (2012) *The Arab Awakening: Islam and the New Middle East* (London: Allen Lane).

Sadat, Mir and Daniel Jones (2009) 'US Foreign Policy Toward Syria: Balancing Ideology and National Interests', *Middle East Policy*, Vol. XVI, No. 2.

Simpfendorfer, Ben, 'China's historic return to the Gulf', in Jeffrey Macris and Saul Kelly, eds., (2012) *Imperial Crossroads. The Great Powers in the Persian Gulf* (Annapolis: Naval Institute Press).

Willis, Michael (2012) *Politics and Power in the Maghreb: Algeria, Tunisia, and Morocco from Independence to the Arab Spring* (London: Hurst & Co.).

About the Contributors

Mohammed Turki Al-Sudairi is a Saudi graduate of Georgetown University's School of Foreign Service. He is currently pursuing a double master's degree from Peking University (PKU) and the London School of Economics (LSE) in International Affairs. His dissertation for PKU dealt with Saudi influences on the Development of Chinese Salafism, a paper in which he utilized extensive Arabic, Chinese, and English sources. He is affiliated with the Gulf Research Centre, and has written on a variety of topics including Sino-Middle East relations, Islam in China, and Saudi politics. His most recent work includes a monograph on Sino-Israel Relations through the Prism of Advocacy Groups (Durham, 2013).

John Duke Anthony is Founding President and CEO of the National Council on US-Arab Relations, Member, US Secretary of State's Advisory Committees on International Economic Policy and Sanctions, and was Founding Chairman of the Advanced Arabian Peninsula Studies Seminar, US Department of State. He created and taught the first academic courses on the Arabian Peninsula and the Gulf States at an American university. In 2000, King Muhammad VI knighted Dr Anthony with Morocco's Highest Award for Excellence. His most recent writings are "Future Significance of the GCC" (Abu Dhabi: 2012), and "ISIS, The GCC, and The United States" (Washington: 2015).

Cinzia Bianco is an analyst for the Mediterranean and Gulf Programme at the NATO Defence College Foundation. Previously she has been a contributor for the *Euro-Mediterranean Forum*, a project of the 2014 Italian Presidency of the European Union. In 2013 she held a research fellowship in the GCC region for the European Commission's project "Sharaka" specialising on relations between the European Union and the Gulf countries. Her most recent works include "EU-GCC Cooperation in an Era of Socio-Economic Challenges" (Istituto Affari Internazionali, 2014). She holds a Master's degree in Middle East and Mediterranean Studies from King's College London.

David B. Des Roches is Associate Professor at the Near East South Asia Center for Strategic Studies at the National Defense University in Washington. He previously worked in a variety of positions in the Office of the Secretary of Defense, culminating as Director of Arabian Peninsula Policy. He also worked in the White House Office of National Drug Control Policy during the Clinton Administration. His research interests include non-traditional defence issues and emerging threats.

Steven W. Hook is Professor of Political Science and past department chair at Kent State University. He is the author of several books, including *US Foreign Policy: The Paradox of World Power* (Washington, D.C.: CQ Press, 2014, 4th ed), co-author of *American Foreign Policy Since World War II* (CQ Press, 2016, 20th ed., with John Spanier), and *National Interest and Foreign Aid* (Lynne Rienner, 1995). His journal articles have appeared in *World Politics*, *International Studies Quarterly*, *Foreign Policy Analysis*, and other leading journals. He is a past president of the Foreign Policy Analysis sections of the American Political Science Association and the International Studies Association.

Saul Kelly is Reader in International History, King's College London. His recent publications include, 'Vanishing Act: Britain's Abandonment of Aden and Retreat from the Gulf', in Clack & Johnson, *At the End of Military Intervention* (OUP, 2014) and 'Desert Conquests: Early British Planning on the Future of the Italian Colonies, June 1940-September 1943', *Middle Eastern Studies*, Vol. 50, No. 6, (2014).

Flynt Leverett is Professor of International Affairs and Asian studies at Pennsylvania State University. He served for eleven years in the US government as senior analyst at the CIA, on the State Department's Policy Planning Staff, and as senior director for Middle East affairs at the National Security Council; he resigned in 2003 over disagreements with Middle East policy and the conduct of the "war on terror." He is a Visiting Scholar at Peking University's Institute for International and Strategic Studies, Senior Fellow at Renmin University of China's Chongyang Institute for Financial Studies, and co-author of *Going to Tehran: Why America Must Accept the Islamic Republic of Iran*.

Hillary Mann Leverett is Visiting Scholar at Georgetown University's Alwaleed bin Talal Center for Muslim-Christian Understanding. She has served at US embassies throughout the Middle East, at the US Mission to the United Nations, at the National Security Council, and on the State Department's Policy Planning Staff. From 2001-2003, she negotiated for the US government with Iranian officials over Afghanistan, al-Qaida, and Iraq. She is a Visiting Scholar at Peking University's Institute for International and Strategic Studies, Senior Fellow at Renmin University of China's Chongyang Institute for Financial Studies, and co-author of *Going to Tehran: Why America Must Accept the Islamic Republic of Iran*.

Tim Niblock is Emeritus Professor of Middle East Politics at the University of Exeter, having previous served as Director of the Institute of Arab and Islamic Studies in the

University (1999-2005), and Director of the Centre for Middle Eastern and Islamic Studies at the University of Durham (1993-1998). He has also held visiting positions at the Chinese Academy of Social Sciences, Northwest University (Xibei) University and Shaanxi Normal University in China. His most recent books (co-edited) are *Asia-Gulf Economic Relations in the 21ˢᵗ Century: the Local in Global Transformation*, (Berlin: Gerlach Press, 2013), and *Security Dynamics of East Asia in the Gulf Region* (Berlin: Gerlach Press, 2014).

Girijesh Pant is Professor School of International Studies at Jawaharlal Nehru University. He is presently working in the Energy Studies Programme of the University with a focus on energy transition regimes, focussing on India and China. He specialises on the political economy of development, West Asian affairs, global energy affairs, and India's energy security. He has held positions as a Senior Fulbright Scholar, Dean of the School of International Studies (JNU) and Vice Chancellor at Doon University and at GGD University in Chhattisgarh, as well as Chair in the Centre for West Asian Studies (JNU). An edited volume of his on India's Emerging Energy Relation is in the press.

Gareth Stansfield is Professor of Middle East Politics and the Al-Qasimi Chair of Arab Gulf Studies at the University of Exeter. He is also a Senior Associate Fellow and Director of Middle East Studies at the Royal United Services Institute (RUSI). He is currently an Honorary Research Fellow attached to the Middle East and North Africa Research Group of the Foreign and Commonwealth Office. A regular commentator and adviser on Middle East politics, focusing in particular on the politics and political economy of Iraq, the Kurdish regions of the Middle East, dynamics of Gulf/Arabian peninsular security, and questions of post-conflict stabilization and nation/state building.

Degang Sun is Professor of International Relations at the Middle East Studies Institute of Shanghai International Studies University, China. He was an academic visitor to the Middle East Centre, Oxford University, and Oxford Centre for Islamic Studies (2012-2013). His research interest is outside powers and the Middle East. His most recent works are *Quasi-alliance Diplomacy in Theory and Practice: An Empirical Studies of the Relations between Great Powers and the Middle East* (Beijing: World Affairs, 2012); "China's Response to the Revolts in the Arab World: A Case of Pragmatic Diplomacy", (*Mediterranean Politics*, Vol. 19, No. 1, 2014, with Professor Yahia Zoubir); and "China's Economic Diplomacy towards the Arab Countries: Challenges Ahead?" (*Journal of Contemporary China*, forthcoming, with Professor Yahia Zoubir).

Yahia H. Zoubir is Professor of International Relations and International Management, and Director of Research in Geopolitics at KEDGE Business School, Marseille, France. His forthcoming coedited book is entitled *North African Politics: Continuity and Change*

(2015). He has coauthored, *Global Security Watch: The Maghreb* (2013) and is coeditor of *North Africa: Politics, Region, and the Limits of Transformation* (2008). He edited and was the main contributor of *North Africa in Transition-State, Society & Economic Transformation in the 1990s* (1999). His publications have appeared in major US, Canadian, European, and Middle Eastern scholarly journals, as chapters in edited volumes, and in various encyclopaedias.